Contents

Introduction: The Forgotten Mothers of the Constitution   1

Part I: Origins

1: The Pioneers   9
2: The Instigators   21
3: The Reformers   32

Part II: Contestations

4: The Globalizers   45
5: The Framers   57
6: The Mothers   68
7: The Breadmakers   83

Part III: Transformations

8: The Change Agents   97
9: The Game Changers   114

Part IV: Persistence

10: The Resurrectors   129
11: The Rectifiers   142
12: The History Makers   158

Epilogue: The Unstoppables   172
Acknowledgments   184
Notes   189
Index   225

WE THE WOMEN

THE UNSTOPPABLE MOTHERS OF THE EQUAL RIGHTS AMENDMENT

JULIE C. SUK

Skyhorse Publishing

Visit our website at www.skyhorsepublishing.com.

10 9 8 7 6 5 4 3 2 1

Library of Congress Cataloging-in-Publication Data is available on file.

Cover design by Brian Peterson

Print ISBN: 978-1-5107-7178-9
Ebook ISBN: 978-1-5107-5592-5

Printed in the United States of America

For my mother and my sisters,
who seem to know exactly when to be unstoppable.

Introduction
The Forgotten Mothers of the Constitution

1. Equality of rights under the law shall not be denied or abridged by the United States or by any State on account of sex.

2. Congress shall have the power to enforce, by appropriate legislation, the provisions of this Article.

3. This Amendment shall take effect two years after the date of ratification.

—Equal Rights Amendment to the US Constitution

THE YEAR 2020 MARKS THE 100th anniversary of the passage of the Nineteenth Amendment, guaranteeing women's constitutional right to vote. But how far have we really come?

After the adoption and ratification of the Nineteenth Amendment, a bold group of women proposed the Equal Rights Amendment (ERA). Women have been fighting for the ERA for almost a century, believing that the Constitution should recognize their equal rights, not only as voters, but as full persons and citizens. It took Congress almost forty-nine years to adopt it in 1972. The fight for ratification in the states took another forty-eight years, culminating in Virginia's historic ratification in January 2020. Virginia was the crucial thirty-eighth state needed to add sex equality to the US Constitution.

Why have women persisted to ratify the ERA? Why did it take so long? Is it too late to add the ERA to the Constitution? And what could it do for women?

We the Women answers these questions. It tells the stories of the women who made the ERA—its "founding mothers"—and the women who would benefit most from the ERA—the mothers of the next generation of Americans who have long navigated women's changing roles in American society. Their efforts to establish women's constitutional right to equality have been disrupted and delayed along the way. Their ordeals are largely forgotten. But women have not given up on constitutional change.

Most constitutions around the world declare equality between women and men. But the US Constitution has struggled with its commitment to sex equality. Efforts to add sex equality to the US Constitution, beginning with women's right to vote, have been fraught with controversy and resistance. After a battle that lasted decades, American women achieved the constitutional right to vote when the Nineteenth Amendment was ratified in 1920. Newly armed with votes, a suffragist vanguard introduced an idea that seemed revolutionary in 1923—that women should have rights fully equal to those enjoyed by men. But the revolution became an evolution, persisting across generations, still unfinished.

Even with all the ratifications completed, a cloud of uncertainty hangs over the ERA because Congress set up time limits on ratification that expired in 1982. With only thirty-five states having ratified it by that deadline, three states short of the thirty-eight needed, the ERA was declared a failure and forgotten for a generation. But it made a surprising comeback in 2017, as the Women's March gave Nevada the momentum to ratify the amendment. The #MeToo movement moved Illinois legislators to ratify the ERA in May 2018. Then the "Pink Wave" got a record number of women elected to Congress later that year, resulting in 23.7 percent of Congress being female. That wave spread to Virginia, as more women were elected to the Virginia legislature in November 2019 than ever before. Women, now occupying leadership positions in the Virginia General Assembly, led their state to finally deliver the thirty-eighth ratification, after decades of failed attempts. But opponents—including the Trump Administration—have tried to stop the ERA by saying that it's just too late.

We the Women journeys across a century of women marching, protesting, testifying, resisting, arguing, litigating, and persisting to establish their constitutional rights. It gives voice to their constitutional claims. If and when the ERA is added to the Constitution, our Constitution will officially have founding mothers as well as founding fathers. The ERA will be the only piece of our nation's fundamental law that was *written by women* after suffrage, *adopted by women* leading the way in Congress, *given meaning by women* lawyers and judges, and *ratified by women* lawmakers in state legislatures of the twenty-first century. Opponents and onlookers have tried to stop these women at every turn. They made the ERA controversial by saying that it would be bad for mothers.

It is time to bury that myth as the ERA comes back to life.

Women are marching forward with a stronger, better vision of a twenty-first century ERA. The ERA matters, not only because of what it will do as law, but because of who is making it matter, and how they seek to improve democracy by making it law. American women have been challenging male abuses of power and changing the Constitution to make it respond to women's needs. They are overcoming the barriers built by legal precedents and political machines. The ERA is paving new legislative paths to women's empowerment—especially for mothers and mothers-to-be, whose needs have been left behind by the progress of gender equality.

The ongoing struggle for constitutional change seeks to address the gender inequalities that remain in the twenty-first century despite the major gains of the twentieth. The ERA returned to the political hopper on the heels of the Women's March and continued to gain support because of the #MeToo movement. From unequal pay to unequal power, women remain unequal because of their traditional role in childbearing and childrearing. Women are paid less than men, are more likely to lose their jobs when they have children, are targets of sexual abuse, and are less likely to hold positions of power because they are—or might become—mothers. *We the Women* shows how women made and remade the ERA over the generations as a response to the disadvantaging effects of motherhood. The next frontier of equal rights must remember its heroic mothers—the mothers of the Constitution and the mothers of the kids next door—who are often forgotten.

Virginia's ratification gave rise to an unprecedented situation in American constitutional history. For the first time, a constitutional amendment that has cleared both hurdles required by Article V of the Constitution—adoption by two-thirds of Congress and ratification by three-fourths of the states—was not officially added to the Constitution because of a congressionally imposed deadline. Congress has the power to lift this deadline. After the multigenerational struggle of the women who wrote, adopted, and ratified the Equal Rights Amendment, opponents' reliance on a deadline to abort these efforts is part of the problem that the ERA seeks to solve: the failure to respect women's work equally to that of men.

Part One, "Origins," explores how the Equal Rights Amendment began. Why did some women demand equal rights and why did others object? It introduces the women who launched the women's rights movement in America and then pursued a constitutional amendment to guarantee women's suffrage. From the pioneers at Seneca Falls in 1848 to the suffragists who testified before Congress for decades before the suffrage amendment was adopted and sent to the states for ratification, these brave women always saw their right to vote as only one of many rights that ought to be equal. After winning suffrage, some of these women introduced another constitutional amendment—the Equal Rights Amendment—to pursue this goal. Meanwhile, some suffragists focused on social reforms to improve the lives of mothers and their children and questioned the benefits of an ERA. Their intent was not to stop the fight for equal rights, but to postpone a constitutional amendment until a moment when American judges were ready to cooperate. Part One explains the thinking of the Pioneers, the Instigators, and the Reformers of the ERA.

Part Two, "Contestations," answers the questions of why and how women fought for the ERA in Congress in the 1970s. It focuses on the women who turned the tide for the ERA, making it a serious prospect for the nation. After World War II, the reformers who advocated for working mothers began to warm up to the idea of an ERA, especially key women of color who saw women's rights through the broader lenses of international cooperation and racial justice. Then, building on the civil rights movement, the first women of color elected to Congress advocated fiercely for the ERA and persuaded many bipartisan allies to fight the few congressmen who opposed the ERA. Nonetheless, this small minority of ERA opponents in Congress—including a known segregationist—convinced conservative women to crusade against ratification in a few battleground states. The STOP-ERA movement took off, warning that the ERA would destroy American motherhood. The ratification process stalled for forty years. Part Two tells the stories of the Globalizers, the Framers, the Mothers, and the Breadmakers.

Part Three, "Transformations," addresses the questions of what the ERA could do for women, and why it should never be too late to ratify it. It turns to the women lawyers who used the ERA to change the constitutional landscape they already inhabited. Women lawyers and judges imported the ERA's goals into their applications of the Fourteenth Amendment's Equal Protection Clause. These successes began to create the impression that the ERA was no longer needed. But the Fourteenth Amendment did not stretch far enough to address discrimination against pregnant women and mothers. The quest for ratification also exposed the undemocratic processes in state legislatures dominated by men. So women in Congress kept the ERA alive by extending the ratification deadline, resisting their colleagues' insistence that the game was over. Part Three explains the strategies and arguments of the Change Agents and the Game Changers.

Part Four, "Persistence," articulates the twenty-first century meaning of the ERA, through the women who gave it new life since 2017. With women elected to office in record numbers, state legislatures kept ratifying the ERA, even though opponents told them it was no longer necessary and also too late. In Nevada, Illinois, and Virginia, these women lawmakers saw the ERA as a new beginning to meet women's needs. The political and moral momentum of the ERA helped them introduce ambitious legislation to implement real equality for women. They saw their work not as revolutionary, but as continuing the work begun by the founding fathers—and mothers—who came before them. They tackled unequal pay, violence against women, unequal motherhood, and reproductive injustice. Part Four reveals the tribulations and triumphs of the Resurrectors, the Rectifiers, and the History Makers.

The ERA can improve women's lives in the twenty-first century, once it overcomes the remaining obstacles to its completion. *We the Women* excavates the ERA's past to guide its future.

PART I

ORIGINS

1
The Pioneers

REMEMBER THE LADIES.

That's what Abigail Adams wrote to her husband, John Adams, in a letter admonishing him during his trip to Philadelphia in the spring of 1776. John Adams went on to become the second president of the United States, and he was one of the fifty-six men attending the Second Continental Congress, a convening that would produce the Declaration of Independence, with his signature on it. Abigail knew that those men—colonists like her husband—were growing increasingly resentful of the king of England, whose laws denied them voice and representation. She understood that there would soon be a new constitution for a new nation. For this new code of laws, she wrote, "Do not put such unlimited power in the hands of the husbands." She channeled the revolutionary fervor that gripped her husband and the men who were about to declare this nation's independence from the tyranny of the king. "Remember, all men would be tyrants if they could," she warned. "If particular care and attention is not paid to the ladies, we are determined to foment a rebellion, and will not hold ourselves bound by any laws in which we have no voice or representation."[1]

We know what happened on July 4, 1776. The Declaration of Independence was signed by John Adams and fifty-five of his compatriots—the Founding Fathers of the United States of America. Its most famous line is still recited by children in civics classrooms across America over two centuries later: "We hold these truths to be self-evident, that all men are created equal."

The Founding Fathers did *not* remember the ladies.

When the new Constitution of the United States was adopted in 1789, it began:

> We the People of the United States, in Order to form a more perfect Union, establish Justice, insure domestic Tranquility, provide for the common defence, promote the general Welfare, and secure the Blessings of Liberty to ourselves and our Posterity, do ordain and establish this Constitution for the United States of America.

Were "We the Women" included in "We the People"? That Constitution was signed by thirty-nine men. The word "he" appeared twice, to refer to a representative elected to Congress and then to refer to the president. The word "she" never appeared. And the Founding Fathers made the Constitution very hard to change. Amendments required two-thirds of both houses of Congress and three-fourths of the states. The Constitution made the slave trade unamendable until 1808. The Founding Fathers made a Constitution that could not change unless an overwhelming consensus supported it—that is, an overwhelming consensus of those who could vote. Slaves could not vote, and the Constitution protected the slave trade, counting an enslaved African American as only three-fifths of a person. The Constitution did not mention women.

Or did it? The preamble said that "We the People" would secure the blessings of liberty to "our Posterity." Surely women would have to be involved to make these future generations of "We the People."[2] But the laws in place at that moment did not give women any rights. Women couldn't vote, or own property, or enter into contracts, or sue, or refuse to have sex with their husbands. Mothers did not have legal authority over their own children—only fathers were legal guardians. The legal system assumed that women would reproduce, and that they did not need rights because their husbands' rights would cover them.[3]

And the ladies fomented a rebellion.

Their rebellion was not a revolutionary war. Without guns or rights, it took the women a while. But the rebellion spanned across generations and made changes to American society that were even more revolutionary than the shift from king to Constitution. Changes that would make it possible, centuries later, for revolution-minded women like Abigail Adams to be in the Congress making the laws, rather than staying home with the children, raising our posterity for the blessings of liberty, while writing letters that could be forgotten.

A first major step of that rebellion was the Declaration of Sentiments, proclaimed in 1848 at the first Women's Rights Convention at Seneca Falls. Abigail Adams had been dead for thirty years by then. The Women's Rights Convention was the brainchild of Elizabeth Cady Stanton and Lucretia Mott, who had met at the World Antislavery Convention a few years before. Because they were women, they were excluded from participation in the proceedings of the abolitionist convention. So they began to organize together for women's rights.[4]

Elizabeth Cady Stanton was the daughter of a judge and the wife of a lawyer. Surrounded by legal minds, she developed one of her own and concluded that the laws would need to be rewritten to improve women's lives.[5] She started by rewriting the Declaration of Independence. Just as the Declaration had denounced the tyranny of England over the American colonies, her Declaration of Sentiments denounced the tyranny of man over woman. "We hold these truths to be self-evident: that all men and women are created equal," it declared. The Declaration of Sentiments presented a list of grievances about the law's exclusion of women from rights, such as the right to vote, the right to own property, the right to work, the right to be educated, and the right to raise one's own children. Sixty-eight women signed the Declaration of Sentiments at Seneca Falls on July 19, 1848. Thirty-two men signed, too.[6]

For Lucretia Mott, an equal partnership with men was important to the future of women's rights. Mott believed that beyond voting and rewriting the laws, women needed to be equal participants alongside men in all other aspects of society. She had grown up near Cape Cod, where women like her mother ran the stores while the men were out at sea.[7] Such equal participation by women in trade and commerce sustained the town's whaling economy. Lucretia Mott had equality in her bones—and by the age of twenty-eight, she became an ordained minister in the Quaker faith, one of the few that ordained women. After signing the Declaration of Sentiments, Lucretia Mott offered an additional resolution that was adopted by the convention's attendees, "for the securing to woman an equal participation with men in the various trades, professions, and commerce." The Lucretia Mott resolution at Seneca Falls was the seed that germinated, seventy-five years later, into the Equal Rights Amendment to the US Constitution.

More immediately, the convention at Seneca Falls launched the women's suffrage movement, which culminated in the ratification of the Nineteenth Amendment to the US Constitution in 1920. It took over seventy years following Seneca Falls to secure women's constitutional right to vote.[8] The goal of full equality of rights in other areas of life—property, work, education, and family—also born at Seneca Falls, was not even proposed as a constitutional amendment until after the success of suffrage in 1920. The Equal Rights Amendment then took almost a hundred additional years—until 2020—to get adopted and ratified by a sufficient number of states. The rebellions that Abigail Adams predicted took several generations of women to foment.

Lucretia Mott and Elizabeth Cady Stanton did not stop after Seneca Falls. They kept organizing, but Elizabeth Cady Stanton missed the 1850 Women's Rights Convention because she was pregnant. In 1851, Elizabeth Cady Stanton met Susan B. Anthony. While Elizabeth Cady Stanton was the intellectual—thinking and writing while raising small children at home—Susan B. Anthony was the activist. Susan B. Anthony chose not to marry or have children, devoting her time to organizing and traveling across the country to give speeches for women's equal rights.[9] They thought that women had a shot at legal equality when the Constitution was being amended after the Civil War. Ratified in 1868, the Fourteenth Amendment to the Constitution guaranteed "equal protection of the laws" to all "persons." But just as the Founding Fathers used the word "he" to refer to representatives in Congress and to presidents in 1789, the Fourteenth Amendment's drafters inserted the word "male" into the US Constitution for the first time, to describe the citizens who were entitled to vote. The words "he" and "male" remain in the text of the Constitution to this day—they have never been removed or replaced.[10]

If there was any uncertainty as to whether the Fourteenth Amendment made women equal in rights to men, the Supreme Court cleared things up in 1873 by saying "No." The Supreme Court upheld the state of Illinois's decision to deny Myra Bradwell a license to practice law on the grounds that she was a married woman.[11] Mrs. Bradwell had studied law and passed the bar exam, and had hoped that the Fourteenth Amendment would prevent Illinois from excluding her from the legal profession. The Supreme Court said that admission to the bar of a state was not a privilege or immunity of citizenship protected by the Fourteenth Amendment.

One justice wrote the concurring opinion that reveals what those men on the Supreme Court were thinking: "Man is, or should be, woman's protector and defender. The natural and proper timidity and delicacy which belongs to the female sex evidently unfits it for many of the occupations of civil life."[12] They were also worried about what would happen to family life in the home if women had the same rights as men. "The constitution of the family organization, which is founded in the divine ordinance, as well as in the nature of things, indicates the domestic sphere which properly belongs to the domain and functions of woman-hood."[13] For nearly one hundred years, the Supreme Court continued to say that the Fourteenth Amendment allowed discrimination against women.

The constitutional amendment guaranteeing women the right to vote was first introduced in Congress in 1878, thirty years after Seneca Falls. By then, Elizabeth Cady Stanton's seven children had grown to adulthood, so she was more available to travel to give suffrage speeches. Testifying at Congress's first hearing on the constitutional amendment for women's suffrage, Stanton scrutinized the Constitution's preamble, just as she had done with the Declaration of Independence thirty years before. "We the people," she began, reading another sentence that generations of American children recite in their classrooms year after year. Then Cady Stanton asked, "Does anyone pretend to say that men alone constitute races and peoples? When we say parents, do we not mean mothers as well as fathers? When we say children, do we not mean girls as well as boys? When we say people, do we not mean women as well as men?"[14] Many laws in place at the time answered "No." The grievances in the Declaration of Sentiments, which she had written as a young woman, remained unresolved.

In 1880, Susan B. Anthony testified before Congress at another hearing on the suffrage amendment. She pointed out that women had been asking men for "equality of rights" for "the other half of the people" for thirty years.[15] A generation had gone by since Seneca Falls. During those years, she had tried to get women included in the Fourteenth Amendment, without success. When the Fifteenth Amendment established the right of citizens to vote regardless of race, she opposed it because it did not include women.[16] Then, she showed up to the polls and voted anyway, and was arrested and fined.[17] She wanted to believe that the Constitution's promise of freedom provided "me and all women the enjoyment of perfect equality of rights everywhere under the shadow of the American flag," but thirty years of experience had proven her wrong. That's why it was time to "make more Constitution."[18]

Lucretia Mott died later that year. By the time the suffrage amendment was adopted by Congress and ratified in 1920, Susan B. Anthony and Elizabeth Cady Stanton were also gone. If Susan B. Anthony had lived fourteen more years, she would have turned 100 when the Susan B. Anthony Amendment—as the suffrage amendment was called—became law.

Why did it take so long?

Women got the right to vote by persuading men to give it to them. It took time for men to agree to share their power. Like the revolutionary men who declared our nation's independence from Britain in 1776, American women rejected "taxation without representation." But instead of resorting to a violent war against the tyrannous regime, women resisted male tyranny by playing by the rules of peaceful change, namely Article V of the Constitution, which lays out the rule for constitutional amendments. Following Article V meant persuading two-thirds of both houses of Congress—elected mostly by men, since women could only vote in fifteen states by 1919 (which was why they wanted a constitutional amendment)—and three-fourths of state legislatures—also elected mostly by men, for the same reason.

It was an uphill battle. The suffrage amendment was introduced many times in Congress for several decades before it was finally adopted by two-thirds of both houses of Congress. Although the Senate Committee on Privileges and Elections held a hearing on the proposed suffrage amendment in 1878, it was not brought to a vote. The Senate formed a Woman Suffrage Committee in 1882, and more hearings ensued for over thirty years.

From 1887 to 1919, the full Senate debated and voted on the suffrage amendment five times before it garnered the two-thirds majority required by Article V. In all but one instance, the suffrage amendment got a majority of the men voting, but less than two-thirds. In the last two attempts before its successful adoption on June 4, 1919, the suffrage amendment fell two votes short of two-thirds on October 1, 1918, and one vote short on February 10, 1919.[19]

It was not easy for women to get the right to vote without the right to vote.

In the House, the proposed suffrage amendment faced other barriers. Then, as now, the Judiciary Committee held the power to decide whether any constitutional proposal gets considered. The Judiciary Committee was hostile to women's suffrage, so the chances of getting the bill out of that committee to the floor of the House for a vote were slim. John E. Raker, a pro-suffrage congressman from California, proposed the creation of a new committee on Woman Suffrage. Only then could the suffrage bill get out of committee and be heard by more elected representatives. A leading voice that made this maneuver possible was that of Congresswoman Jeannette Rankin, the first woman ever elected to Congress. She was elected from Montana, where women could vote under state law since 1914, largely owing to her efforts as a suffragist. Once the Woman Suffrage Committee was formed by a majority vote of the House of Representatives, it opened the first week of 1918 with hearings on the suffrage amendment.[20]

But there were no women in the United States Congress in 1919 when it adopted the Nineteenth Amendment. Jeannette Rankin was the only congresswoman who ever voted on the constitutional amendment for women's suffrage, but her vote was cast in the House in the year that the suffrage amendment fell one vote short in the Senate. In 1919, the year that the Nineteenth Amendment finally won two-thirds of both the House and the Senate, Jeannette Rankin had lost her seat in the House while making an unsuccessful bid for the Senate. So it was an all-male Congress that took that necessary step for the Nineteenth Amendment.

That necessary step happened because a new generation of women continued the work started by Lucretia Mott, Elizabeth Cady Stanton, and Susan B. Anthony. Carrie Chapman Catt succeeded Susan B. Anthony as president of the National American Women's Suffrage Association. Catt was a great political strategist who got involved in both state and international women's suffrage movements. Not all suffragists supported America's entry into World War I, but Catt did.[21]

The two-thirds vote in each house of Congress came within reach because of World War I. In January 1918, Catt testified before the House Committee on Woman Suffrage, pressing the same argument that Elizabeth Cady Stanton had made forty years earlier. "We women utterly refuse to recognize that the men of this country are the people of this country," she declared. "Men and women together are people. And when a question is submitted to men alone, it may be constitutionally and legally adopted, but it is not adopted by a democratic process."[22] The argument was the same, but World War I gave it a new significance. Women's suffrage was not only about women; it was about the future of modern American democracy. The nation was fighting to make the world safe for democracy. What credibility would it have if it continued to deny the vote to half its citizens? With the men fighting in the front lines abroad, the war required women to do some of men's work in industry on the home front. Suffragists argued that if the government needed women's contributions to win the war, women would need to win the vote to contribute to government, if it was still a democracy.

The devastation caused by World War I transformed the stakes of women's suffrage. Anna Howard Shaw, a suffrage leader who was mentored by Susan B. Anthony at the turn of the century, told Congress in 1918 that once the war was over, "many women of this country will be both father and mother to fatherless children, and these women and their children will have no representatives in this Government, unless they are represented through the mothers who have given everything that the Government might be saved and democracy might be secured."[23] Shaw, like Susan B. Anthony, did not live to witness the success of her efforts. At the age of seventy-two, in the summer of 1919, the punishing schedule of travel for suffrage speeches was too much; she developed a fatal case of pneumonia just as Congress sent the Nineteenth Amendment to the states for ratification.

Nevertheless, Shaw drew attention to one of the most compelling arguments for women's rights: support for mothers. The

Nineteenth Amendment owes its ratification to the persuasive force of motherhood. After fiercely contested battles in many states, the Nineteenth Amendment was finally ratified in August 1920 because Tennessee delivered the final ratification needed to make three-fourths of the states. Opponents of suffrage in the Tennessee House of Representatives had postponed consideration of the ratification bill many times before it finally went up for a floor vote. On the floor, the ratification of the suffrage amendment in Tennessee came down to one vote.

That vote was for a mother. Harry Burn, the youngest person ever elected to the Tennessee legislature at the age of twenty-four, betrayed his anti-suffrage allies at the last minute and voted for suffrage. His mother had written him a letter saying, "I have been watching to see how you stood, but have noticed nothing yet. Don't forget to be a good boy and help Mrs. Catt put 'Rat' in Ratification!"[24] When it came down to it, Harry Burn said "aye" to votes for women.

As for Mrs. Catt, the journey to the "Rat" in Ratification had to overcome major obstacles. One of them was a poison pill that she vehemently rejected: a proposal to put a seven-year time limit on the ratification of the suffrage amendment. The idea came from the Eighteenth Amendment, prohibiting the manufacture and sale of alcoholic beverages throughout the United States, which had just been adopted and sent to the states for ratification in 1917. Prohibition was the first amendment in our Constitution's history that had a seven-year deadline on ratification. Opponents of suffrage tried to put the same time limit on the suffrage amendment.

Picking up on the highly contested debates over the Prohibition amendment, Catt testified in Congress that the seven-year time limit was unconstitutional and therefore rejected its validity for the suffrage amendment. It was "two amendments bound up in one" and not acceptable.[25] Catt compared the American amendment process to the constitutional change unfolding in other countries. The suffrage struggle had been going on throughout the world for fifty years, with some countries coming out ahead of the United

States because "our country seems more averse to changing its Constitution than many regarded as more conservative."[26]

Catt was referring to the cumbersome requirements of amending the Constitution in accordance with Article V. She believed that a ratification deadline would be unconstitutional, because deadlines put further barriers on constitutional change than those already cumbersome barriers explicitly stipulated by Article V. A deadline was "two amendments in one" because it altered the amendment procedure required by Article V. A deadline would make the Constitution even harder to change than it already was, rendering it impossible for those excluded from equal rights to seek inclusion.

Although the ratification time limit had prevailed with regard to the Prohibition amendment, it did not prevail when proposed with regard to suffrage the very next month. On January 10, 1918, within a week of Catt's remarks about the seven-year time limit in the House committee hearing, the suffrage amendment was debated on the House floor. A suffrage opponent proposed that the exact same deadline language from the Prohibition Amendment be copied into the suffrage amendment. He made clear that, with or without the deadline, he would not be voting for women's suffrage.[27]

But Congressman Burton French of Idaho—a state where women had been voting since 1896—objected to putting a deadline on women's suffrage. "[I]t may prolong the fight looking to the granting of suffrage," he warned. Some state legislatures had arcane rules that could slow down their efforts to ratify women's suffrage.[28] Many states imposed waiting requirements on failed ratifications of constitutional amendments. If a ratification vote on a federal constitutional amendment failed once, some states had rules that prevented those amendments from being reintroduced for a ratification vote for several years thereafter.[29] Many states also had constitutional provisions excluding women from the right to vote. With women not voting, and with mandatory waiting periods for the reintroduction of ratification bills, the poisonous potential of a seven-year deadline on women's suffrage was clear.

Such a poisonous deadline was not added to the Nineteenth Amendment. Many of the congressmen who voted for the deadline then voted against the women's suffrage amendment a few moments later. Proposing the deadline was just another attempt to stop women from voting. Nonetheless, the House adopted the Nineteenth Amendment by a vote of 274–136 that day. Because the Senate vote in 1918 fell two votes short of the two-thirds majority required by Article V, the Nineteenth Amendment did not go to the states for ratification that year. However, the issue of whether to impose a ratification deadline was rejected and settled in 1918. Although the deadline was raised on the House floor in May 1919 before the House adopted the suffrage amendment again, there was no debate and it was rejected without comment.

The Senate finally adopted the Nineteenth Amendment on June 4, 1919, and sent it to the states for ratification. If Tennessee legislator Harry Burn had disregarded his mother's advice in August 1920, it is possible that the Nineteenth Amendment would have stalled for another generation. And that would bring us back to Abigail Adams's warning with which we began: Women forgotten by the law will foment a rebellion until they get voice and representation in lawmaking. Even if it takes generations. After suffrage was won, Carrie Chapman Catt wrote, "It was a continuous, seemingly endless, chain of activity. Young suffragists who helped forge the last links of that chain were not born when it began. Old suffragists who forged the first links were dead when it ended."[30] By the time women's suffrage was secured in the United States, twenty-six other countries had achieved it already.

With Tennessee's ratification of the Nineteenth Amendment in 1920, women won the right to vote at last. But this victory did not end the fight for women's constitutional rights.

2
The Instigators

ON AUGUST 18, 1920, TENNESSEE became the final state needed to
ratify the Nineteenth Amendment, giving every American woman
the right to vote. That day, Alice Paul unfurled a celebratory flag
with thirty-six stars, one for each ratified state, from the balcony
of the National Woman's Party headquarters in Washington, DC.

Alice Paul founded the National Woman's Party—the organization that introduced parades, protests, prison time, hunger
strikes, and confrontations with the president to the quest for
women's suffrage. Schooled in the militant tactics of the British
suffragettes, Alice Paul and her allies got impatient with the older
generation of suffragists like Carrie Chapman Catt, who had inher-
ited the National American Woman's Suffrage Association from
Susan B. Anthony. They had been struggling for women's right to
vote for generations. Alice Paul did not want to wait any longer. She
masterminded the attention-grabbing suffrage parade on the eve of
Woodrow Wilson's inauguration in 1913, down to the detail of
selecting the strikingly beautiful suffragist lawyer Inez Milholland
to lead the procession on a white horse. Then, she started her own
party to organize the "Silent Sentinels"—suffrage activists who

silently picketed the White House all day, six days a week, in 1917. These protests led to the arrests of suffragists for obstructing traffic. Alice Paul went to jail herself and went on a hunger strike for the suffrage cause. Her extreme tactics and single-minded focus brought a dramatic sense of urgency to the push for the Nineteenth Amendment.[1]

As each state ratified the amendment, Alice Paul sewed a star onto the National Woman's Party flag herself. For a woman who endured force feedings for suffrage, Tennessee's thirty-sixth ratification star marked a victory at the end of a hard-won fight that was personal as well as political. In a photo of Alice Paul, seated and staring intensely at the star that she is sewing on the party's flag, suffragist lawyer and co-conspirator Crystal Eastman is watching Alice Paul with a smile, standing to her left, head moving forward.[2]

"Now at last we can begin," Crystal Eastman wrote, shortly after the Nineteenth Amendment was ratified.[3] Crystal Eastman and Alice Paul began writing the Equal Rights Amendment to the US Constitution after the Nineteenth Amendment took effect.[4] Eastman was part of the Feminist Alliance,[5] a Greenwich Village group that instigated the proto-Equal Rights Amendment in 1914. The Feminist Alliance wrote a letter to President Woodrow Wilson urging a constitutional amendment to prohibit sex discrimination in all civil and political rights,[6] even before the suffrage amendment was adopted. In 1920, armed with the constitutional right to vote, women could now pursue what they were really after: freedom.

Crystal Eastman was a brilliant graduate of NYU Law School—second in the class of 1907—during an era when very few women became lawyers. Complementing Alice Paul's relentless drive to pursue a goal and get things done, Crystal Eastman brought intellectual depth, the experience of lawyering in the industrial workplace, and the personal juggle of marriage and motherhood to the post-suffrage women's rights agenda. The year that women got the vote, Eastman helped found the National Civil Liberties Bureau, an organization that defended a broad range of constitutional rights and later became the American Civil Liberties Union (ACLU).[7]

With Crystal Eastman's imprint as a drafter, the ERA was part of a comprehensive revolutionary vision of real freedom for women.

For Eastman, the next steps for women after suffrage would be choice in occupation and economic independence. How would they achieve them? By breaking down all remaining barriers, actual and legal, to women's full participation in various professions. "It must be womanly as well as manly to earn your own living, to stand on your own feet," Eastman explained. And this was not going to happen simply by opening up these professions to women. Men would have to change, too: "And it must be manly as well as womanly to know how to cook and sew and clean and take care of yourself in the ordinary exigencies of life."[8]

The Equal Rights Amendment, like the suffrage amendment, was a necessary component of this broader equality agenda. Crystal Eastman explained in 1924 in *The New Republic* that the ERA would accomplish three things. First, it would sweep away any common-law precedents that made women dependent on and inferior to men. Second, it would be a bill of rights against sex discrimination; for instance, a woman teacher would have the right not to be fired from her job upon marriage. Third, it would mean that industrial legislation could not treat women workers as children or minors. Eastman clarified that "[g]enuinely protective legislation would probably be extended to include men and thus all element of tyranny removed from it."[9] Many states enforced laws preventing women from performing certain jobs, serving on juries, owning their own earnings, or exercising equal parental authority over their own children. The Equal Rights Amendment would establish women's status as equal citizens. It would permanently inscribe that status into the Constitution.

World War I made women's increased participation in the economy necessary. As Anna Howard Shaw predicted in her testimony about suffrage, the war produced thousands of widows who were left to scramble for a living, having to take up the dual roles of father and mother to their children overnight. In addition to the ERA, Crystal Eastman identified four major components of women's pursuit of freedom after suffrage: (1) equal pay; (2) an equal education of boys and girls toward liberation from traditional gender roles; (3) voluntary motherhood, including access to birth control; and (4) a "motherhood endowment"—in other words, paid maternity leave.

Seventy-five years after the women at Seneca Falls declared that "all men and women are created equal," the Equal Rights Amendment was first introduced in Congress in December 1923 by Representative Daniel R. Anthony Jr., who happened to be Susan B. Anthony's nephew. The proposed constitutional amendment read, "Men and women shall have equal rights throughout the United States and every place subject to its jurisdiction. Congress shall have the power to enforce this article by appropriate legislation."[10] Just as the suffrage amendment was known as the "Susan B. Anthony Amendment" to honor her legacy, the Equal Rights Amendment was called the "Lucretia Mott Amendment" to take up Lucretia Mott's resolution at Seneca Falls in 1848. That resolution sought to make women equal participants with men in "the trades, professions, and commerce."

In Congress, the first hearings on the ERA were held by the House Judiciary Committee in 1925. Crystal Eastman's ideas made their way into the testimony of Mary Murray, a war widow and mother of five who had become a transit worker. "We working women, because we are mothers, potential and actual, say it makes it all the more imperative we be free to have the same chance as men to earn a good wage, to give opportunity to our children to get food, a good education, and a good environment."[11] A constitutional amendment would get rid of all the laws that held working mothers back from the work and resources they needed to support and raise their children.

But by the time the ERA was being heard in Congress, Crystal Eastman was living in England. She was married to an Englishman. Under federal law at the time, a female citizen would lose her US citizenship upon marrying a foreigner, even though a male citizen retained his US citizenship if he married a foreigner. Crystal

Eastman moved to London to join her husband, along with their six-year-old son and one-year-old daughter, in 1922.[12] Days later, Congress changed the Citizenship and Nationality Law to enable women who married foreigners to retain their citizenship, just like men who married foreigners.[13] But there remained many other laws that discriminated against women and hindered them from living as equal citizens. By 1923, Alice Paul and the National Woman's Party made the Equal Rights Amendment their single-minded focus. It was a blanket solution to all these discriminations.

With Crystal Eastman overseas, Burnita Matthews provided the legal brains behind the ERA in Congress, testifying on behalf of the National Woman's Party at nearly all the hearings of the 1920s and early 1930s. Matthews later became the first woman appointed to a federal district court judgeship, in 1949.[14] Matthews was from Mississippi and had spent her childhood accompanying her father to the local court, where he was the clerk. Her father sent her brother to law school, while sending her to music school so that she could make a living as a piano teacher.[15] When World War I sent men into combat, she took the opportunity to look for a civil service job in Washington, DC.[16] There, she enrolled in law school and picketed the White House for women's suffrage with Alice Paul. She joined the National Woman's Party and eventually became its chief lawyer.

In the 1925 ERA hearings, Burnita Matthews questioned the idea that fathers should have greater parental rights than mothers over their children because fathers supported the children economically. Matthews said that "the mother's service to the child is worth just as much as the support of the father." Matthews was talking about the service mothers provided—uncompensated—in raising children within the family. And she pointed out the hypocrisy of a system that did not recognize that service, but nonetheless held women liable for child support. That was the law in many states at the time. Furthermore, in some states, married women did not own the money they earned if they worked for pay. The law made those earnings the husband's property. An ERA would entitle women to own their own earnings, and this would enable a mother to care for her own children if she could spend her own earnings as she saw fit.[17]

In the 1920s congressional hearings, the National Woman's Party pointed to the worldwide spread of constitutional sex equality, as evidenced by European constitutions, as an argument for the Equal Rights Amendment. Equal rights for women were in seven new constitutions adopted after World War I.[18] This point was made several times in congressional hearings throughout the 1920s and 1930s, supported by a leaflet citing the constitutions of Germany, Lithuania, Estonia, and Austria.[19]

The National Woman's Party sought an ERA to ensure that women would not be excluded from the good jobs and schools that were essential to their livelihood. They also wanted the ERA to give mothers the same authority over their own children as fathers. But the question arose as to whether the ERA would require law to treat men and women the same in all situations. What about laws that guaranteed minimum wages for women, or required safe working conditions tailored to their capacity to bear children? Women who worked in factories, often because they were poor and needed the income, relied on these laws to protect their means of survival. A "blanket" amendment by definition would cover everything, wouldn't it?

With Crystal Eastman away in England, the National Woman's Party struggled with the question of whether the ERA would strike down industrial legislation that protected women workers from unhealthy working conditions or exploitation.[20] Many states had laws that required hours, conditions, and minimum wages for work that applied only to women workers. In New York, for instance, a 1912 law limited women's hours in factories to nine a day and fifty a week. In 1913, a new law in New York prohibited women from working at night. These laws grew out of massive strikes protesting overwork and unsafe working conditions. In New York, 146 women workers died in the Triangle Shirtwaist Factory fire of 1911, where unsafe working conditions led to a fire while overworked women workers were locked into the building by the employer, thus prevented from easily evacuating once the fire began.[21] By 1917, at least twenty states had laws imposing a maximum number of hours of work that employers could require of women workers. Several states also required employers to pay minimum wages to women, set by the state's minimum wage commission.[22]

These laws covered women only, because the US Supreme Court had routinely struck down laws that covered working men since 1905. In *Lochner v. New York*, the Supreme Court struck down a New York state law that limited the working hours of (male) bakers, holding that the Fourteenth Amendment entitled workers and employers to decide for themselves—exercising the freedom of contract—how long to work.[23] That decision is among the most infamous decisions of the Supreme Court, known to American law students today as belonging to a canon of wrongly decided cases like *Dred Scott v. Sandford*, which legitimized slavery, and *Plessy v. Ferguson*, which legitimized racial segregation.[24] *Lochner* legitimized the employer's ability to demand anything of employees without state intervention. The *Lochner* era ended with the New Deal in the 1930s, when a new generation of Supreme Court justices switched course and upheld laws that protected workers from the demands of corporations, laws that required minimum wages, maximum hours, and overtime pay.[25]

Nonetheless, while *Lochner* was the law of the land, advocates for workers' rights tried to get around it by enacting laws that protected women only. *Muller v. Oregon*, decided in 1908, upheld an Oregon law that punished employers when they made women work more than ten hours a day in mechanical establishments, factories, or laundries. Curt Muller, the owner and operator of a Portland laundry, brought a constitutional challenge to the law after he was convicted and fined $10 for requiring a female employee to work more than ten hours in a day. The US Supreme Court acknowledged *Lochner*, which protected the working man's freedom of contract against laws limiting men's hours of work. But in *Muller*, the Supreme Court noted that *Lochner* did not require the same approach to women's work. Women did not even have the vote, let alone any other legal rights, so the court concluded that women were vulnerable and therefore should be protected by law from exploitation, especially forms of exploitation that harmed women's reproductive health as mothers.

In *Muller*, the Supreme Court said: "That a woman's physical structure and the performance of maternal functions, place her at a disadvantage in the struggle for subsistence is obvious. This is especially true when the burdens of motherhood are upon her."[26] Because women had always been dependent on men, the court concluded that "some legislation to protect her seems necessary to secure a *real equality of right*."[27] That meant that laws entitling women workers to shorter hours of work and guaranteeing minimum wages were allowed, but such laws could not apply to men, who were considered strong enough to fend for themselves.

This changed after the Nineteenth Amendment went into effect. In 1923, the Supreme Court ended *Muller v. Oregon*'s exceptional protection of women workers, and struck down a District of Columbia law requiring minimum wages for women workers. The case of *Adkins v. Children's Hospital* held that the women's minimum wage law violated the Fifth Amendment, and recognized women's freedom of contract. The court cited the newly ratified Nineteenth Amendment to suggest that women now enjoyed equal status to men and therefore no longer needed any special labor protections. "In view of the great—not to say revolutionary—changes which have taken place . . . in the contractual, political, and civil status of women, culminating in the Nineteenth Amendment, it is not unreasonable to say that these differences have now come almost, if not quite, to the vanishing point."[28]

The *Adkins* decision positioned the Nineteenth Amendment in opposition to labor protections for women in industry. The Supreme Court applied *Lochner* equally to women in industry, leaning on the newly ratified women's suffrage amendment. The court described *Muller v. Oregon* as manifesting an "ancient inequality of the sexes" that "has continued 'with diminishing intensity,'" suggesting that women's vulnerability to exploitation was primarily in the past. But the real consequence of the *Adkins* decision for ordinary working mothers was that their wages plummeted. Before *Adkins*, the minimum wage was $16.50 a week. Women made $8.00 a week after *Adkins*, without the protection of a minimum wage law.[29]

Alice Paul was a consultant to the lawyers who represented the employer, Children's Hospital, in the *Adkins* case. She helped the employers' lawyers link equal rights for women to the liberty of contract pronounced by *Lochner*. Justice George Sutherland, the author of the Supreme Court's 5–3 decision in *Adkins*, had advised Alice Paul on the drafting of the Equal Rights Amendment before being nominated to the Supreme Court.[30] The Equal Rights Amendment was introduced in Congress eight months after the *Adkins* decision. The supporters of the ERA had to explain whether the ERA would destroy special protections for working mothers, and if so, why.

At the ERA hearings in Congress, Burnita Matthews presented the National Woman's Party position—that laws requiring hours, conditions, and minimum wages for women actually prevented women from securing employment and promotion.[31] The logic behind this was that if an employer was not free to extract unlimited hours of work from women at whatever wage they would agree to, but was free to do so with regard to working men, the employer would never hire any women. Women would then be worse off than they would have been without those minimum wage and maximum hour laws—they would lose all opportunity to men. Based on this logic, Alice Paul and the National Woman's Party believed that laws that offered special protections to women workers should be struck down by the ERA.[32]

Crystal Eastman had a different answer. "The Equal Rights Amendment would not affect existing labor legislation," she insisted, "except to establish the principle that industrial legislation should apply to all workers, both men and women, in any given occupation and not to women workers alone."[33] She was actually an expert on industrial legislation, having played a leading role in writing New York's first workers' compensation law. She had written a trailblazing book on the subject.[34] Eastman believed that the ERA would not strike down minimum wages for women, for instance—it would require minimum wages for women and men alike. Her view must have informed the drafting of the ERA.

In the 1925 hearing, Burnita Matthews acknowledged that one way of respecting equal rights would be for the laws to include men in the protections reserved for women workers. At the same time, she cited *Adkins v. Children's Hospital* with approval. Between two radically different ways of getting to equality—*Adkins'* abolition of labor protections for both sexes, or Eastman's expansion of labor protections to include both sexes—the National Woman's Party said that both would be acceptable under the ERA. Although Crystal Eastman returned to the United States in 1927, she died at the age of forty-six of kidney failure before the Senate Judiciary Committee's ERA hearings in 1929. Throughout the 1920s and 1930s, Matthews repeated the National Woman's Party position—that the ERA could strike down labor protections for women.

This was not a popular position with women. There was only one woman in Congress when the ERA was introduced. Mae Nolan succeeded her husband, a California representative in the House of Representatives who died in office in 1922. Although Mae Nolan was assigned to the Woman Suffrage Committee when she first took office, she had the opportunity to chair the Committee on Expenditures in the Post Office, becoming the first woman to chair any congressional committee. Nolan cited her new leadership responsibilities as a reason to resign from the Woman Suffrage Committee and to avoid involvement with the ERA. Nolan's constituents included labor groups that were concerned about the ERA's potential to strike down labor protections for women. Although she was the only woman in Congress, she insisted publicly that there was no need for a congresswoman to focus on women's issues. "A capable woman is a better representative than an incapable man, and vice versa," Nolan said. "After all, the chief responsibility in legislative matters rests with the electorate. If it is alert, informed, and insistent, it will get good representation in Washington from either a man or a woman Member of Congress."[35]

By contrast, throughout her career, Burnita Matthews never questioned the validity of favoring capable women, even though she advocated for an ERA that could strike down special protections for women. Many years later, she reflected on her decades-long career as a federal judge and bragged that she always hired women as her law clerks. "[W]hen a woman makes good at something, they always say that some man did it," she noted. "So I just thought it would be better to have women. I wanted to show my confidence in women."[36]

The Equal Rights Amendment was instigated by women, written by women, and justified by women after they got the constitutional right to vote. It is the only amendment that has been ratified by thirty-eight states about which this can be said. Every other amendment to the Constitution was made by men. It's about time we have female authors of the supreme law of the United States of America.

3
The Reformers

FOR SOME OF THE WOMEN who worked to get the Nineteenth Amendment added to the Constitution, the Supreme Court's citation of a women's suffrage amendment to strike down the minimum wage law for working women was outrageous. Social reformer Florence Kelley described *Adkins v. Children's Hospital* as the case that protected "the inalienable constitutional right of American women to starve."[1]

By overruling the precedent of *Muller v. Oregon*, the Supreme Court was throwing cold water at three decades of Florence Kelley's work for working women. Kelley was a suffragist who had spent her career helping women working in factories for low wages. Her awareness of working women's issues grew out of her years as a sociology graduate student in Europe, where she went because American universities were not awarding PhDs to women.[2] In the 1890s, she became Chicago's first chief factory inspector, a job that enabled her to see the conditions that these women endured. This experience moved her to campaign for an eight-hour workday and a minimum wage, which she believed essential to working mothers' survival. She went on to become the head of the National

Consumers' League, an organization devoted to protecting workers through the political pressure of organized consumer action.[3]

Florence Kelley was the invisible force behind the Supreme Court's 1908 decision in *Muller v. Oregon* to uphold maximum hours laws for women. The Supreme Court's opinion in that case relied heavily on the brief for the state of Oregon, which Florence Kelley had hired the prominent lawyer Louis Brandeis to write. The "Brandeis Brief," as it came to be known, was actually drafted by Brandeis's niece, Josephine Goldmark, who worked for Florence Kelley at the National Consumers' League.[4] Louis Brandeis went on to become a Supreme Court justice, and the Brandeis Brief went on to become an exemplar of sociological jurisprudence, a method of legal argument that relies on social facts, evidenced by scientific data.[5]

While working on the suffrage campaign, Kelley had simultaneously lobbied to get a DC minimum wage law enacted—the very law that the Supreme Court struck down in *Adkins*. For someone who had spent her career trying to improve the lives of disadvantaged women, the *Adkins* decision was a perversion of the Fifth, Fourteenth, and Nineteenth Amendments by the men on the Supreme Court. Kelley opposed the "so-called Equal Rights Amendment," suspecting that judges would interpret it to attack more of her life's work.

Florence Kelley was not alone.[6] Most women's organizations opposed the ERA when it was first introduced. The National Woman's Party was the only women's organization that supported the Equal Rights Amendment in 1923. After the Nineteenth Amendment went into effect, women's organizations that had fought for suffrage now focused on other issues. The National American Woman's Suffrage Association became the National League of Women Voters. Florence Kelley's organization, the National Consumers' League, joined with many of these former suffrage groups to focus on the needs of women beyond the vote. They formed the Women's Joint Congressional Committee (WJCC) to draw Congress's attention to women's issues in Washington, and to advocate for public policies that would respond to women's needs.

While the National Woman's Party was drafting the Equal Rights Amendment as the next step after suffrage, the WJCC focused immediately on the problem of maternal mortality. Some 23,000 mothers had died in 1918; more than 250,000 infants died each year. In a multinational study of twenty comparable industrialized nations, the United States ranked seventeenth for maternal mortality and eleventh for infant mortality. In families living in poverty, one baby in six died within the first year. Eighty percent of pregnant women received no advice or trained care.[7]

Florence Kelley chaired the subcommittee of the WJCC focused on maternal and infant health. She succeeded at building coalitions and bipartisan support. The Sheppard-Towner Maternity and Infancy Protection Act was adopted in November 1921, a little over a year after the Nineteenth Amendment was ratified. Senator Morris Sheppard was a Democrat from Texas who had also sponsored the bill that became the Prohibition Amendment to the US Constitution, prohibiting the manufacture and sale of intoxicating beverages, for which the Woman's Christian Temperance Union—the largest women's political organization in America—had advocated for decades.[8] Sheppard was a vocal supporter of organized labor and was known to link the interests of wage earners to the national interests of the United States more broadly. The other sponsor, Horace Mann Towner, was a Republican congressman from Iowa. The Sheppard-Towner Act provided funding to state governments to reduce maternal and infant mortality. After the vote, the Sheppard-Towner Act was the first success of women's political organizing. It provided pregnant women with reproductive healthcare to increase the chances of survival, both for mothers-to-be and for their gestating babies.

When it came to the health of mothers and babies, a broader coalition of women contributed their efforts and support, beyond those who led the drive for suffrage. The fact that nearly every women's organization supported the bill was noted by the members of Congress who adopted it.[9] The WJCC approached every member of the Senate and most of the members of the House of

Representatives. They worked not only with the suffrage organizations on the campaign, but also with the National Congress of Mothers and Parent-Teacher Associations and the Woman's Christian Temperance Union.

The Sheppard-Towner Act drew so many votes in Congress that it could have been a constitutional amendment. Only seven members of the Senate and thirty-nine members of the House voted against it. Even several congressmen who had spoken against the bill in floor debates ended up voting for it in the end. In a strange twist, the only woman in Congress, Representative Alice Robertson of Oklahoma, a Republican who had opposed woman's suffrage, voted against the maternity bill. President Warren Harding signed the Sheppard-Towner Maternity and Infancy Act into law on November 23, 1921,[10] recognizing the political force of the women's suffrage amendment.

The Sheppard-Towner Act led to the creation of 3,000 child and maternal health centers throughout the country, by way of federal grants to the states. These centers were staffed by public health nurses and midwives who educated women about prenatal and infant care. Sheppard-Towner was federal legislation that pursued a substantive policy goal—reducing maternal and infant mortality—which required the appropriation of federal funds and collaboration between the federal and state government. The policy goal was implemented by state and local government agencies, not by federal judges.

Despite the broad political coalition that initially supported it, the Sheppard-Towner Act was short-lived. It was only in effect from 1922 to 1929. Opponents attempted to kill it through litigation. Harriet Frothingham, a member of the National Association Opposed to Women's Suffrage (NAOWS), brought a lawsuit arguing that the federal program to reduce maternal and infant mortality violated states' rights and therefore was contrary to the Tenth Amendment of the US Constitution.[11] The Tenth Amendment simply states: "The Powers not delegated to the United States by the Constitution, nor prohibited by it to the States, are reserved to the States respectively, or to the people." The Supreme Court eventually dismissed Frothingham's case in June 1923, holding that it did not have jurisdiction. But the lawsuit emboldened others to attack the protection of mothers and babies. The American Medical Association opposed Sheppard-Towner, claiming that it was the first step towards socialized medicine.[12] The post-suffrage momentum around reducing maternal mortality died down. In 1926, Congress agreed to renew Sheppard-Towner for a few years, but mandated that the law would expire in 1929.

When the ERA was introduced in 1923, one question that arose was whether it would allow special benefits for mothers, including those provided by the Sheppard-Towner Act. Crystal Eastman had written in 1920 that women's equality after suffrage should include a "motherhood endowment." Burnita Matthews, speaking for the National Woman's Party, argued in ERA hearings before Congress that the Equal Rights Amendment was perfectly compatible with the Sheppard-Towner Act. Her reasoning was that Sheppard-Towner benefited boy babies as well as girl babies, and therefore treated the sexes equally.[13] Nonetheless, Florence Kelley accused the National Woman's Party of complicity with the opponents of Sheppard-Towner.

Kelley believed that women's economically subordinate status, stemming largely from their biological and social function as mothers, made them susceptible to exploitation and abuse at the hands of employers. For Kelley, both the Sheppard-Towner Act and minimum wage legislation were public policies that made up for the particular difficulties women faced because of their biological role as mothers. Women were vulnerable to exploitation not only because of biology, but also because they lacked the political power that would come with the right to vote. They were generally not represented by unions that could bargain for better wages and working conditions. Kelley believed that the elected officials had an obligation to adopt laws protecting those who were excluded by law from the means of protecting themselves.[14] In many states, the legislatures had fulfilled this obligation by enacting labor legislation protecting women from overwork and guaranteeing women a minimum wage. Judges would then interfere by striking these laws down, based on a flawed commitment to "freedom of contract" that they found in the Fourteenth Amendment.

In 1929 ERA hearings before a subcommittee of the Senate Judiciary Committee, Kelley explicitly linked maternal mortality to the need for protective labor legislation for women: "There are every year from 23,000 to 26,000 deaths of mothers consequent upon childbirth and the diseases and incidents connected with it. . . . Is there any answer to the question, 'What corresponding dangers are there suffered by men?' How can it be said in the presence of these deaths that the resisting power of women is identical with the resisting power of men under the strains and hazards of industry?"[15]

Kelley opposed the ERA because she feared that the justices who were willing to strike down the women's minimum wage in *Adkins* would be likely to use the ERA for a similar purpose. She called out the ERA's supporters—namely the National Woman's Party—for cozying up to the corporations that were lobbying against minimum wage laws for women.[16] There was no male equivalent to maternal mortality, which was severely exacerbated by overwork in industry. If a judge applied an equal rights amendment to require the identical treatment of women and men, women would lose out. The language of "the so-called equal rights amendment" was just too vague. "Equal rights among whom?" Kelley asked. "Everyone has talked about equality, but no one seems to have dwelt much upon the people concerned."[17]

Dorothy Kenyon asked the same question. Kenyon was a trailblazing lawyer who went on to argue equal protection cases on behalf of women for the ACLU[18]—the organization that Crystal Eastman cofounded. Kenyon noted that the language of the amendment was difficult to interpret and subject to many possible interpretations. Therefore, "The equal rights amendment would operate like a blind man with a shotgun. No lawyer can confidently state what it would hit."[19] Kenyon raised the question as to what the standard of equality would be. The standards could be "high or low." It would be up to courts to decide. To the extent that the amendment gave Congress the power to enforce equal rights, Congress could decide to get rid of labor legislation to make women equal to men, on the one hand, or to extend protective legislation to make men equal to women, on the other hand. ERA proponents said that both approaches were valid interpretations of the ERA. But for the advocates of working women, only the latter approach was acceptable, and only the former approach was likely to be taken by the judiciary, given the composition of the Supreme Court at that moment. With the broader constitutional order hostile to labor rights, Kenyon knew, as Florence Kelley did when she worked on the *Muller* litigation two decades prior, that equal rights would most likely destroy rather than save labor regulation.

Congressional hearings in 1931, after the expiration of the Sheppard-Towner Act, more explicitly engaged the conflict between equal rights and maternity protection. The National Consumers' League claimed that "votes for women enabled women to use the ballot to achieve maternity and infancy legislation." Now, they characterized the ERA as rolling back the achievements of the Nineteenth Amendment. "It is precisely the development of legislation adapted to their needs which enabled women to enter and to continue in industry until they now number 8,500,000 employed. To adopt the [equal rights] amendment would be to reverse this process."[20]

The primary objection to the ERA, as developed in the submissions of Florence Kelley, Dorothy Kenyon, the National Consumers' League, and the National League of Women Voters, was that the ERA in the hands of the incumbent and life-tenured American judiciary would destroy labor laws without replacing them. And if that happened, there was nothing women could do about it. With suffrage, they could vote for politicians who would respond to their needs. But if the politicians adopted laws to protect women that judges were going to strike down, women would be back to square one.

The women who objected to the ERA in the 1920s believed that a constitutional guarantee of equality would be empty without legislation that helped the least advantaged—working women. If the ERA jeopardized such legislation, it was not worth fighting for. The National Woman's Party believed that the total absence of labor protection was better than protection for women only, whereas Florence Kelley and all the other women's groups regarded the total absence of labor protection as destructive to working mothers, and immeasurably worse than women-only protections. The disagreement among women that weakened the ERA in the 1920s was shaped by the power of the men on the Supreme Court. Five of the nine justices—all men—wrote the law in *Lochner* that defined the horizon of legal possibility into which the ERA was launched. The Supreme Court's decision in *Adkins* exemplified how constitutional rights could become shotguns in the hands of blind men, and in its aftermath, women were left with lower wages and no protection. For Kelley, beyond the issue of labor rights, *Adkins* also exemplified the "monopoly of jurisprudence by men." "No woman has participated in the minimum wage case at any of its stages," she lamented.

The solution? "[W]omen need votes, *and* wage statutes, *and* unions, *and* women judges."[21] An important insight that grew out of the Supreme Court's invalidation of a minimum wage for women workers was that women needed to be in positions of decision-making power in order to protect their interests.

The goal of putting more women into positions of political power flowed naturally from the suffrage agenda. In addition to *Adkins*, the Nineteenth Amendment triggered legislation in some states requiring parity between women and men in politics. Indeed, these laws began to be adopted before the Nineteenth Amendment was adopted and ratified, but they rode the tide of the suffrage movement, which had already established votes for women in some states. The first statute mandating women's representation in decision-making bodies was adopted by Colorado in 1910. The Colorado legislature made equal representation by men and women on party committees part of the new primary law. Between 1910 and 1920, Michigan and Nebraska followed.[22] By 1929, eighteen states had some form of equal representation rule for political party committees.[23] These state statutes were known as fifty-fifty plans.

In the 1930s, these statutes were challenged in litigation invoking the First and Fourteenth Amendments of the federal Constitution. One New York court invalidated a fifty-fifty rule, citing the Nineteenth Amendment to support its decision. The court read the Nineteenth Amendment as "wiping out all distinction between sexes so far as voting and qualifications for public trust and office are concerned."[24] This court opinion suggests that Florence Kelley and Dorothy Kenyon were reasonable to fear that judges would interpret the ERA to wipe out all sex distinctions. Between the Nineteenth Amendment and the New Deal, decisions like *Adkins* made it unlikely that the judges in power at the time would have interpreted the ERA favorably toward laws to overcome women's disadvantage.

The Reformers who opposed the ERA in the 1920s were not that far off from the Instigators who wrote and supported it. Crystal Eastman, who wrote the ERA, and Florence Kelley, who opposed it, both wanted the law to work for working mothers. Like Crystal Eastman and Alice Paul, who both spent years in England engaging the women's movements abroad, Florence Kelley had spent many years in Switzerland and Germany, learning about how law could work for working mothers.

The voices of opposition to the ERA were not saying "no" to equal rights; they were saying "not now, not here" to the constitutional amendment at a particular moment in American legal history. The women who opposed the "so-called equal rights amendment" did so primarily in the name of preserving real equality of rights for women. This was evidenced by their support for constitutional equal rights in other countries. In a pamphlet opposing the ERA, the National League of Women Voters contrasted what was likely in the United States with the "equal rights" guarantees found in European constitutions that were embraced by the National Woman's Party.

For instance, the German constitution said that "men and women have fundamentally the same civil rights and duties," the

League of Women Voters pointed out. "Germany has freely enacted legislation making special provision for women as to overtime work, night work, employment in mines and lead processes, maternity, benefits for employed women, and the like." The German constitution acknowledged that the relationship of men and women to actual situations and conditions of life was not always identical, and therefore permitted legislation that took differences into account to make women equal in effect. Other countries' constitutions operated differently from the US Constitution—they empowered the legislative rather than the judicial branch. The League of Women Voters understood that, outside the United States, constitutions "partake far more of the nature of general principles which the legislative branch of the government is free to interpret and develop with great flexibility."[25]

In a spirit of more ambitious reform to the benefit of women, those who opposed the ERA in the 1920s admired an ERA in a different constitutional context—that of Germany after World War I. Germany's constitution did not put a powerful supreme court in charge of giving meaning to constitutional rights upon litigation. Instead, it enshrined equal rights as a statement of general principles and foundational values. Within this constitutional context, an ERA would not be a weapon destructive to laws that women needed.

The arguments and concerns of ERA skeptics improved the ERA over time. The ERA was not ratified and handed over to the *Adkins* court to interpret, and this gave the ERA room to grow as the composition of the Supreme Court changed. By the end of the 1930s, New Deal legislation on minimum wages and maximum hours withstood the logic of *Adkins*. The Supreme Court upheld the Fair Labor Standards Act, adopted in 1938. The League of Women Voters came to support the ERA in the 1950s, as did Dorothy Kenyon by 1970,[26] after the nine men on the Supreme Court changed their approach to laws protecting workers.

In the years that followed, ERA proponents broadened their vision and won the hearts of a broader diversity of women by the time of its adoption in 1972. When we cast Crystal Eastman, Alice

Paul, and the National Woman's Party as the "founding mothers" of the ERA, we should not see Florence Kelley, Dorothy Kenyon, or the League of Women Voters as the "antis."

Rather, the opponents of the 1920s and 1930s were founding mothers, too. At the least, they are the founding "aunties," rather than "antis." The forty-nine years between the ERA's introduction and adoption in Congress saw the genesis of a 1970s ERA that was more responsive to the needs of more women, especially working women and mothers.

The ERA got postponed because of serious questions about whether it would undermine or improve working women's and mothers' lives. In the twenty-first century, feminist lawyers continue to ask whether the ERA will help women who attempt to juggle motherhood with work outside the home.[27] For many working mothers, that juggling act was and remains one of necessity rather than choice. Law could either ease that juggle, or intensify it. Which kind of law would the ERA be, under life-tenured judges who were hostile to workers' rights?

Champions of real equality for women opposed the ERA in the 1920s because they thought women deserved something better than a shotgun wielded by judges to strike down laws they didn't like. In the era of the ERA's introduction, the Reformers were doing more than testifying against the ERA; they were broadening the principle of equal rights. In the same year that the ERA was introduced, Florence Kelley began to pressure the Women's Joint Congressional Committee—made up of white women's groups—to include the National Association of Colored Women. She succeeded in 1924. Kelley was already working with leaders of African American women's groups as a board member of the National Association for the Advancement of Colored People (NAACP), which she helped to found in 1909. Like ERA framer Crystal Eastman, who founded the organization that became the ACLU, Kelley saw women's equal rights as embedded in a world of other struggles for justice. It would take another world war for the ERA to inch ahead with this broader vision.

PART II

CONTESTATIONS

4
The Globalizers

THE ERA TOOK A NEW turn in the 1940s. World War II sent men into combat overseas, and women stepped into men's jobs on the home front to provide necessary support for a nation at war. By 1944, the Republican and Democratic parties both embraced the ERA in their platforms. After the Holocaust and the atrocities of war, the United Nations Charter proclaimed a new world order committed to human rights, including "the equal rights of men and women."[1] All the countries that rewrote their constitutions after the war included a provision recognizing women's equality. In the United States, more women's organizations began to support such a provision for the US Constitution. And in 1945, the National Association of Colored Women took a stand in favor of the ERA, through the congressional testimony of its founder, Mary Church Terrell.

Mary Church Terrell was born in Tennessee in 1863. Both her parents were enslaved. The National Association of Colored Women was one of several organizations that she helped to form in her lifetime. The NACW was founded in 1896, the year that the Supreme Court decided the infamous case of *Plessy v. Ferguson*.[2]

That case put the Supreme Court's stamp of approval on Jim Crow segregation; it held that "separate but equal" train cars were allowed under the Fourteenth Amendment's Equal Protection Clause. Through the NACW, Terrell crusaded against racial injustice for over fifty years. She died at the age of ninety in 1954, two months after the Supreme Court finally decided *Brown v. Board of Education*,[3] which struck down racial segregation in public schools.

Terrell was also a cofounder (with Florence Kelley) of the National Association for the Advancement of Colored People (NAACP). In her autobiography, she wrote, "A white woman has only one handicap to overcome—that of sex. I have two—both sex and race. I belong to the only group in this country which has two such huge obstacles to surmount. Colored men have only one—that of race."[4] Before critical race scholars like Kimberlé Crenshaw coined the term "intersectionality" much later in the twentieth century to give a name to this challenging dynamic,[5] Mary Church Terrell navigated the intensified disadvantages of both race and sex that befell black women. She worked on anti-lynching campaigns with the NAACP, while she led the NACW to support the women's suffrage movement.

Terrell also helped form Delta Sigma Theta, a sorority that began at Howard University in 1913 to empower black women. Delta Sigma Theta faced a serious dilemma when Alice Paul organized the history-making suffrage parade that year. Paul insisted that black women march at the back of the parade, to avoid offending the sensibilities of white women from Southern states. One black woman, Ida B. Wells, a well-known journalist and activist, took offense and simply ignored Paul's instruction. Wells integrated herself into the Illinois women's delegation in the middle of the parade. By contrast, Terrell cooperated with Paul's plan of racial segregation that day. She marched in the back of the parade with Delta Sigma Theta, the black sorority that she was mentoring to fight discrimination. Terrell later remarked that if Alice Paul could have gotten the Nineteenth Amendment passed without enfranchising African American women, she might have done so.[6]

Nonetheless, Terrell looked beyond Paul's racism and supported the National Woman's Party in its final push for suffrage. In 1917, she took her daughter Phyllis to join Paul's picket line for the suffrage amendment outside the White House. Although Terrell managed not to get arrested on the days she picketed, she proudly received the "Jailed for Freedom" pin from the National Woman's Party, awarded in 1921 to all the women who picketed in 1917, in recognition of their sacrifices that contributed to the Nineteenth Amendment victory.

A quarter century after she received the suffrage pin, Terrell testified in Congress to support the Equal Rights Amendment. In 1945 and 1948, she represented NACW before the House and Senate judiciary committees. Although Terrell was supporting an amendment that Alice Paul championed, her arguments *for* the ERA sounded like Florence Kelley's arguments *against* the ERA. Like Kelley, Terrell put the needs of working mothers front and center. The two perspectives intersected through the experiences of women of color. For Terrell, a major problem to which the ERA could offer some solutions was the dual role that women increasingly played, as breadwinners and caregivers for their families. "Today, thousands of women are obliged to support themselves and their families entirely or help to do so. Today, women sorely need help to discharge their duties and obligations to their families which the equal rights amendment could so easily afford."[7] Terrell proposed that the ERA would help support working mothers.

Terrell's belief that the ERA could afford support to mothers most likely grew out of her global perspective on women's constitutional rights. In her 1948 ERA testimony, she pointed out that the newly enacted Japanese constitution contained an equal rights provision[8] that gave Japanese women advantages and opportunities denied to American women. Terrell had been traveling and studying the globe for sixty years by then. She had studied ancient Greek in college at Oberlin in the 1880s, which led her on a tour of Europe after graduation, with the plan of studying abroad for a year.

She settled in Paris at first, boarding with a French widow and her niece, where she studied French. But she found that Paris was a big city for an American girl to navigate alone. So she went to the Swiss Alps, where she boarded with a family of four, and attended a girls' school where she studied French. After that, her longest period of study was in Germany, where she lived with a German Jewish family in Berlin. There, she became fluent in German and well-versed in German literature, music, and drama, and she encountered people from all over Europe, two of whom proposed marriage to her. Finally, she moved on to Florence, Italy, where she lived with an Italian widow and her twelve-year-old son. She ended up staying in Europe for two years instead of one. When it was time to return to the United States, she remarked, "Life had been so pleasant and profitable abroad, where I could take advantage of any opportunity I desired without wondering whether a colored girl would be allowed to enjoy it or not, and where I could secure accommodations in any hotel, boarding house, or private home in which I cared to live. I knew that when I returned home I would face again the humiliations, discriminations, and hardships to which colored people are subjected all over the United States."[9]

It was a few years after her return from Europe that she established the National Association of Colored Women. Upon her immediate return, she married Robert Terrell, who went on to become one of the first African American judges in a DC court. In the first five years of their marriage, she had two pregnancies that resulted in miscarriage, and then a third pregnancy leading to the birth of a baby boy who died two days after he was born. Terrell experienced a "maternal instinct" that was "abnormally developed," and she was overcome with grief over her miscarriages and her baby's death. It was around this time that she threw herself into women's clubs working on suffrage and was befriended by Susan B. Anthony and Carrie Chapman Catt. She organized the first secular national meeting of African American women in the United States. When the organization was formed, Terrell referred to it as her "baby." Two years later, she had a baby daughter, Phyllis.

Because of all of her suffrage work, Terrell was invited in 1904 to address the Congress of the International Council of Women in Berlin. When she first received this invitation, she was extremely flattered and excited, but not sure if she would be able to accept. She worried about her motherly duties. "Even if I could scrape together the money, how could I summon courage enough to leave my family? Especially my small daughter!"[10] she wondered. Her husband was supportive and offered to take care of Phyllis at home, but Terrell was tempted to take her daughter on the trip at the last minute. It was only after her husband argued her out of it "by showing how impossible it would be for me properly to attend to the business for which I was making the voyage and to care for a little girl among strangers at one and the same time" that she finally relented and traveled back to Germany by herself.

Terrell attended the Berlin conference along with Susan B. Anthony, Carrie Chapman Catt, and women's rights activists from around the world. Although she prepared her public address on "The Progress of Colored Women" in advance in English, she surprised and delighted the audience by delivering it in German instead. In that speech, she explained that were it not for the Union Army in 1865, she would still be enslaved on a plantation. But within fifty years of slavery, African American women had become "a great power for the good." How? The National Association of Colored Women was establishing "day nurseries for children of colored workers," teaching communities about household affairs, providing classes in English and German, and building homes for "fallen women and seduced girls." "In short," she noted, "we did everything that was in our power."[11] Black women were doing everything they could to take care of the children and the vulnerable. They were the heroic mothers of their communities.

At the Berlin conference, Terrell was in the company of German leaders of the women's movement, including Helene Lange, who spoke about the quest for women's suffrage in Germany.[12] Lange was a leader of the Federation of German Women's Organizations and the treasurer of the International Council of Women. With her partner in life and work, Gertrud Bäumer, Lange had published the mammoth *Handbook of the Women's Movement* in 1901,[13] which argued for the rights of working women as well as the rights of mothers over their children. Bäumer later became the president of the Federation of German Women's Organizations and, more importantly, was one of the women elected to the parliament that adopted the German constitution of 1919, the first constitution in the world to guarantee equal rights between women and men. Shortly after the 1904 conference in Berlin, Bäumer wrote that the importance of what women could do, what they could contribute to society as equals, stemmed from their female nature as mothers.[14] The German constitution's provision on equal rights for women—which Bäumer had a hand in making—was then cited by the National Woman's Party in 1925 hearings on the ERA as an example of the twentieth-century constitutions that were recognizing women's equal rights.[15] Dating back to 1904, and possibly earlier, American women like Mary Church Terrell were already engaging these ideas with German women on the international scene. In 1919, she gave another speech in German at the International Congress of Women in Zurich, where resolutions were adopted promoting peace, women's suffrage, equal rights in marriage, and economic support for mothers.

The German constitution adopted at Weimar in 1919 had several provisions that addressed the rights of women. Article 109 had the provision that we would call the German ERA: "All Germans are equal before the law. Men and women have basically the same rights and duties of citizenship."[16] There were other provisions that enlarged women's rights. Article 128 prohibited the exclusion of women from the civil service: "All citizens, without distinction, are eligible according to their abilities and accomplishments, in accordance with law. All regulations making exceptions against female civil servants are abolished." Article 119 said, "Motherhood is under state protection and welfare." The preceding clauses of Article 119 stated: "Marriage, as the foundation of the family and the preservation and expansion of the nation, enjoys the special protection of the constitution. It is based on the equality of both sexes. It is the task of both the state and communities to strengthen and socially promote the family. Large families may claim social welfare."[17]

The German constitution of 1919 is part of the history of the American Equal Rights Amendment, because both the proponents of the ERA and the women who opposed it in the 1920s took some inspiration from Germany. Although the German constitution of 1919 did not survive World War II, German women lawyers participated in the adoption of a new West German constitution that replaced the 1919 constitution in 1949.[18] The guarantee of equal rights between women and men endured in the West German constitution—known as the Basic Law—that was adopted at Bonn in 1949 and remains in force in the unified Germany today. Article 3.1 says, "Men and women shall have equal rights," Article 3.3 says, "No person shall be favored or disfavored because of sex," and Article 6.4 says, "Every mother shall be entitled to the protection and care of the community." These provisions have been interpreted to require German law to provide paid maternity leave and protections for pregnant workers in the workplace.

Germany was not the only country that enshrined equal rights for women and men in its constitution after World War II. As many witnesses pointed out during the congressional hearings on the ERA in 1945 and 1948, the Charter of the United Nations was signed on June 26, 1945. The preamble included the principle of equal rights of men and women, which was then written into almost every constitution that was made in that period. Women were elected to constituent assemblies in France and Italy and became constitution-makers. Like their German counterparts, they cared about the relationship of equal rights to working motherhood and put both equal rights and motherhood protection into their countries' postwar constitutions.

In France, where Mary Church Terrell had settled to study French fifty years earlier, women fought to protect motherhood in the constitution they helped to write after World War II. After suffrage was won in 1946, Gilberte Roca from the Communist Party echoed Crystal Eastman's sentiment that "the right to vote is only the beginning of equality." Like Crystal Eastman and Alice Paul in America, Roca believed that the next step for the voting woman was equal rights, because "she remains a diminished citizen if, to take a few examples, she cannot, because she is married, open a bank account, sell her own belongings without the consent of her husband, if she does not have access to all the careers and she cannot freely engage in commerce or a profession because her husband is opposed to it, ultimately, if she does not have the same rights as the father over her children."[19] These were the same legal disabilities that the National Woman's Party had in mind when they introduced the ERA in the United States, some vestiges of which remained when the ERA was adopted fifty years later.

French feminists like Roca, who participated in the French parliamentary assembly that adopted the post–World War II Constitution, embraced a vision similar to Crystal Eastman's in her writings about the American post-suffrage moment. Roca said, "[I]f women rejoice that their rights are being recognized, they know that it is not enough to grant women equality of rights, but that it is also necessary to give her the possibility of exercising them."[20] For a woman to fully exercise her role as a citizen, she would have to be able to combine working with being a mother. Motherhood was important, not only to a woman's enjoyment of life, but to the nation's postwar aspirations for population growth.

If the new constitution would take care of the French people's posterity, just as the US Constitution's preamble aspired to do for the American people, there was no avoiding the role of mothers. Roca argued that the preamble's guarantee of health and material security to mothers laid the foundation on which the legislature would then have to regulate work in mothers' favor, improve housing, and institute a system of nurseries, childcare centers, afterschool programs, and cafeterias—in short, "all the undertakings that will allow the woman to be no longer a servant but the guardian of her household and to participate with all of the might of her intelligence and her heart in the French rebirth."[21]

In Italy, too—where Terrell completed her years of study abroad—women got elected to the constituent assembly that wrote the constitution in 1947. Women from across the political spectrum argued that equality and the protection of working mothers ultimately benefited the entire nation. Article 37 of the Italian Constitution of 1947 states: "Working women are entitled to equal rights, and, for comparable jobs, equal pay as men. Working conditions must allow women to fulfill their essential role in the family and ensure appropriate protection for the mother and the child." Angelina Merlin, one of twenty-one women elected to the constituent assembly to draft the new Italian Constitution, proposed Article 37 because "Protecting the mother means protecting society at its roots . . . through the mother, one guarantees the future of society."[22] The Italian constitution, like every other, was concerned with ensuring good lives for its people's posterity.

This global historical context lay beneath the two points that Mary Church Terrell made in her 1948 testimony supporting the ERA: First, that women needed the ERA to support themselves and their families, while also fulfilling their duties to raise their families; second, that other constitutions around the world, including specifically Japan's, had equal-rights provisions that American women still did not enjoy. The first point, about the juggle of working motherhood, came out of her own experience of cherishing motherhood, and juggling that intense maternal instinct with work she pursued equally passionately as an advocate for women's rights and racial justice. Terrell made the pursuit of women's rights more global, both by broadening their connection to racial equality and the plight of working mothers and, literally, by making global connections with women's rights advocates from Germany and other countries.

By the end of World War II, ERA advocates stood on stronger moral terrain than ever before. The ERA would not only end specific antiquated laws about women's property rights, but would also constitutionalize moral propositions of human rights that the whole world now embraced—equality between women and men, and nondiscrimination on grounds of sex. The experience of the

Holocaust and the growing struggle against Jim Crow in the United States strengthened the moral imperative to oppose discrimination.

Arguments against the ERA changed, too.[23] Labor organizations continued to express some concern about the need for special labor protections that the ERA might endanger. But skeptics moved beyond the issue of women-only protective labor laws. The National League of Women Voters worried that the ERA would end husbands' obligation to support their wives, alimony for abandoned wives in the case of divorce, and pensions for widows. The National League of Women Voters had given "unequivocal support" to the UN Charter, but its president argued that "the equal rights amendment is not the proper method in this country for reaching the goals set forth in the United Nations Charter."[24]

Nonetheless, the post–World War II moment enabled unprecedented steps forward for the ERA. For the first time ever, the ERA got a debate on the Senate floor in 1946. Only thirty-eight senators voted for it[25]—a majority of those voting but short of the two-thirds required by Article V. There were no women senators at the time. In 1948, hearings on the ERA before subcommittees in both houses of Congress were combined with hearings on a women's status bill that proposed to create a presidential commission on the status of women. The commission would collect data on the economic, political, and civil status of women and establish a policy determining permitted and prohibited sex distinctions. In these hearings, opponents of the ERA became proponents of the proposed women's status legislation, which they believed would better realize the equal rights between women and men proclaimed in the UN Charter.[26]

In the 1940s, women elected to Congress began to support the ERA. Katharine St. George, a congresswoman from New York, testified in support of the ERA before a subcommittee of the House Judiciary Committee in 1948. She argued that it was time for women to take their place on equal footing with men. She directly addressed the question of whether the ERA would allow special treatment for mothers: "Much is made of the hazard and handicap of maternity," she said. "Maternity is not a disease, it is a natural and perfectly normal function." Treating maternity as a normal function would mean providing maternity benefits and bonuses for the time that women workers in industry needed to be absent to fulfill the normal function of maternity. For St. George, providing maternity bonuses was no different from providing soldier bonuses. "[T]his in no way conflicts with the idea of equality," she declared.[27]

In that congressional session, a compromise emerged on the Senate floor. The ERA bill included a rider introduced by Senator Carl Hayden of Arizona. The "Hayden rider" read: "The provisions of this article shall not be construed to impair any rights, benefits, or exemptions now or hereafter conferred by law upon persons of the female sex."[28] Once the ERA was written with a protection for motherhood in it—somewhat similar to the European constitutions—the ERA reached its next milestone. For the first time, a two-thirds majority of the Senate adopted it. In 1950, sixty-three senators voted in favor, comprising two-thirds of those present.[29] In 1953, two-thirds of the Senate adopted the ERA again, again with the Hayden rider in place. This time, the ERA got seventy-three votes.[30] The ERA first began to garner support sufficient to be passed by one house of Congress when it was clearly understood to permit some protection of women because they were mothers.

By then, there was one woman in the Senate—Republican Margaret Chase Smith of Maine, who had been in the House of Representatives from 1940 to 1948. Her political career began as the widow of a congressman when she was elected to her deceased husband's seat in the House. She sponsored the ERA bill in 1945 and made a statement supporting it to the House Judiciary Committee in 1948.[31] Then, she was elected to the Senate in 1949, where she opposed the Hayden rider. Many women who supported the ERA believed that the rider would weaken the ERA by over-protecting women. Nonetheless, Smith still voted for the ERA with the Hayden rider in place, believing that a weak ERA was better than no ERA. There were nine women in the House, including Katharine St. George and other ERA supporters. But the ERA did not get debated on the floor of the House, even after two-thirds of the Senate had adopted it twice in the 1950s.

It was not the women or their concerns about overprotection that held up the ERA in the House. It was Emanuel Celler, chair of the House Judiciary Committee from 1949 to 1973, and his all-male committee. Celler kept the ERA locked up in committee for over a decade, preventing consideration by the full House of Representatives. While two-thirds of the Senate adopted the ERA twice after World War II and sent it to the House, the House did not act, largely due to the way Celler exercised his power as committee chair.

After the ERA was broadened, globalized, and clarified with regard to maternity, it is very likely that two-thirds of the House would have followed the Senate to adopt it. But a small group of men on the House Judiciary Committee used their discretionary power to stop that from happening. It would take nothing short of a political storm to thrust the ERA out of their hands.

5

The Framers

IN THE 1960S, THE CIVIL rights movement swept across the nation, bringing new momentum to the Equal Rights Amendment. But to make things happen, momentum needs feet that can move on the ground and hands that can shake to make deals. Martha Griffiths, a Democratic congresswoman from Michigan, brought that sparkling combination of political instinct, legal acumen, and drive to make the law change. As the fiftieth anniversary of women's constitutional right to vote approached in the summer of 1970, she decided it was time to liberate the ERA from the men who were holding it captive.

Martha Griffiths was a lawyer, judge, and state legislator before being elected to Congress in 1955. She graduated from the University of Michigan Law School in 1940, along with her husband, her college debate teammate who persuaded her to go to law school. They were the first married couple to graduate from Michigan, a law school that her husband chose over Harvard because it admitted women while other law schools did not.[1]

With a partner in law and in life, Griffiths was no stranger to sparring and collaborating with men. She learned how to maneuver a man's world through strategy and persuasion. Neither she nor any of the ten women in the House could vote on the fate of the ERA unless and until the bill could be rescued from the stranglehold of Emanuel Celler, the octogenarian chair of the House Judiciary Committee. So Griffiths studied up on parliamentary procedure.[2] She spent months collecting signatures from her fellow representatives on a petition to discharge the ERA from the grip of the House Judiciary Committee so that the ERA's supporters in the House could at least have a shot at persuading the rest of the democratically elected body. She needed half of the members of the House—218 signatures—to make this happen.

The Senate Judiciary Committee's Subcommittee on Constitutional Amendments held hearings on the Equal Rights Amendment in early May of 1970. Feminist activists Betty Friedan and Gloria Steinem testified in support of the amendment, as did the chairwoman of the President's Task Force on Women's Rights and Responsibilities and the chairwoman of the Citizens' Advisory Council on the Status of Women. Both of these groups had issued reports proposing legislative changes to promote women's equality, including passage of the ERA.

With a combination of determination, charm, and *realpolitik*, Griffiths cornered her colleagues and convinced them, one by one, to sign her petition. When she got to 218, she demanded an hour of debate about the ERA on the House floor. It was August 10, 1970, two weeks before the nation would celebrate the Nineteenth Amendment's fiftieth birthday.

"Give us a chance to show you that those so-called protective laws to aid women—however well-intentioned originally—have become in fact restraints, which keep wife, abandoned wife, and widow alike from supporting her family," she said.[3] Even before the beginning of debate—in merely asking for time to persuade everyone about the ERA—the first thing Griffiths mentioned was wives supporting families.

The case for the ERA was simple. An Equal Rights Amendment would eradicate the remaining legal vestiges of women's inferior status in society. Crystal Eastman had explained this almost fifty years earlier. State laws still excluded women from certain jobs, professions, or jury service, and some restrictions on married women's property rights remained on the books, hobbling women's access to credit and business opportunities. The ERA would end these forms of inequality under the law.[4]

Griffiths knew that in order to succeed, the ERA would have to be a bipartisan effort. So she kept her speech short, and asked her Republican colleague Florence Dwyer to take over in making the case for the ERA. Dwyer had endorsed the ERA since her first term in Congress in 1957, and she had also cosponsored the bill that became the Equal Pay Act of 1963. Dwyer, unlike Martha Griffiths, was a mother. Indeed, being a mother had enabled her path to politics, which began in her local Parent-Teacher Association, which led her to the Northeastern Republican Club, which led her to the New Jersey state legislature in 1950 and to Congress in 1957. In taking the floor to support the ERA discharge petition, Dwyer said that the ERA was needed to stop "laws prohibiting women from working in certain occupations and excluding women from certain colleges and universities and scholarship programs to laws which restrict the rights of married women and which carry heavier criminal penalties for women than for men." At the same time, Dwyer was equally emphatic in stating, "But it does not—and this deserves special emphasis—it does not obliterate the differences between male and female."[5] Dwyer was not a lawyer, but she had taken classes at Rutgers Law School and she understood that equal rights under the law did not have to mean identical treatment in all circumstances.

Dwyer's speech on the House floor embraced the recommendations of the Citizens' Advisory Council on the Status of Women as well as the recommendations of the President's Task Force on Women's Rights and Responsibilities.[6] Both documents had set forth the legal and policy changes needed to improve women's status in American society.[7] The President's Task Force proposed expanding the Equal Pay Act to cover more employees, public funding for childcare, and the appointment of more women to positions of responsibility in government. For Dwyer, these reports provided the specifics of the ERA's simple command: "[W]omen want only what is their due. They want to be treated as whole citizens. They want to be recognized as having a full stake in the life of our Nation. Consequently, they also want the means necessary to fulfill this role."[8]

In pleading for a floor debate on the ERA, Dwyer assured her colleagues of what the ERA would not do: "It would not take women out of the home. It would not downgrade the roles of mother and housewife. Indeed, it would give new dignity to these important roles. By confirming women's equality under the law, by upholding woman's right to choose her place in society, the equal rights amendment can only enhance the status of traditional women's occupations. For these would become positions accepted by women as equals, not roles imposed on them as inferiors."[9] Immediately following Dwyer's speech, the House voted 333–22 to bring the ERA to the floor for consideration by the full body.

During that hour of debate, other Republican women supported the ERA on behalf of mothers and housewives. Charlotte Reid of Illinois said that the ERA would support all women's choices: "An abiding concern for home and children should not restrict their freedom to choose the role in society to which their interests, education, and training entitle and qualify them."[10] Reid had been in Congress since 1963. Like Mae Nolan forty years earlier, Reid was a widow who had run for her deceased husband's seat and won.

Margaret Heckler, a Republican from Massachusetts, spoke proudly from her experience as a mother of three: "I do not have any desire to become one of the boys," she said.[11] In her testimony in support of the ERA to the Senate judiciary subcommittee three months earlier, Congresswoman Heckler had compared American women to women in other countries. She challenged the assertion that American women "enjoy greater freedom than women of any other nation," because "[m]any countries we consider 'underdeveloped' far surpass America in the quality and availability of child care available to working mothers, in enlightened attitudes about employment leave for pregnancy, and in guiding women into the professions."[12]

Catherine Dean May, a Republican congresswoman from Washington state, argued that the ERA was needed because the Founding Fathers wrote the Constitution when the common law denied legal personhood to women. May insisted that the ERA would be compatible with special laws for mothers. Echoing Katharine St. George's comparison of motherhood bonuses to soldier bonuses two decades earlier, May pointed out, "No one questions special laws for veterans, or for the blind, or for various segments of our society—it would certainly not be inconsistent to still have special laws for mothers or mothers-to-be."[13]

After one hour of persuasion, with statements by Republican and Democratic congresswomen alike, the opponents attempted to recommit the ERA to the House Judiciary Committee, with instructions to hold hearings. But that motion failed by an overwhelming majority, with only 26 congressmen voting for it, and 344 members of the House against it. That meant that the resolution was still discharged from the House Judiciary Committee by Griffiths' discharge petition, and eligible for a floor vote by the entire body of the House. By a similarly overwhelming majority of 352 votes in favor and only 15 votes against, the House took the historic vote to adopt the Equal Rights Amendment that began its modern path to ratification.

Even though there was only one hour of debate, the women of the House covered a lot of ground. They talked about the inequalities that affected married women, widows, mothers, and pregnant women and girls. All the women present voted in favor of the ERA. The 352 votes in favor of the ERA constituted 96 percent of those present and voting, and 81 percent of the total composition of the House, well above the two-thirds threshold required by Article V. The ERA then moved to the Senate for consideration.

But things went very differently in the Senate that fall. After the commemorations of the Nineteenth Amendment's fiftieth anniversary died down, the Senate took up the ERA bill on the floor in October 1970. The Senate, unlike the House, allows for unlimited debate,[14] and the ERA got much more than an hour on the floor. Hours of debate with exclusively male voices ensued. There were ninety-nine men in the Senate, and only one woman—Margaret Chase Smith of Maine. Once a sponsor of the ERA in the House, she was the first woman to serve in both houses of Congress, from 1940 to 1948 in the House and 1949 to 1972 in the Senate. In 1964, she became the first woman to seek the nomination of a major political party for the presidency. She lost the Republican nomination, which went to her Senate colleague, Barry Goldwater. By 1970, Smith was nearing the end of her long Senate career. She voted for the ERA, but she did not speak when the Senate took up the ERA in the 1970s, even though she had testified in 1948 as a member of Congress in support of the ERA at committee hearings, and had voted twice in favor of the ERA in the 1950s.[15]

Some of the most vocal senators in the room had filibustered the Civil Rights Act of 1964, the landmark legislation that prohibited race and sex discrimination in employment and several other areas of life.[16] One participant in the Civil Rights Act filibuster, Democratic senator Sam Ervin of North Carolina, was especially opposed to the ERA. He had a lot to say about it, and a slew of changes he wanted to propose to the ERA bill that Martha Griffiths had successfully guided to a 96 percent positive vote in the House.

In the Senate, the primary sponsor of the ERA bill was Birch Bayh, a Democrat from Indiana who had championed the Civil Rights Act of 1964.[17] Marlow Cook, a Republican senator from Kentucky, served with Birch Bayh on the Senate Judiciary Subcommittee on Constitutional Amendments. Cook championed the women who had moved the ERA in the House, and he urged his fellow senators to heed the legislative history that these female framers had already created.

Senate ERA proponents recognized Martha Griffiths and Florence Dwyer as the authorities that would shape the ERA's meaning and guide its future interpretation. Senator Cook pointed out that the words of the ERA would get their meaning from congressional intent. Cook urged that the specific meanings be found in the speeches of the ERA's proponents in the House, and the hearings before the Senate subcommittee.[18] Reading the legislative history created by the women in the House, Cook reiterated that the ERA would not lead homemakers to lose alimony in divorce, or cause mothers to be drafted, or deny social security benefits to husbands with working wives. Florence Dwyer's contributions on the House floor provided reassurance to Cook that the role of the homemaker would not be downgraded. With that, Cook tried to calm the fears of the ERA's opponents.[19]

Bayh and Cook knew that any significant changes made by the Senate to the bill already passed by the House would, in effect, kill the ERA. By the time the ERA bill got debated on the Senate floor, it was October, and elections for many seats in Congress were less than a month away. Time was running out. On any bill, if the Senate did not pass the same version that the House had adopted, the normal course of action would be a conference committee to reconcile the two versions of the bill. With elections around the corner, it was clear that if the Senate did not adopt the version of the ERA that the House had adopted in August 1970, there would be no time for a conference committee to produce a reconciled bill. The ERA bill would die and would go back to square one. It would have to be reintroduced by the next Congress after elections.

The opponents of the ERA in the Senate, though small in number, took advantage of this situation. Time was on their side. Senator Sam Ervin proposed a few seemingly minor procedural changes to the House's ERA resolution. The House resolution placed no time limit on the states' ratification, and made the effective date of the amendment only one year after ratification. In the Senate, Sam Ervin introduced an amendment that would impose a seven-year deadline on ratification and increase the delay in effective date from one year to two years.

Ervin packaged these seemingly minor procedural changes with a major substantive change that he knew would be a deal-breaker for the ERA's proponents. In addition to the seven-year deadline and the increased delay in effective date, Ervin's amendment package included the following sentence: "This article shall not impair, however, the validity of any law of the United States which exempts women from compulsory military service."[20] Ervin wanted it to be clear that the ERA would not require women to be drafted. At the very least, he wanted to preserve the possibility for Congress to pass laws exempting women from mandatory military service. In the event of a draft, that would mean men would have to serve, and women would only serve if they wanted to.

The exemption that Ervin was proposing was similar to the Hayden rider included in the ERA bills that the Senate adopted in the 1950s. It was also similar to the existing laws about compulsory jury service. Under the laws of several states, men were automatically included in jury pools and would be required to serve if called. By contrast, women could serve on juries if they voluntarily signed up for jury service; it was not mandatory for women. In effect, this meant that far fewer women were on juries, which could sometimes work to the disadvantage of female criminal defendants when they did not get a jury of their peers. The Supreme Court had blessed these asymmetrical jury laws in *Hoyt v. Florida* in 1961 on the grounds that "woman is still regarded as the center of home and family life," and therefore should be relieved of civic duties like jury service.[21] This was the kind of law—and Supreme Court decision—that Martha Griffiths wanted the ERA to stop.

When confronted with Ervin's proposal to exempt women from the military draft, Senator Bayh resisted the effort to change the ERA that the House had already adopted. First, Bayh argued that the military exemption was unnecessary because the language of the ERA did not assume the identical treatment of women and men with regard to the draft. But more importantly, Bayh tried to expose Ervin's proposal as a covert attempt to kill the ERA: "What we are proposing—and I think we need to recognize this," said Bayh, "is that if we accept a significant amendment such as this, we are greatly increasing the probability that this measure would have to go to the conference committee."[22] Bayh made it explicit that changing the House's ERA in this way at that moment would stop it from being sent to the states for ratification. Nonetheless, Ervin's package of changes to the ERA was adopted by a slim majority of those voting (though a minority of the total number of senators), 36–33.

Other senators then added a provision to the House resolution that bundled the ERA with the constitutional right to voluntary prayer in public buildings,[23] a constitutional amendment that had been proposed without success in the past. Ervin and his allies also tried, unsuccessfully, to add a constitutional provision that would have ended busing to integrate schools in the South.[24] It was open season: Skeptics of the ERA could game the unlimited time for debate and the limited time available for a conference committee to change the ERA bill to score political points—there would be no time to act on them anyway. The Senate changed the House's ERA to include a seven-year deadline on ratification, a two-year delay in effective date, a provision allowing women's exemption from military service, and a right to voluntary school prayer in public buildings. But the Senate did not ultimately vote on this amended ERA resolution before the session of the 91st Congress ended. The ERA went to the legislative graveyard. After elections in November, Congress was in a lame-duck session for the rest of the year, with no real prospects for getting anything done.

Ervin stopped the ERA from advancing in 1970, but Martha Griffiths did not give up. When the 92nd Congress began in January 1971, she reintroduced the ERA immediately. Griffiths was determined to get the ERA passed by both houses this time. Just as she found ways to get the discharge petition signed and to collaborate with the Republican women in the House, she looked for a way to win the support of the men of her own party, like Celler and Ervin, who had pulled the brakes on the ERA in the past. Even if they weren't going to support the ERA, she needed to get them to back down, at least a little bit, by showing that she was will- ing to play ball. Her new bill included the seven-year deadline on ratification and the two-year delay on effective date. She was trying to avoid Ervin's trapdoor to the legislative graveyard this time, by showing that she was listening to the skeptics' concerns. In March 1971 hearings before a House judiciary subcommittee, Griffiths said she incorporated "minor technical changes" to the ERA resolution as "an effort to gain united support for the Amendment."[25] Of the Senate's changes to the House ERA bill that had garnered 96 percent of her chamber, Griffiths was flexible about the seven-year time limit and the additional year's delay on the effective date, but she was rigidly against the military draft exemption and the school prayer provision.

Griffiths spent her political capital to save the substantive positions that were much more important to her than the deadline. She made sure that no qualifying language exempting women from military service would be part of her ERA resolution. But to move that point forward, she decided to give an inch on the seven-year ratification deadline. It felt minor at the time, because Griffiths predicted with confidence that the ERA would be ratified in less than seven years. When Griffiths testified before the House Judiciary Committee in March 1971, she explained, "I don't really feel you have to have 7 years. I don't feel you have to have that but for some people they prefer it so that I will be glad to support the 7 years because I think that if we pass it throughout this body it is going to be passed through the States in far less than 7 years."[26]

It is clear that Griffiths accepted the seven-year time limit because she was saving her political capital for substance rather than procedure. After witnessing 96 percent of her colleagues in the House vote for the ERA in 1970, she reasonably predicted that three-fourths of the states would ratify the ERA within two years. She did not see the seven-year time limit as much of a compromise, so she focused on fighting off the other Senate amendments that she found far more objectionable, particularly the military exemption. Griffiths's prediction was reasonable at the time, but it turned out to be a miscalculation with serious consequences for the ERA's future success.

Notwithstanding this slight modification of the ERA resolution that got debated on the House floor in October 1971, nothing had changed in Martha Griffiths's substantive case for the ERA since August of the previous year. Many members of the House repeated their speeches and statements to articulate the goals and meaning of the ERA that they had adopted on August 10, 1970. What did change was the time and words the women in Congress spent to defeat the vigorous efforts by Ervin's allies in the House to reinstate a military draft exemption for women as an amendment to the ERA.

Ervin sent the ERA to the legislative graveyard in 1970, but the women of Congress brought it back to life in 1971. From 1970 to 1972, a small number of men in the Senate played their powerful hand to change the ERA's political stakes. Nevertheless, the founding mothers of the ERA persisted.

THE FRAMERS · 64

6

The Mothers

PATSY TAKEMOTO MINK WAS THE first woman of color ever elected to Congress. She was a third-generation Japanese American who had served in Hawaii's state legislature before a new congressional seat in the House of Representatives was created for Hawaii in 1964. She ran a grassroots campaign for that seat, relying on small donations. Against the odds, she won, in the year that Congress passed the landmark Civil Rights Act that banned race and sex discrimination in employment. She moved to Washington with her husband and twelve-year-old daughter, where she advocated fiercely to expand opportunities for women and girls.[1]

Patsy Mink knew something about getting shut out of opportunities, and what to do about it. When she was a sophomore in high school, her father and other members of her community got arrested because of their Japanese ancestry after the United States entered World War II. When she attended college at the University of Nebraska, she was assigned to a separate dorm for foreign and nonwhite students, and encountered fraternities and sororities that excluded students of color. Many people suffered those blows of discrimination in silence, but not Patsy Mink. While America was at war with Japan, she got herself elected student body president of her high school. At the University of Nebraska, she gave speeches and wrote letters to protest the housing segregation policy, which the university ended before she graduated.

Mink went to law school at the University of Chicago, but after graduation, she had trouble finding a job. Law firms did not want to hire her, not only because she was a woman, but also because she was married—in a mixed-race marriage, which was additionally disfavored—and the mother of a young child. She did not let the discrimination stop her. She became the first Japanese American woman to practice law in Hawaii by passing the bar and opening up her own law office. Representing women in divorce and adoption cases, she got to know the problems facing real families. When she launched her political career, she was a natural at going door to door to talk with voters.

Within a few years of Mink's arrival in Washington in 1965, she was joined by Shirley Chisholm, the first African American woman to be elected to Congress in 1968. Well before becoming colleagues in the House, Mink and Chisholm seemed to share a political philosophy, which Chisholm summed up when she said, "If they don't give you a seat at the table, bring a folding chair."[2]

Chisholm was a teacher from Brooklyn, New York, where she had run a childcare center for many years before getting involved in state politics. Only a few months after taking her seat in the House of Representatives, she reintroduced the Equal Rights Amendment, asking, "If women are already equal, why is it such an event whenever one happens to be elected to Congress?"[3] Chisholm went on in 1972 to seek the Democratic nomination for the Presidency, becoming the first African American woman to do so. Mink, too, ran a limited presidential campaign in 1972. The nomination went to George McGovern, but these two women made a major crack in the highest glass ceiling, which would remain unshattered for at least another fifty years.

Together, Mink and Chisholm gave the ERA a legal and political infrastructure focused on disadvantages with which they were acutely familiar because of their experiences. Both had competed in elections against men of their own race, and Chisholm admitted, "in the political world I have been far oftener discriminated against because I am a woman than because I am black."[4] That statement was copied into the Senate Judiciary Committee's favorable report on the ERA three years later[5] and quoted abundantly during the floor debates that resulted in the ERA's adoption by Congress. Their vision of the ERA responded to the unique problems of working women, including mothers, and moved the women in the House to defeat the crippling amendments that the ERA's opponents introduced.

When Martha Griffiths's discharge petition led to the first floor debate in the House on August 10, 1970, Patsy Mink expressed her unequivocal belief that the ERA would guard, rather than threaten, any existing legal protections that were helpful to women. Any law that conferred rights, benefits, or privileges to one sex would have to be construed to apply to both sexes.[6] Like Crystal Eastman almost fifty years before, Mink believed that women would fare better if their protections could be kept and expanded to men, rather than abolished.

Mink's strong stance on labor protections for women was a response to some feminists from labor organizations who had objected to the ERA in hearings before a subcommittee of the Senate Judiciary Committee a few months before. Myra Wolfgang, a well-known labor leader, had testified, "The working mother has no 'wife' to care for her or her children. She assumes the role of home maker and worker and must perform both these roles in a 24-hour period. Even in the two-parent households, there is an unequal division of domestic chores."[7] Some states still prohibited employers from requiring women to work overtime, and regulated employment before and after childbirth. Wolfgang noted, "It would be desirable for some of these laws to be extended to men, but the practical fact is that an equal rights amendment is likely to destroy the laws altogether rather than bring about coverage for both sexes."[8]

By the time Mink argued for expanding rights rather than abolishing them to achieve equality, she had waged and won other battles in Congress on behalf of working mothers. She was the leading female voice in the January 1970 Senate Judiciary Committee hearings successfully opposing the nomination of Judge Carswell to the US Supreme Court. Judge Carswell had voted against rehearing a lower court's decision in *Phillips v. Martin Marietta*,[9] one of the first sex discrimination cases to reach the Supreme Court under the Civil Rights Act of 1964. In that case, the employer had refused to hire a woman, not just because she was a woman, but because she was a mother of preschool-age children. Judge Carswell had affirmed a decision saying that the employer's exclusion of mothers of young children was not sex discrimination, since the employer employed women who were not mothers.

During the Carswell hearings, Mink pointed out that the employer in that case hired men with preschool-age children, and therefore, refusing to hire a woman with preschool age children was discrimination on the basis of sex. She characterized Judge Carswell's vote as "a vote against the right of women to be treated equally and fairly under the law." Why? "Four million working mothers in this country have children under the age of 6 years."[10] In becoming a leading voice on behalf of working mothers against Carswell's confirmation, Patsy Mink contributed to Carswell's defeat in the Senate, paving the way for the nomination and confirmation of Justice Harry Blackmun. (Shortly thereafter, Justice Blackmun became the author of *Roe v. Wade*, establishing women's constitutional right to choose an abortion.)

In the ERA debate a few months later in August 1970, Republican women like Florence Dwyer and Margaret Heckler emphasized the ERA's compatibility with the enduring role of mothers and homemakers. Two weeks after the House's first adoption of the ERA, the needs of mothers and homemakers became the focus of protests across the nation. Commemorating the fiftieth anniversary of the women's suffrage amendment, the Women's Strike for Equality brought women out into the streets across the country.

Betty Friedan, the bestselling author of *The Feminine Mystique*, had ignited women across America who were demanding liberation from their traditional roles as homemakers. She led the National Organization for Women in arranging marches in New York, San Francisco, and points in between.[11] Friedan's call for a "women's strike" was for women to stop working—at home and at work—to demand "the new social institutions that are needed to free women, not from childbearing or love or sex or even marriage, but from the intolerable agony and burden those become when women are chained to them."[12] The strike's organizers planned "baby-ins" near the demonstration sites, where children would be left while their mothers participated in the strikes, to draw attention to the need for day-care centers. One of the planners was Bella Abzug, then a Democratic candidate for the House of Representatives. She envisioned a march that would be "a statement, and commitment from the Women of America that the oppressed majority are coming into their political own."[13]

In New York City, 50,000 women gathered in what was the largest march for women's rights.[14] Bella Abzug's speech before the crowd in Bryant Park called for the implementation of the strike's three major demands: free and legal abortion; the establishment of community-controlled, twenty-four-hour day-care centers for the children of working mothers; and equality of educational and employment opportunity. "We mean to have it now!" she declared.[15] Eleanor Holmes Norton, then the chair of the New York City Commission on Human Rights (and now congresswoman for the District of Columbia), called on the Senate to pass the Equal Rights Amendment that the House had adopted just two weeks before. She stressed that a mandate to prevent job discrimination against women "is an empty mandate unless the women have a place to leave their children."[16]

The Women's Strike for Equality joined the demand for equal rights in employment and education with the demand for affordable, sustainable, high-quality childcare. These were not two independent goals; childcare was a necessary precondition of women's advanced education and employment at levels equal to men. In San Francisco, Judy Syfers, a housewife-turned-activist, gave a speech, "I Want a Wife," which poignantly articulated this point: "I belong to that classification of people known as wives. And not altogether incidentally, I am a mother. . . . I, too, would like to have a wife. . . . I would like a wife so that I can become economically dependent on myself, and, if need be, support those dependent upon me. I want a wife who will work and send me to school. And while I am going to school I want a wife to take care of my children."[17] As the floor debates in the House two weeks before had illustrated, women from both political parties saw equal pay and childcare as crucially linked to the goals of the Equal Rights Amendment. A few months later, Bella Abzug was elected to the Congress that would adopt the ERA.

For the working mother who had no wife, the law would have to provide the support that she needed to be equal to men. The ERA would be the beginning, rather than the end, of this political, legal, and social transformation. It would have to catalyze public policies that would do more than a wife could. Childcare was a major component. Since 1969, childcare had been the subject of congressional hearings that had preoccupied the congresswomen who became the most ardent proponents of the ERA. Patsy Mink had served, along with fellow House Democrat Edith Green, on the House committee that held hearings on the Comprehensive Preschool Education and Child Day-Care Act in 1969. Shirley Chisholm testified at several hearings on those childcare bills.

Chisholm reported that "one of the things that we are not really doing in our Nation is really meeting the needs of the working-women of this country."[18] She said, quite bluntly, that "the day-care disaster we face in the United States is the result of America's tradition of discrimination against women." Increasingly, women were breadwinners, just like men, and this was even more true of poor women. Chisholm then argued that the day-care disaster, unequal pay, and women's underrepresentation in leadership were all part of a pattern. "Look around you," she said. "Out of 435 Members of the House, 10 are women." Why this severe underrepresentation?

Female responsibility for children, Chisholm insisted. "It takes two people—one male and one female—to make a baby." Yet law and public policy made it "just as difficult as possible for women to work: rotten wages, poor day-care services, limits on training programs, and little opportunity for advancement."[19] Chisholm's childcare testimony pointed out that Russia, Scandinavia, Israel, and many other countries had comprehensive day care funded by government.[20] The legislation that Patsy Mink's committee was proposing, and for which Shirley Chisholm was advocating in hearings, would have provided funding for high-quality day-care centers for all children—not only the poor.

In between this childcare hearing and the ERA floor debate in August, Patsy Mink and Edith Green were busy hosting hearings of the House Committee on Education and Labor on Title IX of the Education Amendments Act. Eventually adopted in 1972, Title IX states: "No person in the United States shall, on the basis of sex, be excluded from participation in, be denied the benefits of, or be subjected to discrimination under any education program or activity receiving Federal financial assistance."[21] It has been interpreted to go beyond prohibiting discrimination; it measures equality by rates of actual participation by the underrepresented sex—usually women and girls. It is also the primary source of law for addressing sexual harassment and violence on campus.

Patsy Mink is often referred to as the "Mother of Title IX" because she was a principal driving force of the law in Congress. Upon her death in 2002, the statute was renamed the Patsy Takemoto Mink Equal Opportunity in Education Act to recognize her legacy. Held in June 1970, the hearings on Title IX featured some of the same witnesses who had testified in support of the ERA before the Senate just a month before, including Virginia Allan, chair of the President's Task Force on Women's Rights and Responsibilities. Republican congresswomen Catherine May and Margaret Heckler also testified in support of Title IX, as did Martha Griffiths. Mink's statement during these hearings focused on specific manifestations of gender inequality in education: underrepresentation of women in both the faculty and student ranks and disparity in pay between male and female faculty. What was wrong with these forms of inequality was not only the unfairness to women, but that "our society is denied full use of our human resources," by way of this "glaring favoritism" for men.[22] In the education realm, Mink believed that Congress had a particular obligation to take legislative action to eliminate the "glaring favoritism" that benefited men for generations. It is clear that the framers of the ERA saw statutes like Title IX and the Comprehensive Child Development Act as cut from the same cloth as the Equal Rights Amendment.

Unlike Florence Kelley in the 1920s, or Myra Wolfgang in May 1970, Patsy Mink did not allow her appreciation of protections for working women to destroy her support for the ERA. At first, she wanted language in the ERA specifying that existing privileges for one sex would be applied to both sexes equally, but she did not condition her support of the ERA on such an amendment. She didn't have to, because the proponents of the unmodified ERA coalesced around her vision of how the ERA would work. The language of the Equal Rights Amendment by itself does not require the expansion of rights to achieve equality, but the legislative history strongly favors this interpretation. Mink announced that she would vote for the simple ERA, without the clarifying language that she proposed, because "[i]t would be my hope that the legislative record that is being made today will serve to give us this judicial construction which we intend."[23]

For the ERA's proponents, the amendment was not only about these specific legal puzzles, but about establishing a new constitutional sensibility around the full participation of women in every aspect of social, economic, and political life. As Shirley Chisholm put it, "The time is clearly now to put this House on record for the fullest expression of that equality of opportunity which our founding fathers professed. They professed it, but they did not assure it to their daughters, as they tried to do for their sons. The Constitution they wrote was designed to protect the rights of white, male citizens."[24] The ERA provided an opportunity to correct and perfect the

Founding Fathers' work. "[T]here were no black Founding Fathers, there were no founding mothers—a great pity, on both counts. It is not too late to complete the work they left undone. Today, here, we should start to do so."[25] The women in Congress—and especially these two women of color—were talking about a new constitutionalism that would include people excluded by the Founding Fathers.

But they faced resistance in the House by men who feared the consequences of this new constitutional vision. After a burial in the Senate's legislative graveyard in 1970, and a resurrection brokered by Martha Griffiths for reintroduction in the House in 1971, the ERA had been through some changes. By the time the House Judiciary Committee reported the ERA and sent it to the floor for a vote, Republican congressman Charles Wiggins of California had tacked on an amendment reminiscent of Sam Ervin's attempt to exempt women from the draft. The Wiggins amendment had been endorsed by a divided House Judiciary Committee that summer. It read: "This article shall not impair the validity of any law of the United States which exempts a person from compulsory military service or any other law of the United States or of any State which reasonably promotes the health and safety of the people."[26]

Like the Ervin amendment that had stopped the ERA from going to the states for ratification in 1970, the Wiggins amendment proposed to allow Congress to exempt women from the military draft, and further to allow Congress and state legislatures to make sex distinctions when reasonable to promote health and safety. The well-being of families and children animated these concerns: If the ERA required mothers to be drafted, and prohibited special accommodations for pregnant women, families and children would face new harms. In voicing these concerns, proponents of the Wiggins amendment claimed that they supported the ERA in principle: "the proposed Constitutional amendment would be a means of articulating a National Policy against sex discrimination which is needed and has not yet been fully articulated by the judicial system."[27] Nonetheless, the Wiggins amendment was rejected by the House, with 87 members in favor of it and 265 against. Some, but not all, proponents of the Wiggins amendment went on to vote in favor of the ERA without the Wiggins language.

In the October 1971 floor debates leading to the ERA's adoption by both houses of Congress, the women of the House rallied against the Wiggins amendment. Within this debate, these congresswomen articulated a sophisticated constitutional theory that is often forgotten in discussions of the ERA today. Shirley Chisholm called out the Wiggins amendment as "a parliamentary trick meant to permit Members of this body who are opposed to equality for women, to appear to vote for it." She argued that "[t]here is no truth whatever to the assertion, on which much of the support for the Wiggins version rests, that the equal rights amendment in its unmodified form would sweep away laws that the States have passed for the protection of women." By this time, Chisholm, like Republican senator Marlow Cook, interpreted the ERA in original form as preserving and expanding, rather than abolishing, any special rights enjoyed by women only: "The State laws that are in question fall into two classes," she explained. "Either they guarantee to women benefits that should be guaranteed to men as well, or they deprive women of rights that men are allowed to exercise."[28] The ERA would not require the eradication of special rights for one sex; it would require such rights to be extended to both sexes.

Patsy Mink described the Wiggins amendment as "highly mischievous." In the guise of preserving special protections for women, it made the ERA "worthless and demeaning and destructive to women." In exposing the Wiggins amendment as a wolf in sheep's clothing, Mink also advanced a different vision of how constitutional rights would work. The Wiggins amendment assumed that the guarantee of equal rights would move judges to abolish all sex distinctions, thereby necessitating language allowing exceptions. But because women were already included in the Equal Protection Clause, in Mink's view, the ERA was redundant as a legal tool for judges. Nevertheless, the ERA was still necessary because "the courts have refused to acknowledge this right in case after case which have been brought to the courts' attention."

Against this landscape, the purpose of the ERA was "to underscore this fundamental human right which I believe is guaranteed by the Constitution but which courts have denied." The ERA would ignite new governmental action, in addition to extinguishing old sex distinctions. "It may be redundant to have this constitutional amendment, but there are worse things than redundancy, among them the lack of action by our executive, legislative, and judicial bodies to put into effect the equal rights safeguards already in the Constitution." Mink envisioned the *lack of governmental action* in all three branches as the problem that made the ERA necessary. She explained: "The equal rights amendment as originally offered will awaken our somnolent public servants to the fact that women are people and fully entitled to equal protection of the laws. Adoption of the amendment would, I also agree, leave us the formidable task of seeking extensive legislation and judicial actions to implement it in all States and local jurisdictions across the country."[29]

At that moment, Patsy Mink saw the ERA as "constitutional backing" for transformative laws like Title IX and the Comprehensive Child Development Act.[30] Title IX was passed in June 1972, three months after the ERA was sent to the states for ratification. Mink had made her legislative theory of constitutional rights more explicit in her testimony before the House judiciary subommittee's 1971 hearing on the ERA. Mink said that there were three general approaches to injustice: (1) a constitutional amendment in the form of the ERA, (2) judicial attacks on discriminatory laws under the Fifth and Fourteenth Amendments, and "(3) passage of Federal and State legislation to prohibit overt discrimination and to eliminate situations which are discriminatory in effect." Mink noted, "While these approaches are not mutually exclusive—and indeed, could be attempted simultaneously—it is my belief that the most immediate progress is attainable through the third alternative, direct legislative enactments."[31] The ERA would provide a compass for these legislative projects, and the legislatures would be looking not only to repeal laws that distinguished by sex overtly, but also to change situations where women were disparately impacted or

THE MOTHERS • 79

burdened. On the House floor, Mink said that "No constitutional provision claiming to pronounce equality for all with the Wiggins amendment will guarantee equality in fact."[32] Implicitly affirming Mink's vision, the Senate Judiciary Committee report sending the ERA to the Senate floor in March 1972 cited the Title IX hearings as a source of evidence for the problems that were driving the quest for the ERA.[33]

This vision of the ERA—as a necessary foundation for legislators implementing real equality on the ground—was amplified by other women in the House. Martha Griffiths, like Patsy Mink, acknowledged the possibility that judges would simply interpret the ERA in the same way that they interpreted the Equal Protection Clause. So why was the ERA needed? Griffiths believed that it would send an important message to the Supreme Court, saying, "Wake up! This is the 20th century. Before it is over, judge women as individual human beings. They, too, are entitled to the protection of the Constitution, the basic fundamental law of this country."[34] Then, with the Supreme Court's eyes wide open, Griffiths agreed with Mink that the ERA would be in the hands of legislators, not judges. Griffiths had introduced her discharge petition in August 1970 by saying, "[T]his is not a battle between the sexes—nor a battle between this body and women. This body and State legislatures have supported women. This is a battle with the Supreme Court of the United States."[35]

Ella Grasso, newly elected to Congress from Connecticut in 1970, also reinforced the conviction that the political branches of government, not the courts, would give effect to the ERA. "History shows that women cannot rely on the courts to achieve their rights," she noted. "Indeed, Congress must provide the constitutional framework upon which to build a body of law to achieve the goal of equal rights. Our responsibility is clear."[36] Grasso would go on to become the first woman governor of Connecticut in 1975.

Although it was possible for that body of sex equality law envisioned by Grasso, including Title IX, to emerge even without an ERA, there was an important connection between the ERA's text and these legislative agendas. Section 2 of the ERA grants Congress the power to enforce the ERA. It is noteworthy that, of all the changes that the Senate inserted into the House's ERA of 1970—the seven-year ratification deadline, the military draft exemption for women, the school prayer provision, and the two-year delay before the effective date of the ERA—Martha Griffiths resurrected only two of them from the legislative graveyard: the seven-year deadline and the two-year delay for the effective date. Of these, only the two-year delay was actually inserted into the text of the proposed constitutional amendment itself. (The ratification deadline was in the resolution proposing the ERA.) This distinction is important, because ultimately, Griffiths embraced the two-year delay on effective date, while she was less enthused by the seven-year ratification deadline.

In ERA hearings, Griffiths noted that the purpose of the two-year delay was to give the states as well as the federal government the time to review their own laws. During that period, before judges could start enforcing and interpreting the ERA, Congress and the states would repeal or replace laws that abridged women's equality of rights. Doing so would give the legislative branches the opportunity to lead the courts in defining the meaning of the ERA. By enacting legislation to implement equal rights, legislatures could build robust legislative records illuminating why some laws would be repealed while others would be kept and expanded, and what to do about policies that unintentionally disadvantaged women. Unlike courts, legislatures could replace discriminatory laws by designing public policy respectful of equal rights, rather than simply striking down laws. Griffiths also made clear that the law could continue to treat pregnancy and motherhood differently. "[Y]ou would have to have some distinction in laws that apply to mothers, to pregnant women, because men aren't pregnant,"[37] she said. That, too, would be up to the legislatures.

Democratic congresswoman Bella Abzug, who went from being a Women's Strike organizer to a congresswoman from New York within a year, became a powerful voice for the working mothers' ERA.[38] In her testimony at ERA hearings in March 1971,

Abzug echoed Patsy Mink's remarks during the Carswell hearings and Shirley Chisholm's contributions to the comprehensive childcare hearings. Abzug framed the ERA as an amendment that working mothers needed. A major factor perpetuating inequality was the lack of childcare: "Those of us in Congress should be particularly concerned that we have the large female work force that I have described . . . yet, to this day, in 1971, we don't have a universal child-care system. . ." Abzug explained that "millions of women are working because they have to; and it is not only women who have to sacrifice as a result of this, but it is the children, who are the future of our society, who are being penalized by what is essentially a very sexist, which means a male-thinking society."[39] Through these words, Abzug brought a central demand from the Women's Strike for Equality to the congressional consideration of the ERA: the need for a publicly supported childcare infrastructure to support real equality of opportunity for women.[40]

In the floor debate, Abzug, too, opposed the Wiggins amendment by pointing out that protective labor laws prevented women from "enjoying the full fruits of their labor." On the ground, special labor laws for women only "excluded women from more lucrative jobs." These laws gave women special treatment they did not need, while withholding the one form of special treatment that women actually needed—maternity leave. Abzug said, "[S]ome States require that women, unlike men, be given chairs for rest periods but I want any Member to show me what States provide a guarantee of security for maternity leave so that women will still have jobs to return to after giving birth."[41] In connecting maternity leave to the ERA, Abzug assumed that the ERA would be compatible with maternity benefits for women only, as did the Senate Judiciary Committee's 1972 report sending the ERA to the Senate floor: "'Equality' does not mean 'sameness,'" it explained. "As a result, the original resolution would not prohibit reasonable classifications based on characteristics that are unique to one sex. For example a law providing for payment of the medical costs of child bearing could only apply to women."[42]

Congresswomen across the political spectrum unified against the Wiggins amendment. Louise Hicks, a conservative Democrat who opposed busing for racial integration, objected to the Wiggins amendment because she believed that mothers with family responsibilities would be exempted from the military draft regardless.[43] Republican Margaret Heckler voted against the Wiggins amendment because she firmly believed that the ERA could recognize difference without it. Heckler told personal stories of her experiences as a woman politician who was also a mother. During one of her first congressional campaigns, she ran into an opponent she had defeated in a primary for Congress. That opponent said, "If I had known you were a mother, that race would have really been different." Ultimately, for Heckler, the ERA was not needed to get sameness to overcome difference—it was needed to overcome these attitudes. There was no need to modify the ERA to do just that.[44]

The women of the House soundly defeated the Wiggins amendment. The unmodified ERA bill passed the House on October 12, 1971, in a vote of 354–24. The Senate followed suit, adopting the same unmodified ERA on March 22, 1972 by a vote of 84–8. That's 93 percent of the House and 92 percent of the Senate. Within a year, thirty states had ratified the ERA, with six years to get the eight remaining states. The ERA seemed unstoppable.

But some of the men who voted against the ERA were really determined to stop it. After losing by a landslide in the Senate, Sam Ervin declared that time would be his "best friend and weapon" in defeating the ERA in the states. [45] And then he found an even better friend and weapon—a formidable mother of six—who was ready for combat.

7

The Breadmakers

BY 1972, PHYLLIS SCHLAFLY WAS a household name. As Patsy Mink was campaigning in 1964 for the seat that would make her the first woman of color ever elected to Congress, Schlafly became a bestselling author. Her book, *A Choice Not an Echo*, called upon the true conservatives of America to take back the Republican Party from the moderates prone to compromising with liberals.[1] The book started with a speech that she wrote to boost Senator Barry Goldwater's campaign for the presidency. Determined to get the word out as quickly as possible, Schlafly just published the book herself. She set up her own publishing operation in January 1964, and by August, her book had sold 1.6 million copies and helped Barry Goldwater win the Republican nomination. Goldwater did not win the presidency, but Schlafly's book laid the groundwork for a conservative movement that became unstoppable. In 1972, Schlafly turned her attention to the Equal Rights Amendment.

In the Senate, there were only eight men who voted against the ERA in 1972. Barry Goldwater was one of them. The ERA drew overwhelming support from most Republicans and Democrats in the Senate, well beyond the two-thirds required by the Constitution.

But this landslide did not happen without a long and drawn-out fight. Opponents packed the legislative record with hours and pages of rousing speeches, which went straight from the *Congressional Record* to Phyllis Schlafly's operation for mass distribution. Thus the STOP-ERA movement was born.

Senate rules made it possible for a small minority of vocal skeptics to help themselves to generous portions of air time on the floor and prolong the debate. Senator Sam Ervin had effectively stopped the ERA in the Senate in October 1970 with his very long justifications for the military exemption amendment. Martha Griffiths did not give up the ERA fight, and neither would he. When he returned to the Senate floor in March 1972, he was armed with an even longer list of changes to propose to the ERA adopted by the House, and a lot to say about each one.

Ervin's colleagues in the Senate smelled the threat of filibuster in the air. They knew that Ervin was no novice to the Senate filibuster—many of them were there in 1964 when Ervin was one of the Southern senators who filibustered the Civil Rights Act in an attempt to kill antidiscrimination protections for racial minorities and women. In opening the ERA debate on March 15, 1972, Senator Birch Bayh said, "I am convinced that the Senator from North Carolina is sincere in his determination not to participate in any delaying or dilatory tactics."[2] Senator Bayh limited ERA debate to sixteen hours. Ervin agreed, but his ERA speeches occupy more pages of the *Congressional Record* than the ERA speeches of all of the women in the House combined. Even when Ervin was not himself speaking, the ERA debates in the Senate were almost exclusively devoted to the amendments he proposed.

Ervin was back with the same amendment from 1970 that would allow Congress to exempt women from the military draft. Believing in the separation of church and state, he had opposed the school prayer amendment when it was originally proposed. And he did not try again to propose to end busing to integrate schools. But there were other issues that he thought would get his colleagues worked up. He proposed an amendment saying that the ERA would not require same-sex marriage. He tried another amendment that looked a lot like the Wiggins amendment that had failed in the House, generally allowing state and federal laws that protected women. And another that explicitly said that fathers could be required to pay child support. And another protecting the privacy of women and men, intended to preserve single-sex bathrooms. And finally, an amendment that said that the ERA would not disturb rape laws.[3]

Ervin claimed to speak on behalf of mothers and homemakers. In October 1970, he memorably quoted a Spanish proverb, "An ounce of mother is worth a pound of priest,"[4] practically etching it on the ERA's tombstone as he sent it to the legislative graveyard. Ervin claimed that the ERA "seeks to rob the wives, the homemakers, the mothers, the working women, and the widows of America."[5] In response to ERA proponents' efforts to challenge the exemption of women from jury service, Ervin insisted that these laws enabled women to say, "Treat me like a mother."[6]

Phyllis Schlafly had not given much thought to what the ERA would mean for mothers until after she took in Ervin's objections. As the ERA was being debated in Congress in 1970, Schlafly ran for a congressional seat in Illinois held by George Shipley, a Democrat who voted for the ERA in the House. She did not make an issue of the ERA in that campaign, which focused on reforming welfare and foreign policy. Shipley made an issue of Schlafly's motherhood—he said Schlafly should "quit attacking my foreign-aid votes and stay home with her husband and six kids." To that, Schlafly shot back, "My opponent says a woman's place is in the home . . . . But my husband replies that a woman's place is in the House – the U.S. House of Representatives."[7] In the same election season, Bella Abzug was using that as her campaign slogan across the country in the race that she won in New York, following her leading role in the Women's Strike for Equality. Schlafly lost her 1970 bid for Congress, but she cut her teeth at campaigning and organizing.

During this time, she recalled years later, "I figured ERA was something between innocuous and mildly helpful." But after the

House voted to adopt it in 1971, a friend urged Schlafly to debate a feminist about the ERA. Schlafly's initial reaction was, "I don't even know which side I'm on."[8] So she read about the ERA debates in Congress, and by February 1972, she wrote to Sam Ervin wishing him success in defeating the ERA in the Senate.[9] She took over Ervin's motherhood rhetoric in her article, "What's Wrong with Equal Rights for Women?" which she published in her own newsletter, *The Phyllis Schlafly Report*. Her argument was simple: Women had babies and men didn't. It followed, then, that the single greatest achievement in the entire history of women's rights was the right to bear and raise children, and to "be supported and protected in the enjoyment of watching her baby grow and develop." That was one fact of life that no law or political movement could change, Schlafly concluded. "Of all the classes of people who ever lived, the American woman is the most privileged. We have the most rights and rewards, and the fewest duties."[10] Schlafly warned that the ERA would destroy the privileged status of American women.

When the ERA returned to the Senate floor in March 1972, Senator Ervin invoked a Yiddish proverb that said, "God could not be everywhere, so he made mothers."[11] Ervin insisted that the ERA would absolutely prohibit any difference in the treatment of men and women. But Ervin's account of what the ERA would do was an invented caricature. It did not line up with the picture of the ERA that its framers in the House and proponents in the Senate articulated. ERA proponents wanted to outlaw discrimination against women, but nobody wanted an ERA to abolish all sex distinctions. In fact, neither proponents nor opponents of the ERA questioned the continued desirability of maternity leave to cover pregnancy and childbirth, separate bathroom facilities for women and men, and rape laws.

Furthermore, congresswomen from both political parties—Florence Dwyer, Patsy Mink, Margaret Heckler, and Bella Abzug—put forth an ERA that would help working mothers as well as homemakers. They described inequalities that stemmed from motherhood and homemaking as problems that the ERA would overcome. Ervin did not even recognize these congress-women's contributions as he attacked the ERA. And because these Congresswomen were all in the House and not the Senate, there was no direct confrontation between them in a legislative debate on the floor. Ervin conveniently ignored what they had said and written.

When all of his proposed amendments failed, Senator Ervin then attempted to package all of them into one amendment, and proposed that *both* the simple ERA *and* this ERA package full of exceptions be sent to the states for ratification, to see if any of them would be ratified by three-fourths of them. That proposal, too, was rejected by an overwhelming majority of the Senate. Hours upon hours were spent considering all of Senator Ervin's proposals, before they were all soundly defeated. Ultimately, eighty-four senators embraced the simpler ERA that the House had adopted, with no qualifying language.

Does that mean that the senators who voted for the ERA were in favor of drafting women, same-sex marriage, fathers not pay-ing child support, unisex bathrooms, and the repeal of rape law? Absolutely not. In floor debates, the eighty-four senators who voted for the ERA had a wide range of opinions on these issues. Some expressed no opinion at all. Therefore, we cannot say with con-fidence that the senators who voted for the ERA fully endorsed the significant social and cultural changes that Ervin's amendments tried to prevent. The rejection of Ervin's amendments was simply a rejection of Ervin's caricatured portrait of the ERA as an amend-ment that would require women and men to be treated exactly the same in all possible circumstances. If the ERA did not require rigid sex-blindness in the first place, Ervin's amendments making excep-tions to it would be unnecessary and irrelevant. In voting for the ERA without Ervin's amendments, the senators advanced an ERA that was primarily a statement of general principle, a proclamation of women's status as equals. They were not voting for an ERA that required a unisex approach to everything, and therefore they did not need to vote for the amendments that spelled out its exceptions.

The best evidence supporting this account of the ERA's meaning in the Senate can be found in a speech by John Sherman Cooper, a Republican senator from Kentucky. Cooper explained that Ervin's amendments were all premised on one possible interpretation of the ERA, and not its necessary legal meaning. Statutes could resolve these specific questions and conflicts, but a constitutional amendment would be a declaration of women's equality and entitlement to rights. But then, why would a constitutional amendment be necessary? Wasn't it purely symbolic? Cooper acknowledged that he was somewhat "doubtful that the amendment is really needed." But he voted for it anyway out of respect for women. "I have the belief that the women of this country believe it is needed, and that they want Congress and the State legislatures to express their full equality. I shall vote for the measure."[12] By this time, Senator Cooper had earned the admiration of a young Mitch McConnell, who had interned in the senator's mailroom. McConnell wrote years later in his autobiography that his deep respect for Senator Cooper stemmed largely from Cooper's brave leadership in breaking the Senate filibuster over the Civil Rights Act of 1964.[13]

There was one woman in Congress who voted against the ERA in 1971: Leonor Kretzer Sullivan, a Democrat from Missouri. Her words, like Ervin's, found their way into Phyllis Schlafly's writings against the ERA. Congresswoman Sullivan was elected to Congress a year after her husband died in office in 1951. Sullivan's remarks and vote against the ERA may seem surprising in light of her record in Congress of supporting policies in favor of working women. She supported income tax law reforms that enabled widows and working mothers to make deductions for childcare, and she also opposed cuts to the Women's Bureau of the Department of Labor.

In many respects, Sullivan was a holdover from the Florence Kelley era: like Kelley, she was an advocate for consumers, and helped pass several consumer protection laws. On the floor of the House, she said, "I trust I will not be accused of being a 'male supremacist' because I cannot vote for the so-called equal rights amendment." Sullivan expressed concern that the ERA would impose equal legal obligations on mothers and fathers to support their spouses and children, particularly upon desertion. "One of the most serious of all of our social problems is the disregard by millions of American men of their obligations for the support of their families, even under threat of prosecution." She was worried about fathers neglecting their obligations to support their children. She did not think the Constitution should make it "impossible for our courts to punish a deserting father for failure to at least try to support his children." She warned that this could then accelerate "the process of family disintegration."[14] A few years later, Phyllis Schlafly would quote Sullivan in a book she wrote to rally the STOP-ERA movement.[15] The "STOP" in "STOP-ERA" stood for "Stop Taking Our Privileges." She used Sullivan's words to say that the ERA would end husbands' financial support of their wives and children—a great privilege that American women enjoyed.

In March 1972, Senator Sam Ervin did not convince most of his Senate colleagues that the ERA would destroy American motherhood. But he convinced Schlafly, who proved more effective than the men in the Senate at stopping the ERA. Ervin and Schlafly formed a strategic collaboration to stop ERA ratification, beginning with Ervin's home state of North Carolina. There, the senator had privileges that enabled him to send mail to constituents at the taxpayers' expense, which he shared with Schlafly. Schlafly edited his anti-ERA speeches in Congress into readable format to be delivered to the North Carolina electorate.[16] Schlafly then arranged for Ervin's edited speeches to go out to STOP-ERA activists and legislators in twenty-four states.[17]

Schlafly inspired American mothers and homemakers throughout the Midwest and the South to become politically active, to stop the ERA from being ratified. Schlafly disseminated Ervin's speeches to these new audiences of women who could now have a say on what their Constitution would do. The STOP-ERA campaign materials, made from Ervin's floor speeches in the Senate, told a story of forgotten mothers: Ervin proposed amendments to the ERA in Congress to try as hard as he could to make sure that the

ERA would put mothers on the pedestal that they deserved. That pedestal would protect mothers from the unpleasantries of military service, bathrooms shared with men, deadbeat dads, and rape.

Schlafly wrote that the rejection of all of Ervin's amendments "constitute an impressive legislative history of what ERA is intended to accomplish. They reveal the radical changes in society that ERA will compel."[18] Because Ervin's amendment exempting women from military service failed, for instance, Schlafly claimed that the ERA would most certainly require women to be drafted. Similarly, Schlafly claimed that laws that helped wives or mothers would automatically be defunct under the ERA, that bathrooms would be integrated, and that laws criminalizing rape would be dead letter.

Schlafly essentially rewrote the ERA's legislative history for her readership. Her version omitted and departed from what ERA proponents in Congress actually said in response to the Wiggins and Ervin amendments. The bipartisan supporters of the ERA did not reject those amendments because they embraced Wiggins's and Ervin's depiction of what the ERA would do. They rejected these efforts to modify the ERA because they believed that a constitutional amendment for women's equality would simply state a foundational principle. It would not resolve all the specific policy questions involving sex distinctions in the law. As for the military draft, most of the ERA's vocal proponents were critical of the Vietnam War and against the military draft for men and women alike. In fact, with waning popular support for the war, the draft ended in 1973. The mothers of the ERA wanted to nourish the legal and political conditions by which women—most of whom were wives, mothers, homemakers, or all of the above—could participate equally in shaping the life of the nation. Yet the actual legislative history, featuring the well-reasoned arguments of women lawmakers, was successfully distorted and then forgotten. Schlafly became the self-proclaimed champion of American mothers and wives, and she turned the ERA into the enemy of mothers, rather than a constitutional home for them.

Although thirty states ratified within a year of Congress's adoption in 1972, Schlafly had already organized STOP-ERA chapters in twenty-six states by early 1973. Each STOP-ERA chapter was headed by a chairwoman handpicked by Schlafly. These organizations flourished in Arizona, Florida, Illinois, Louisiana, Missouri, Ohio, Oklahoma, and Virginia.[19] With the exception of Ohio, none of these states ratified the ERA within seven years of its adoption by Congress. ERA ratification began to stall. Nebraska's legislature attempted to rescind its ratification in 1973, followed by Idaho, Kentucky, Tennessee, and South Dakota by 1979. Very few states ratified after 1973. In 1977, Indiana became the 35th state to ratify the ERA, the last state to do so before the 1979 or 1982 deadlines. Lifelong ERA warrior Alice Paul died that year, at the age of 92.

Meanwhile, Schlafly's home state of Illinois became a major battleground. There, she mobilized combat units of housewives to caravan to the state's capitol whenever ERA ratification resolutions were being considered, armed with freshly baked bread and pies. They would affix stickers that said, FROM THE BREADMAKERS TO THE BREADWINNERS.[20] Sometimes they would bring babies wearing "STOP-ERA" badges. They put their Thanksgiving cooking plans on hold to march to the capitol in defense of a woman's "most precious and important right of all"—the right to be a mother.[21]

Schlafly claimed that the ERA would strike down all laws that made husbands liable for the support of their wives, including those that protected alimony for housewives facing divorce. The campaign appealed to middle-aged women who had married young and devoted themselves exclusively to home and family for decades. For housewives who had forsaken career for motherhood, a divorce that treated the spouses the same could mean destitution and the loss of custody over their children.[22]

Schlafly delighted in getting under the feminists' skin and sought out those opportunities. When the pro-ERA National Women's Conference convened in Houston in 1977,[23] Phyllis Schlafly hosted a counter-event that she billed as a "pro-family rally" in Houston's nearby Astro Arena. The National Women's Conference was funded by a congressional act sponsored by Patsy Mink in 1975. Bella Abzug was the chairwoman who planned the conference. Martha Griffiths and Margaret Heckler were there, too. The National Plan for Action that emerged from the conference called for ERA ratification,[24] as well as governmental action in funding and providing childcare,[25] eliminating domestic violence,[26] and helping homemakers displaced by widowhood, divorce, or desertion.[27] It drew 20,000 people.

But another 15,000 people, including many mothers and housewives from across America, converged on the Astro Arena, convinced by Schlafly that the ERA would destroy their families. Phyllis Schlafly promised, "If you stay with us, the equal rights amendment will die 16 months from Tuesday, and then we'll have another party."[28] Because the ERA proponents who were gathered across town that day managed to extend the deadline, Schlafly had her party on June 30, 1982 to dance on the grave of the ERA.[29]

How did Phyllis Schlafly manage to stop the ERA?

It is a simple social fact, not a romantic stereotype, that most American women are mothers. Statistics from 2016 indicate that 86 percent of American women have given birth at least once by the time they have reached the end of their childbearing years at the age of forty-four.[30] In the late 1970s, the percentage of American women who became mothers had peaked above 90 percent. Even when the motherhood rate was relatively low in 2006, the percentage of women who gave birth in their childbearing years was still 80 percent. In almost fifty years of debating, adopting, and ratifying the modern ERA, a significant majority of American women were and remain mothers.

From Crystal Eastman in 1920 to Bella Abzug in 1977, the founding mothers of the ERA envisioned an ERA that would help address the inequalities that women face because they are mothers. They advocated for maternity leave, childcare, and economic security for homemakers. They also advocated for equal educational opportunity, equal pay for equal work, and access to professions that were closed to them in the past.

As the ERA was being ratified by the states, Congress passed Title IX, opening many doors of educational opportunity to women. Congress passed laws strengthening the enforcement of Title VII, which prohibited sex discrimination in employment. Congress had also passed the Comprehensive Child Development Act in 1971, following the House's overwhelming vote, for the second year in a row, in favor of the ERA. The Comprehensive Child Development Act would have made childcare available to all children, and could have significantly eased the burdens on working mothers. But President Nixon vetoed it, and subsequent efforts to reintroduce it were unsuccessful. There were efforts to get paid maternity leave for women in some states, particularly by getting temporary disability benefit programs to cover pregnancy and childbirth. But the Supreme Court held in 1974 that it was perfectly constitutional for a state temporary disability benefit program to exclude pregnancy and childbirth from coverage.[31] The vast majority of women in America were and remain mothers, but the law opened up opportunities to women without removing the barriers to taking those opportunities—barriers that stemmed from motherhood. The revolution begun by Crystal Eastman remained unfinished.

Phyllis Schlafly's STOP-ERA movement offered an alternative: For some mothers, no revolution might have been more appealing than a partial revolution. At the very least, it may have appeared more stable. But it was too late for that—"no revolution" was no longer a realistic option. Phyllis Schlafly stopped the ratification of the ERA, but she did not stop the forward path of change in women's roles in American society that had shaped her own life: She herself worked in an ammunition plant during World War II, ran for Congress twice, went to law school, and traveled around the country giving political speeches, all while raising six children.[32] Women were in new terrains that were sometimes hostile and challenging to navigate, especially with the added burdens of bearing and raising children. Once the STOP-ERA movement launched its attack, the ERA fight became a battle for American motherhood.

Founding Mothers
of the Constitution

The Pioneers

Abigail Adams
1744-1818

Lucretia Mott
1793 - 1880

Susan B. Anthony
1820 - 1906

Elizabeth Cady Stanton
1815 - 1902

Jeannette Rankin
1880 - 1973

Anna Howard Shaw
1847 - 1919

Carrie Chapman Catt
1859 - 1947

The Instigators

Alice Paul
1885-1977

Crystal Eastman
1881 - 1928

Burnita Matthews
1894 - 1988

The Reformers

Florence Kelley
1859 – 1932

Dorothy Kenyon
1888 – 1972

The Globalizers

Mary Church Terrell
1863–1954

Katharine St. George
1894 – 1983

Margaret Chase Smith
1897 – 1995

The Framers

Martha Griffiths
1912-2003

Florence Dwyer
1902 - 1976

Margaret Heckler
1931 - 2018

Charlotte Reid
1913-2007

Catherine Dean May
1914-2004

The Mothers

Patsy Mink
1927-2002

Shirley Chisholm
1924 - 2005

Ella Grasso
1919 - 1981

Edith Green
1910-1987

Bella Abzug
1920 - 1998

Betty Friedan
1921 - 2006

Eleanor Holmes Norton
b. 1937

Louise Hicks
1916 - 2003

The Breadmakers

Leonor Sullivan
1902 - 1988

Phyllis Schlafly
1924 - 2016

The Change Agents

Ruth Bader Ginsburg
1933 – 2020

Pauli Murray
1910 – 1985

The Game Changers

Liz Holtzman
b. 1941

Barbara Jordan
1936 - 1996

Barbara Mikulski
b. 1936

Millicent Fenwick
1910 - 1992

Patricia Wald
1928 - 2019

The Resurrectors

Pat Spearman
b. 1955

Nicole Cannizzaro
b. 1983

Heidi Gansert
b. 1963

Joyce Woodhouse
b. 1944

Yvanna Cancela
b. 1987

The Rectifiers

Heather Steans
b. 1963

Kimberly Lightford
b. 1968

Toi Hutchinson
b. 1973

Barbara Flynn Currie
b. 1940

Mary Flowers
b. 1951

Rita Mayfield
b. 1966

Litesa Wallace
b. 1978

Juliana Stratton
b. 1965

The
History Makers

Jennifer Carroll Foy
b. 1981

Jennifer McClellan
b. 1972

Mamie Locke
b. 1954

Kelly Convirs-Fowler
b. 1981

Danica Roem
b. 1984

Eileen Filler-Corn
b. 1964

The Unstoppables

Kaye Kory
b. 1947

Hala Ayala
b. 1973

Vivian Watts
b. 1940

Jen A. Kiggans
b. 1971

Charniele Herring
b. 1969

L. Louise Lucas
b. 1944

The Unstoppables

Jackie Speier
b. 1950

Carolyn Maloney
b. 1946

Lisa Murkowski
b. 1957

Sheila Jackson Lee
b. 1950

Pramila Jayapal
b. 1965

Rashida Tlaib
b. 1976

Nancy Pelosi
b. 1940

PART III

TRANSFORMATIONS

8

The Change Agents

FORTY YEARS BEFORE SHE BECAME known as "Notorious RBG," Ruth Bader Ginsburg was an ACLU lawyer with a potentially notorious client.

Captain Susan Struck, an unmarried Air Force nurse, had a casual romance and got pregnant while serving in Vietnam. She tried to keep it a secret, but after seven months, people around her figured it out. The Department of Defense immediately sent her to a military base back in the United States and instructed her to get an abortion if she wanted to keep her job. Susan Struck was not planning a life of motherhood, but she was a pro-life Catholic and couldn't bring herself to have the abortion. She had saved up enough sick days to give birth, give the baby up for adoption to a loving family, and then go back to work for the military.[1]

Did the Constitution allow the Defense Department to fire her for getting pregnant and giving birth to a baby?

Ruth Bader Ginsburg believed that it should not. Men in the military became temporarily disabled and took leaves from which they returned. Servicemen became fathers without losing their jobs. Why should it be any different for women who became pregnant?

To Ginsburg, the Air Force was plainly discriminating on account of sex.

But in 1970, when Susan Struck first asked the ACLU to bring her case to court, the US Supreme Court had never regarded sex discrimination as unconstitutional. In 1972, Ginsburg went to work on the brief supporting Captain Struck before the Supreme Court. She intended to persuade the court to rule that what happened to Susan Struck was wrong. Specifically, that firing a pregnant woman for refusing to abort was sex discrimination, contrary to the Constitution.

The Air Force had several policies that were unwelcoming of women, and they caught Congresswoman Martha Griffiths's attention as she argued for the Equal Rights Amendment. At an ERA hearing in 1971, Griffiths pointed out that the Air Force did not hire mothers. The Air Force also required female candidates to submit photos of themselves, which it did not require of men.[2] The Fourteenth Amendment guaranteed "equal protection of the laws" to all persons. Many lawyers—including Griffiths and Ginsburg—believed that discrimination against women should be unlawful under the Fourteenth Amendment.

But in case after case alleging sex discrimination, the Supreme Court had not taken the Fourteenth Amendment in that direction. Instead, the court had permitted the law to discriminate against women because, well, women were different from men. Only women could bear children. A judge ruled in Susan Struck's case that the Constitution allowed the Department of Defense's policy of discharging servicewomen if they got pregnant and gave birth.[3] Throughout the ERA fight, Griffiths contended that judges' failures to read sex equality into the Fourteenth Amendment made the ERA necessary. Even though the Fourteenth Amendment was capable of outlawing sex discrimination, judges—mostly men—needed a wake-up call in the form of a new amendment to open their eyes and minds to that possibility.[4]

Ginsburg authored her brief for Susan Struck within months of Congress's overwhelming majority vote to adopt the ERA. The

ERA had already been ratified by a few states, and was still pending before many of them, so Ginsburg couched her arguments as claims under the existing Constitution—the Fifth and Fourteenth Amendments, which guaranteed due process and equal protection of the law to all persons. Ginsburg wrote, "Heading the list of arbitrary barriers that have plagued women seeking equal opportunity is disadvantaged treatment based on their unique childbearing function."[5]

Throughout history, firing women because of pregnancy or motherhood kept women economically dependent and subordinate in society. Ginsburg's brief also provided some insight into why it was wrong to tell pregnant women to get abortions to keep their jobs. The Defense Department's policy "impels women who seek to pursue a career in the Air Force to remain childless while men in the Air Force are not constrained to avoid the pleasures and responsibilities of procreation and parenthood."[6] Firing pregnant women perpetuated the stereotype that the expectant mother was unfit for a career, and "should be confined at home to await childbirth and thereafter devote herself to child care." As for efforts to glorify women's role as mothers, "The pedestal upon which women have been placed has all too often, upon closer inspection, been revealed as a cage."[7]

Captain Struck's case struck a personal chord for Ginsburg, because she had her own experience of being pregnant on a military base in 1954. Just after their honeymoon, her husband, Marty, was stationed as an army reserve officer at Fort Sill, Oklahoma. She went with him, and got a good civil service job in a federal government office. But when she got pregnant, she was demoted to a position with lower pay and less responsibility. During a prenatal checkup, a doctor diagnosed some complications that might result in birth defects. The doctor urged her to consider an abortion.[8] Ginsburg chose to become a mother, even though staying pregnant meant less income for her family. Abortion was a crime in most states, including Oklahoma, but it was legally permitted on military bases, and even encouraged when the government saw fit.

In the *Struck* case, Ginsburg sensed a history-making opportunity: It could lead the Supreme Court to write a decision outlawing pregnancy discrimination, scrutinizing gender stereotypes, and defending a woman's right to choose whether to become a mother. Three grand principles that women needed to function as truly equal citizens, in one landmark decision. Unlike other cases involving abortion, this case put women who chose to continue a pregnancy—rather than to terminate it—at the center of reproductive freedom. After the ERA's opponents questioned equality for women in the military, this case put servicewomen at the center of equal opportunity. A favorable ruling for Struck would affirm life and motherhood and create constitutional responses to inequalities women faced because of childbearing.

The revolutionary potential of this case was too powerful. The Defense Department decided not to face off against Ginsburg's brief before the Supreme Court. Two years had gone by since Struck gave up her baby for adoption, and the Air Force decided to let her keep her job after all.[9] The Air Force ended its policy of terminating pregnant servicewomen, which also ended the implicit requirement of abortion to keep one's job. That meant that Susan Struck no longer had a Supreme Court case against the Air Force. Ginsburg's brilliant brief in *Struck v. Secretary of Defense* was moot on arrival. It would never shape a Supreme Court decision. In the year that the ERA was adopted by Congress, America did not get the landmark decision addressing a broad range of issues that motivated the ERA's framers and the participants in the Women's Strike for Equality: pregnancy discrimination, gender stereotypes that hampered women's employment opportunities, and the right to bear or raise children.

The man who stopped Ginsburg from shaping a landmark Supreme Court decision in 1972 was Erwin Griswold, the Solicitor General of the United States. He instructed the Air Force to give Struck her job back and to change its pregnancy policy, which killed the Supreme Court case. By handing her client a win, he dealt a blow to the lawyer fomenting major constitutional change.

Griswold was no stranger to Ruth Bader Ginsburg. When Ginsburg had entered Harvard Law School seventeen years earlier, Griswold was the dean who had invited all nine female students to a dinner where he asked them to justify their presence as women taking the places of men at the nation's top law school.[10] By the time Griswold got Ginsburg's brief in the *Struck* case, he knew that Ginsburg's place in the legal world was no longer in question. The previous year, she had persuaded the Supreme Court to take its first step towards constitutionalizing sex equality by unanimously striking down a law that treated men and women differently.

Ruth Bader Ginsburg wrote a winning brief to the Supreme Court in the case of *Reed v. Reed*, which invalidated an Idaho law that preferred males over females as administrators of a deceased person's estate.[11] After the tragic death of a teenage boy, a probate court appointed Mr. Reed, the boy's father, as the administrator of his estate. The mother, Mrs. Reed, believed that the probate court should have appointed her instead. But the court chose Mr. Reed because the Idaho law said, "[o]f several persons claiming and equally entitled to administer, males must be preferred to females."[12] The Supreme Court concluded that a mandatory preference based on sex was "the very kind of arbitrary legislative choice forbidden by the Equal Protection Clause of the Fourteenth Amendment."[13]

The timing of this pivotal decision was not a coincidence. It came down in November 1971, less than a month after the House had adopted the ERA by 93 percent of the vote. Martha Griffiths had criticized the Idaho law during hearings in March,[14] and had even filed an amicus brief along with the National Organization of Women urging the Supreme Court to strike down the law.[15] Equal rights were in the constitutional atmosphere and, by way of its new interpretation of the Fourteenth Amendment, the Supreme Court was catching on.

Ginsburg's brief in *Reed v. Reed* was a *tour de force*. It quoted the Declaration of Sentiments at Seneca Falls in 1848, to explain how nineteenth-century laws did not recognize women as full persons. It pointed out that the Nineteenth Amendment gave women the vote, but only after three-quarters of a century of struggle. The brief included a twenty-page appendix listing many laws in the states that continued to treat women less favorably than men—similar to lists that were submitted as part of the legislative record in congressional floor debates on the Equal Rights Amendment. One section of the brief reads like a treatise on the Supreme Court's Fourteenth Amendment cases, from *Lochner* to *Muller* to *Hoyt v. Florida*, which proponents and opponents of the ERA had been discussing for decades. Ginsburg also referred several times to *A Matter of Simple Justice*, the 1970 report by the President's Task Force on Women's Rights and Responsibilities that urged passage of the ERA and was referenced frequently in ERA hearings and floor debates from 1970 to 1972.

Ginsburg also situated her plea for constitutional recognition of sex equality in the larger global context. The brief cited the West German Constitutional Court's decisions within the last decade striking down similar laws preferring sons to daughters in property inheritance.[16] She also cited the UN Charter.[17] Those two bodies of law—the German constitution and the UN Charter—were part of the ERA's legislative history, as proponents had invoked them in hearings in the 1920s through the 1940s.

In presenting the brief to the Supreme Court in *Reed v. Reed*, Ginsburg did not pretend that this tremendous body of knowledge nudging the law toward sex equality was her work alone. On the cover page of that brief, Ginsburg listed Pauli Murray and Dorothy Kenyon—two trailblazing women attorneys who had pioneered the arguments she was now presenting to the court—as coauthors.[18] Neither Murray nor Kenyon had actually worked on writing the brief, but Ginsburg insisted on acknowledging the women whose past work made her work possible moving forward.

Dorothy Kenyon, as we may recall from chapter 3, was a reformer who opposed the ERA in the 1920s and 1930s, even though she was a fighter for women's equal rights. Before the Supreme Court changed during the New Deal, Kenyon reasonably worried that the ERA would start functioning like a blind man with a shotgun. But in the 1960s, after litigating and losing cases of sex discrimination that she tried to frame using the Equal Protection Clause, Kenyon changed her mind about the ERA. After years of avoiding the blind man with a shotgun, she herself became more militant. "I know exactly how the Black Panthers feel, ignored, passed over, segregated (intellectually at least) and frustrated until they are ready to kill," she wrote to a close colleague. By 1970, she concluded, "It's worth passing the equal rights amendment, if only to stir up the men."[19]

Pauli Murray was the brain behind the "dual strategy" of pressing courts to ban sex discrimination under the Fourteenth Amendment while also pressing Congress to adopt the Equal Rights Amendment.[20] By the time Ruth Bader Ginsburg was writing the briefs in *Reed* and *Struck*, she was operating within the dual strategy that Murray and Kenyon had devised. Ginsburg's arguments were both elaborations of the existing Equal Protection Clause and implicit proposals for the interpretation of the new Equal Rights Amendment.

Pauli Murray was a brilliant African American lawyer who gave a name—"Jane Crow"[21]—to the double handicap of being a woman of color, which Mary Church Terrell identified in 1940 and Shirley Chisholm discussed in Congress in 1970. In her early life, Murray was excluded from several elite universities and law schools, either because she was black or because she was a woman.[22] A paper she wrote as a law student played a crucial role in shaping the legal arguments that ultimately triumphed in *Brown v. Board of Education*. But the men who argued that landmark case did not even tell her that they were using her work.[23] Unlike those men, Ginsburg felt compelled to recognize Murray's crucial intellectual contributions to the legal strategy of *Reed v. Reed*, which ended up succeeding.

Although the Supreme Court did not have the occasion to be persuaded by Ginsburg's brief in *Struck*, she included some of the same arguments when she argued *Frontiero v. Richardson*, another case in which she advocated for a military servicewoman.

The battle for the ERA in Congress focused on whether women could be drafted, with ERA opponents raising fears of a future with women serving in the military. But the reality was that women were already serving in the military, as the *Struck* and *Frontiero* cases demonstrated. In *Frontiero*, the court invalidated a rule that automatically allowed male military personnel to get dependent benefits for their wives, while requiring female military personnel to prove that their husbands were actually dependent on them for over a year and a half in order to qualify for the same benefits.[24] There were no pregnancies or babies in that case, so it did not provide an opportunity for Ginsburg or the Supreme Court to make law about motherhood. Nonetheless, Ginsburg argued that the law in question reinforced traditional stereotypes about men as providers and women as dependents and therefore required greater scrutiny. Ginsburg believed that men should also welcome their liberation from these confining gender stereotypes.[25]

Frontiero was the case in which the Supreme Court finally retracted some of the sex-discriminatory comments that had infected its Fourteenth Amendment opinion a century before. The 1873 case of *Bradwell v. State of Illinois*, saying "Man is, or should be, woman's protector or defender," was quoted with disapproval. Lifting language from Ginsburg's brief, the Supreme Court said in *Frontiero* that its "romantic paternalism" a century before "put women, not on a pedestal, but in a cage."[26] The Supreme Court only had male justices in 1973, but Ginsburg's words remade the law that they wrote.[27] Decades before Ruth Bader Ginsburg got her seat on the highest court of the land in 1993, her voice and legal analysis shaped the law of sex discrimination under the Fourteenth Amendment.

At the end of her oral argument before the Supreme Court in *Frontiero v. Richardson*, Ginsburg notably quoted Sarah Grimké, a nineteenth-century abolitionist who fought for women's equal rights. "I ask no favor for my sex," Ginsburg said, referring to Grimké's writings. "All I ask of our brethren is that they take their feet off our necks."[28] Through this quote, Ginsburg was not only invoking Sarah Grimké, but also the legislative history of the ERA. During the May 1970 congressional hearings, a pro-ERA witness for the Washington, DC organization, Women's Liberation, identified herself as "Sarah Grimké" rather than by her own name, and was accompanied by "Emma Goldman" and "Angelina Grimké," two additional women's rights figures of the nineteenth century. At the ERA hearing, "Sarah Grimké" said, "Equal rights under the law will give women the confidence to struggle further for liberation." With that, she quoted Sarah Grimké's powerful line demanding that men take their feet off women's necks.[29] By repeating this line at her oral argument in *Frontiero*, Ginsburg brought the ERA and its abolitionist origins into the new interpretation of the Fourteenth Amendment that she was urging the Supreme Court to adopt.

It worked. "There can be no doubt that our Nation has had a long and unfortunate history of sex discrimination," the Supreme Court declared in *Frontiero*. Four justices likened sex distinctions to race distinctions, particularly because generalizations about females typically relegated all women to inferior legal status without considering the capabilities of individuals.[30] They even mentioned the ERA to explain the direction they were taking:

> And § 1 of the Equal Rights Amendment, passed by
> Congress on March 22, 1972, and submitted to the legis-
> latures of the States for ratification, declares that "equality
> of rights under the law shall not be denied or abridged by
> the United States or by any State on account of sex." Thus,
> Congress itself has concluded that classifications based
> upon sex are inherently invidious, and this conclusion of a
> coequal branch of Government is not without significance
> to the question presently under consideration.[31]

In *Reed v. Reed* and *Frontiero v. Richardson*, the men on the Supreme Court adopted Ruth Bader Ginsburg's legal analysis—which was closely linked to ERA proponents' case for the ERA—into its new Fourteenth Amendment jurisprudence of gender equality. As the tables of authorities in Ginsburg's briefs will attest, it was work to which dozens of women had contributed over dozens of years.

As one of these women, Pauli Murray believed in the ERA's transformative potential for women of color in particular. "As a constitutional lawyer, a woman and a Negro I can say with conviction that Negro women as a group have the most to gain from the adoption of the Equal Rights Amendment," she predicted, in her statement submitted for the Senate Judiciary Committee hearings in September 1970.[32] Murray's dual-strategy advocacy of the ERA intended to build women's rights on the achievements of the Fourteenth Amendment and the civil rights movement, as cases like *Reed* and *Frontiero* eventually did. But in the ERA, she saw new possibilities and formed new aspirations that went beyond the sex discrimination arguments she had crafted for Fourteenth Amendment litigation.

In her ERA testimony before Congress, Murray said, "[U]nderlying the issue of equal rights for women is the more fundamental issue of equal power for women." The powerlessness began with the sexual violence and forced motherhood experienced by her own family during slavery.[33] In the twentieth century, Murray pointed out that the decades-long ERA debate about protective labor legislation for women did not resonate with black women, because most black working women worked in low-paying private household or service jobs that were left out of labor legislation. In such jobs, the least advantaged women in American societies faced the greatest abuses of power, including sexual violence, as a staple of their economic subsistence.

"I appeal to this Committee and to the United States Senate to use the uniquely human gift of vision and imagination in a creative approach to the Equal Rights Amendment,"[34] Murray said. To her mind, there were serious dangers when women, "more than half the population," were absent from decision-making power in a democratic society. Severe underrepresentation of women in decision-making processes indicated "a society in dangerous imbalance."[35]

Ruth Bader Ginsburg ascended to positions of decision-making power. By 1980, she was a federal appeals court judge. In 1993, she became the second woman justice on the US Supreme Court, two decades after she convinced an all-male court to strike down sex-discriminatory laws.[36] One of her first major opinions as a justice was *United States v. Virginia*, the Supreme Court's landmark decision on sex discrimination. The 1996 decision made it unconstitutional for the Virginia Military Institute—a longstanding male pipeline to power in Virginia—to exclude women: "Today's skeptical scrutiny of official action denying rights or opportunities based on sex responds to volumes of history," Ginsburg wrote for the court. Unless the government could demonstrate an "exceedingly persuasive justification," gender-based governmental action was unconstitutional.[37]

An "exceedingly persuasive justification . . . must not rely on overbroad generalizations about the different talents, capacities, or preferences of males and females," the court explained. At long last, Ginsburg directly authored constitutional law as a Supreme Court justice. And that law now said, once and for all, that sex distinctions "may not be used, as they once were . . . to create or perpetuate the legal, political or economic inferiority of women."[38]

Shortly after *United States v. Virginia* was decided, Justice Ginsburg said, "There is no practical difference between what has evolved and the ERA."[39] Indeed, Ginsburg herself had persuaded the men on the Supreme Court to strike down several additional sex-discriminatory laws under the Fifth and Fourteenth Amendments between *Frontiero* and *Virginia*. But by 1996, the court's sex discrimination cases under the Fourteenth Amendment had not accomplished everything Ginsburg had hoped for in the landmark decision that could have been reached in *Struck v. Secretary of Defense*, or by an ERA that could have been implemented, if it had not been stopped.

The Supreme Court decided several cases in the 1970s that struck down laws that perpetuated gender stereotypes. Anti-stereotyping was one principle that Ginsburg articulated in her

Struck brief in 1972. But another equally important principle—which hit very close to home for Ginsburg—was that excluding mothers and mothers-to-be was unconstitutional. The Supreme Court rejected that principle in a 1974 case that allowed the exclusion of pregnancy from temporary disability benefits. In *Geduldig v. Aiello*, the Supreme Court upheld a California policy of providing paid temporary disability leave to employees for every temporarily disabling condition except pregnancy. Women who had given birth tried to claim these benefits—this was their only hope for a paid maternity leave to recover from childbirth—but the state excluded normal pregnancy and birth from coverage. The Supreme Court concluded that there was no Equal Protection Clause violation.

If the ERA had been in effect, the court could not tolerate pregnancy discrimination so easily, because the framers of the ERA were explicitly concerned with policies that excluded women because they were mothers or mothers-to-be. When Martha Griffiths testified in ERA hearings, one example she gave of a violation of the proposed Equal Rights Amendment was public schools' policies of expelling pregnant students.[40] Griffiths, following Patsy Mink, also criticized the Supreme Court's decision in *Phillips v. Martin Marietta*, in which a working mother had challenged a company's policy of not hiring mothers of preschool-age children.[41] In that case, the Supreme Court said that the employer could justify a policy of hiring fathers, but not mothers, of preschool-age children as a "bona fide occupational qualification" if the employer could show that such mothers were less likely to perform the duties of the job.[42]

The all-male Supreme Court had trouble seeing what was wrong with discrimination against mothers and mothers-to-be. This blind spot remained in *Gilbert v. General Electric*, as the Supreme Court again concluded that pregnancy discrimination was legal, this time under Title VII. The court held that pregnancy discrimination was not sex discrimination when an employer excluded pregnancy from its paid temporary disability benefits program.[43]

Congress disagreed with the Supreme Court and passed the Pregnancy Discrimination Act in 1978. That law clarified Title VII by saying that discrimination by employers because of pregnancy, childbirth, or a related medical condition is sex discrimination.[44] Birch Bayh, the primary Senate sponsor of the ERA in 1972, saw the decision as a reason why the ERA was still needed. "We are still struggling to get those extra three states, and we hope and pray to get them. But until that happens, and even afterwards, I think it is important for Congress to legislate in those areas that are necessary to implement the equal rights amendment."[45] A few weeks before Congress adopted the Pregnancy Discrimination Act, it adopted the resolution to extend the seven-year deadline on ERA ratification.

Pauli Murray believed that the ERA could do more than the Fourteenth Amendment to overcome the power imbalance between men and women. Murray focused on Congress, suggesting that a Congress made up of fewer than one-third women was in dangerous imbalance. The women in Congress who pushed the ERA forward in 1970–1972 made up about 2 percent of Congress; in 2018, women reached an all-time high of 23.7 percent. That represents significant progress over fifty years, but it's still less than one-third. Murray's one-third is not a random standard—she was a lifelong fighter for constitutional change, and in order to change the Constitution, Article V requires two-thirds of Congress to adopt an amendment, which three-fourths of the states then have to ratify. If women are less than one-third of Congress, that means that women don't have the power to block a constitutional amendment. It's mathematically possible for men in Congress to adopt a constitutional amendment by a two-thirds vote without ever consulting any congresswoman. Such an imbalance threatens the democratic process.

Imbalance of power leads easily to the abuse of power. Abuse of male power can be manifested in many different ways. The #MeToo movement has brought the spotlight to sexual violence and harassment. From Harvey Weinstein to elected officials and federal judges, sexual harassment is not only about unwanted sex— it happens when men in positions of power abuse their status to control women's economic destinies. From the rape of black female slaves noted by Pauli Murray, to everyday harassment endured by low-wage working women in the service industry, to the sexual assaults on college campuses and in Hollywood that ignited the #MeToo movement, it is clear that the resurgence of the ERA is as much about empowerment as it is about solving specific legal problems.

In 2019, a group of female students brought a #MeToo lawsuit against Yale University to challenge the sexual violence they experienced at parties hosted by Yale chapters of all-male fraternities. The solution is not criminal punishment for the men, or monetary damages for the women, but a power reset. The plaintiffs wanted a court order "fully integrating women into the governance and all aspects of the operation of the Fraternity" and "fully integrating women in the Fraternities' alumni and career networks."[46]

Delta Kappa Epsilon is one of the fraternities being sued. Its alumni and career network includes former presidents George H. W. Bush and George W. Bush as well as current Supreme Court justice Brett Kavanaugh. The #MeToo movement is calling out the abuse of power manifested in sexual violence, and trying to end the dangerous imbalance of power flagged by Pauli Murray.

The continuing appeal of the ERA to twenty-first century women—especially women of color—is a testament to Murray's vision of the Equal Rights Amendment as going beyond the Fourteenth Amendment to empower women. Pauli Murray was far ahead of her time. After Murray died in 1985, the Fourteenth Amendment began to lose its ability to empower the powerless, because the Supreme Court increasingly used the Equal Protection Clause to strike down race-conscious affirmative action intended to help disadvantaged minorities. In the 1989 case of *J. A. Croson v. City of Richmond*, the Supreme Court struck down a plan in Richmond, Virginia, that boosted minority-owned businesses in government contracting.[47] The Supreme Court used the Fifth Amendment in the 1995 case of *Adarand Constructors v. Peña* to strike down a federal affirmative action policy that gave a leg up to minority-owned businesses in contracting with the government.[48]

Justice Ginsburg steered clear of these rulings when she wrote *United States v. Virginia*. Departing from the race-based affirmative action cases, *Virginia* preserved the possibility of legal sex-based affirmative action and laws that treat men and women differently in order to offset women's disadvantages, including those stemming from pregnancy.[49] Speaking for the court, Justice Ginsburg noted, "Sex classifications may be used to compensate women 'for particular economic disabilities [they have] suffered,'" or "to 'promot[e] equal employment opportunity,'" or "'to advance full development of the talent and capacities of our Nation's people.'"[50]

More so than the Fourteenth Amendment, the ERA is closely connected to the goal of women's empowerment, because of the historical record made by its framers. The ERA could provide much-needed clarification regarding the constitutionality of governmental efforts to overcome a dangerous imbalance of power between women and men. Responding to #MeToo, California passed a new law in 2018 prohibiting corporations doing business in California from having all-male boards of directors.[51] Prior to the adoption of this law, a quarter of companies doing business in California had no women on their boards. The law requires every corporate board to have at least one woman. Boards with six or more members must have at least three women; boards with five members must have at least two; and boards with four members or fewer must have at least one woman. Before the ink was dry, legislators worried that the law would be challenged on Equal Protection Clause grounds because it makes sex distinctions.[52]

Lawsuits have been brought to challenge the constitutionality of the California law. One of them was brought by the Pacific Legal Foundation, the same organization that has challenged race-conscious affirmative action at universities like Harvard. That lawsuit alleged that the California law is a "sex-based classification that violates the Fourteenth Amendment under the Equal Protection Clause."[53] Whether this argument ultimately prevails or not, the litigation indicates that the Fourteenth Amendment has become a natural starting point for those seeking to end, rather than make, creative efforts to empower the disempowered. By contrast, the framers of the ERA intended the ERA to support legislation empowering women to overcome their past exclusions. Patsy Mink believed that the ERA would legitimize "extensive legislation" to implement the principle of equal rights, including federal and state laws "to eliminate situations which are discriminatory in effect."[54]

Meanwhile, in several countries around the world, such as Germany, France, and Italy, new equal rights amendments adopted in the late twentieth and early twenty-first centuries have established the constitutionality of laws to overcome women's underrepresentation in positions of power.[55] Most European countries have laws requiring gender balance for certain leadership roles, such as political parties' lists of candidates for elected office, or corporate boards of directors. The constitutional amendments authorizing those laws have directly transformed the composition of legislatures. Elected legislatures in Europe have more women in them than does the United States Congress.[56] Many countries around the world have had a female head of state, but the United States has not.

Despite significant gains for women, the Fourteenth Amendment has not fulfilled the broader vision of equality that many ERA proponents expressed from the 1920s through the 1970s. From Crystal Eastman and Mary Church Terrell to Shirley Chisholm and Patsy Mink, the founding mothers of the ERA wanted an amendment that would expand the special protections women enjoyed under the law to include men, rather than strike down those protections. But the Supreme Court has not moved in that direction with the Fifth and Fourteenth Amendments. In 2017, its ruling in *Sessions v. Morales-Santana* invalidated a federal immigration law that eased the path to citizenship for children of unmarried American citizen mothers, but not for children of unmarried American citizen fathers.[57] Instead of extending to unmarried citizen fathers the same privilege enjoyed by unmarried citizen mothers, the Supreme Court ruled, "'How equality is accomplished . . . is a matter on which the Constitution is silent."[58]

But the history of the ERA is not silent about it. The ERA's framers intended sex equality to be accomplished by empowering Congress and encouraging state legislatures to repeal laws that discriminate against women. They anticipated the continued legitimacy of sex distinctions based on women's unique physical characteristics, such as maternity leave to cover childbearing. As to single-sex rights or privileges that working women needed, legislatures would be required under the ERA to extend such protections to men.

Through their dual strategy of the Fourteenth Amendment and the ERA, Ruth Bader Ginsburg and Pauli Murray began a process of transformation. Their ideas of sex equality as a constitutional principle made their way into the Supreme Court's sex equality law under the Fourteenth Amendment. The Supreme Court's pivotal sex discrimination decisions of the 1970s, culminating in 1996 in *United States v. Virginia*, can be traced back to the dual strategy. But some of the ideas in Ginsburg's brief in the *Struck* case and in Murray's 1970 ERA testimony met more resistance along the way. The ideas that discrimination against pregnancy was unconstitutional, that there was a constitutional right to choose motherhood, and that equal rights would require mechanisms for exercising equal power—these ideas were introduced in the 1970s struggle for constitutional equality for women, but the men in power were not ready to make them law.

Because of the transformative work that these women lawyers did to get the spirit of the ERA into the Supreme Court's Fourteenth Amendment decisions, the ERA quietly became part of the US Constitution without being fully ratified. Remember Shirley Chisholm's political philosophy—"If they don't give you a seat at the table, bring a folding chair." Owing largely to RBG and the feminists on whose shoulders she stood, the rights of women finally have a seat at the constitutional table. But unless the ERA is added to the Constitution, women's rights will be sitting on a folding chair forever.

9

The Game Changers

CAN THE ERA DEADLINE BE changed? Or eliminated?

Just as Congress sent the ERA to the states for ratification in 1972, a thirty-one-year-old lawyer named Liz Holtzman launched her primary campaign for the Brooklyn congressional seat occupied by eighty-four-year-old Emanuel Celler, the most senior member of the House of Representatives. Celler had been in Congress when the ERA was first introduced in 1923. He had opposed the ERA for decades. From the mid-1950s, he wielded his power as chairman of the House Judiciary Committee to stop the ERA from getting a debate on the floor, year after year, despite the growing and eventually overwhelming support for the amendment.

Celler belittled the young woman seeking to overthrow him, calling Holtzman "a toothpick trying to topple the Washington Monument." She was, after all, running a primary campaign on a shoestring budget out of her parents' basement, relying on conversations with voters in supermarkets and subway stations rather than expensive TV commercials.[1]

Against the odds, Liz Holtzman toppled Celler in the election and became the youngest woman ever elected to Congress. (Since

2018, that honor belongs to Alexandria Ocasio-Cortez, who also ran a successful grassroots campaign at the age of twenty-eight to wrest a seat in the House from a long-serving male incumbent.) As a congresswoman, Holtzman played a critical role on the House Judiciary Committee that brought the articles of impeachment against Richard Nixon in 1974.

In 1977, Holtzman introduced the resolution to extend the time limit on the ratification of the ERA. By 1977, there were thirty-five state ratifications, three states that had attempted to rescind their ratifications, a relentless STOP-ERA operation, and widespread confusion about what the ERA would do. To respond, Liz Holtzman led Congress to extend the time limit by three years. By the time Congress voted to keep the ERA alive, the number of women in Congress had nearly doubled since Congress adopted the ERA in 1972. But of all the women who had led the ERA effort in the House in 1970–1972, only one Democrat, Shirley Chisholm, and one Republican, Margaret Heckler, remained.[2] Liz Holtzman and Margaret Heckler took the collaborative lead to establish a bipartisan Congresswomen's Caucus in 1977. That November, Holtzman presided over hearings in the House Judiciary Committee's Subcommittee on Civil and Constitutional Rights about extending the ERA deadline. When the House voted on the ERA deadline extension in 1978, every single woman in the House supported it, Republicans and Democrats alike.

Before she got to Congress, Liz Holtzman already had a taste for challenging and changing procedures that advantaged those who were already in power. Like so many women who moved the ERA forward before her, Holtzman was trained as a lawyer, and she understood how procedural rules could shape outcomes. In her first election bid for the position of New York State Democratic committeewoman in 1970, Holtzman discovered a law that required the incumbent's name to appear first on the ballot, ahead of other candidates' names. Studies showed that voters who were not familiar with any of the candidates tended to vote for the person at the top of the list. So incumbents won, and candidates challenging the status quo faced a major disadvantage. Holtzman sued the Board of Elections to get the ballot design law struck down as unconstitutional. In the aptly titled case, *Holtzman v. Power* (James Power being the name of the city's election commissioner), a New York court agreed with her and changed the ballot procedure.[3]

Republican Margaret Heckler was Holtzman's ally on extending the deadline. Heckler had spoken from her own experience as a working mother in politics when she advocated for the ERA in the House earlier in the decade. She believed that the ERA deadline should be extended because the ratification process had been flawed in some states. She criticized the games that men in state legislatures had been playing to avoid ratifying the ERA. She was, after all, the congresswoman who said she had "no desire to become one of the boys" in her ERA floor speeches in 1970 and 1971. Confusing messages about what the ERA would do were proliferating. The Congresswomen's Caucus that Heckler organized with Holtzman in 1977[4] was rallying support for the Pregnancy Discrimination Act to protect mothers-to-be from workplace discrimination, while Phyllis Schlafly's STOP-ERA movement was telling state legislators that ratifying the ERA would be bad for mothers. Heckler said that an informed debate about the ERA had not occurred in some states, because legislators in those states were holding up the ratification bills in committees and preventing the ERA from getting an open discussion, despite evidence of widespread popular support. That explained why ratification was taking longer than the ERA's framers had projected.

In floor debates about the deadline, Heckler read from a *Washington Post* editorial that said, "Perhaps fairness is no longer a factor in this fray" to describe the ERA ratification efforts in Virginia.[5] The Virginia House of Delegates' Privileges and Elections Committee had kept the ERA bottled up in committee—just like Celler had done in the House Judiciary Committee for over a decade. In Nevada, Heckler noted, "legislators have used intricate procedural devices to preclude consideration of the amendment."[6] Because state legislators blocked the ERA from consideration,

Heckler suggested that another election cycle would be needed to allow the people to express their will with regard to ERA ratification in those states. Extending the deadline was necessary for states like Virginia and Nevada, where legislative procedures gave incumbent men discretionary power to block amendments that the public might favor.

Holtzman shared Heckler's sense that more time was needed to give the ERA a fair chance to be openly debated and honestly considered by the states. At the House judiciary subcommittee hearings that she convened on the deadline extension, Holtzman said, "the question of equal rights for women is just as vital and alive today as it was in 1972 and the need for the amendment is just as great as it ever was." It had not yet attained thirty-eight ratifications, because, in her view, the amendment "generated substantial interest in the public, but, unfortunately, some misinformation as well."[7]

Backing up Holtzman's push to make more time for democratic debate about the ERA was Barbara Jordan, who had joined the House in the same year as Holtzman. Jordan was the House of Representatives' first African American woman from the South, and the first African American woman to serve on the powerful Judiciary Committee. Jordan grew up in racially segregated Texas, where she was shut out of the University of Texas because of her race. She was a debate champion at a historically black university, where she became a civil rights leader.[8]

Jordan made headlines as a junior congresswoman in 1974 for her televised speech as a member of the House Judiciary Committee supporting the impeachment of President Nixon. During impeachment proceedings, she and Liz Holtzman worked together on the Judiciary Committee to explain why a man who had clearly abused his power should be impeached. Jordan began that speech by explaining that constitutional amendment and change had made her part of "We the People": "We the people. It is a very eloquent beginning. But when the document was completed on the seventeenth of September 1787, I was not included in that 'We the people.' I felt somehow for many years that George Washington and Alexander Hamilton just left me out by mistake. But through the process of amendment, interpretation and court decision I have finally been included in 'We the people.'" With impeachment, she was exercising her duty to inquire into the conduct of public men, and if the Constitution could not stop a president "swollen with power and grown tyrannical," she concluded, "then perhaps that eighteenth-century Constitution should be abandoned to a twentieth-century paper shredder."[9]

Jordan had a constitutional philosophy that was as relevant to the ERA deadline extension as it was to impeachment. She believed in the Constitution's ability to change to include people like her—those previously excluded and disempowered—so that they could put a check on men who abuse power. In that speech, Jordan said, "My faith in the Constitution is whole, it is complete, it is total, and I am not going to sit here and be an idle spectator to the diminution, the subversion, the destruction of the Constitution." She was also willing to abandon the Constitution to the "twentieth-century paper shredder" if it could no longer deliver on its promises. It is not a coincidence that both Jordan and Holtzman made their names early on in their congressional careers for their work on impeachment.[10] Extending the deadline on ERA ratification was another move to stop men in power from abusing it. In 1977, both women attended the National Women's Conference in Jordan's home town of Houston, Texas,[11] shortly after the House Judiciary Committee hearings on the ERA deadline extension began. Jordan spoke at the conference's opening ceremony, and ERA ratification was a major plank of the National Plan of Action that emerged from Houston.[12]

Jordan, like Holtzman and Heckler, was a lawyer by training, and she had a strong legal understanding of the Supreme Court's precedents about amendment deadlines. *Coleman v. Miller* held that "the Congress has the power under Article V to fix a reasonable limit of time for ratification in proposing an amendment,"[13] and that meant Congress had the power to decide not to have a deadline at all when proposing an amendment. Since that case involved a proposed amendment that had no deadline, its technical legal ruling was that Congress could choose not to have a deadline. Another Supreme Court precedent, *Dillon v. Gloss*, said that Congress had the power to put a seven-year deadline in the text of the Prohibition Amendment itself, and pointed to Congress's power over deadlines generally.[14] "What the *Coleman* case says is that we can set the time, and if we can set the time, we can change the time,"[15] Jordan said.

Opponents of the deadline extension accused ERA proponents of foul play. Republican congressman Eldon Rudd of Arizona said, "Three outs, and the inning is over. But they want more than three strikes, and more than three outs, when the game is almost over, and the proponents of the ERA are not winning."[16] The sports analogy carried the weight of academic and legal seriousness because Erwin Griswold, the former solicitor general and dean of Harvard Law School, used it in congressional hearings: "It is a little like extending the time of a football game after fourteen minutes in the final quarter, with the score tied, and one team on the other's one-yard line."[17] Recall from chapter 8 that Griswold was the dean who had demanded that women law students justify their presence at Harvard Law School, and the solicitor general who deprived Ruth Bader Ginsburg of the opportunity to shape a landmark Supreme Court decision that could have helped millions of pregnant women and mothers. Now, he was back to stop Congress from extending the life of the ERA.

Congresswoman Barbara Jordan responded to this argument: "Change the rules in the middle of the game? It is no 'game.'" These men were treating the process of enshrining women's equal rights in the Constitution like a game of baseball or football. That was part of the problem to which the ERA was a response. Was constitutional change a sport, or a process of perfecting humanity? "We are talking about the rights of living, breathing, viable working human beings, individuals," Jordan declared. "We are talking about the Constitution of the United States, something which needs to be done to make it still more perfect. It is no game."[18]

A newly elected Barbara Mikulski, who later became a senator and the longest-serving woman in Congress, was more explicit in diagnosing the threat to the constitutional establishment of equality. She said, "the ratification has become bogged down in State legislatures because of horse-trading."[19] The ERA "has been attacked by the same type of coalition that fought against abolition, fought against suffrage, fought against end to child labor," she pointed out, naming three constitutional amendments, two of which were successful, that did not have ratification deadlines. Ultimately, horse-trading was a threat to democracy, not a normal instance of it: "I think it is time that we bring an end to the efforts of those who would manipulate democracy and extend time to those who would expand democracy."[20]

Mikulski suggested that amendments that expanded who "we the people" are would take a long time because the revolutionary and structural changes they involved were naturally resisted. Competing visions of fairness were at stake. "Is it fair that women have had to wait over 200 years to get full equality in this country? I think that it is unfair that we have had to fight horse-trading State legislators and smear tactics of the opponents." To get at a deeper meaning of fairness, Mikulski warned, "Do not treat this like a term paper for some Yale law review article. Do not become so obsessed with rarefied nitpicking that you lose sight of the point."[21]

But that's not how the opponents saw it. For the opponents of the deadline extension, a constitutional democracy required the rule of law—and this meant enforcing a deadline to ensure that the states were treated fairly. Several congressmen argued, for instance, that it was not fair to states that relied on the ERA being open for ratification for only seven years—and not floating around forever—when deciding to ratify. Perhaps they would not have ratified it if they had known that the process would last longer.

One answer to that argument is that states did not and could not reasonably rely on a forever-unchangeable seven-year deadline because it was not part of the constitutional amendment itself. The ERA's deadline was different in legally significant respects from the deadline that was imposed on the Prohibition Amendment—the subject of the Supreme Court's decision in *Dillon v. Gloss*. The

Prohibition deadline was written into the Prohibition Amendment itself. The Eighteenth Amendment says that prohibition will be "*inoperative unless* it shall have been ratified as an amendment" (emphasis added) by three-fourths of the state legislatures or by state ratifying conventions within seven years.

Patricia Wald, then an assistant attorney general in the Department of Justice, argued in the deadline extension hearings that in these matters, one Congress cannot bind a future Congress. Wald went on to become the first woman judge of the US Court of Appeals for the District of Columbia Circuit in 1979, the court to which Ruth Bader Ginsburg was also appointed in 1980. Wald had a realistic perspective on the passage of seven years for women, especially if they were mothers. She was one of eleven women to graduate from Yale Law School in 1951, after which she landed in a prestigious judicial clerkship followed by a law firm job. She hid her pregnancy while working at the law firm, and then put her promising legal career on hold for ten years to stay home and raise her five children.[22] Recall that Elizabeth Cady Stanton spent the 1850s raising children and not traveling much to advance women's suffrage. Similarly, Pat Wald spent the 1950s raising children and not advancing her legal causes. Wald became an Assistant Attorney General over twenty-five years after graduating from law school.[23]

Interpreting the legislative history of the seven-year deadline on the Prohibition Amendment, Wald argued that in order for a ratification time limit to have any legal effect binding future Congresses, it would have to be put into the amendment text itself, not the proposing resolution. For the ERA, similar to the Twenty-Third, Twenty-Fourth, Twenty-Fifth, and Twenty-Sixth Amendments, the seven-year deadline was placed in the congressional resolution proposing the amendment to the states, rather than in the text of the constitutional amendment.

In response to the notion that changing the time limit was changing the rules of the game because the ratifying states had somehow relied on the ratification period being open for only seven years, Wald noted that none of the states had indicated a reliance on the deadline in the resolutions they submitted to the federal government to certify their ratifications.[24] Wald concluded that because the ERA deadline was not in the amendment text, Congress was always free to revisit it by a majority vote, without following Article V's more onerous requirement for constitutional amendments.

But some members of Congress insisted on requiring a two-thirds vote on changing the deadline. That argument continues to be made in ongoing twenty-first century debates about Congress's power to remove the deadline altogether. On the House floor in 1978, Millicent Fenwick, a Republican and fiscal conservative from New Jersey, pointed out that "[t]he Constitution is explicit where supermajorities are required . . . Article V of the Constitution prescribes a two-thirds vote only when Congress proposes a constitutional amendment. We are not here proposing an amendment. We are merely deciding whether a reasonable time for consideration by the States has passed."[25] Fenwick's distinction, between proposing an amendment and deciding whether a reasonable time has passed, suggested that Congress had the power to decide the legal consequences of delivering a ratification after a time limit that Congress had itself imposed.

Fenwick's understanding of Congress's role was given a more thorough explanation by Ruth Bader Ginsburg, who testified as a constitutional law professor expert in the deadline extension hearings before both congressional chambers' judiciary committees. Ginsburg argued that "the time stipulation is a measure susceptible to alteration based on circumstances evolving since the submission of the amendment."[26] She invoked "the well-established general rule that statutes of limitations may be extended should the legislature determine its initial estimate was inadequate."[27] By this logic, the proposer of the amendment retained the sole authority to decide whether to accept ratifications that came in later than estimated or initially anticipated.

Ginsburg's argument was consistent with ordinary intuitions about deadlines and their consequences, and particularly about whose decision it should be as to what to do about latecomers. To take a mundane example that is familiar to most students, handing in an assignment after its due date can mean that the teacher throws the assignment in the trash bin and gives the student a failing grade without ever reading it or considering the reasons why it's late. But other outcomes are possible, and one might think that a teacher who reacts to a missed deadline in this way is being draconian. The deadline-imposer could react humanely to a missed deadline by considering whether the deadline provided ample time in the first place, the latecomer's reasons for lateness, the importance of the thing that is arriving late, and any negative consequences of accepting a latecomer. In 1977, Ginsburg believed that Congress can and should revisit it because, "In my judgment, Congress miscalculated."[28]

Recall the political maneuvers by a small group of male senators who opposed the ERA that led to Martha Griffiths's inclusion of the seven-year ratification deadline. The deadline was part of a political bargain made under political circumstances in Congress that Pauli Murray would most likely call a "dangerous imbalance." Because a small and vocal minority of senators packaged the seven-year ratification deadline with a military exemption that would have crippled the ERA at its core, Griffiths decided to play the hand she was dealt by agreeing to the deadline. She attempted to save her political capital to save the ERA's core. That was her miscalculation. Ginsburg's argument suggested that a later Congress could recalculate by changing the deadline.

Ginsburg also examined the history of the language used in ratification time limits. Not only did the Eighteenth, Twentieth, Twenty-First, and Twenty-Second Amendments include a deadline in the constitutional text itself, they also used strong language that clearly stated the consequence of missing the deadline by saying that the article would be "inoperative unless" ratified by the requisite number of states in seven years. As for the Twenty-Third and Twenty-Fourth Amendments, adopted in 1951 and 1964, the time limit was placed in the proposing resolution rather than in the proposed constitutional amendment, but the language remained strong and consequential. Those amendments said that the amendment would be valid "only if ratified" within seven years. Then, for the Twenty-Fifth and Twenty-Sixth Amendments, the proposing resolution weakened the language considerably, saying that the amendment would be valid "when ratified" within seven years. That weaker language was used for the ERA resolution. Ginsburg concluded that the proposing resolution was an expression of an "initial judgment as to time," deliberately separated from the text of the proposed amendment submitted to the states for ratification, in order that Congress would retain authority to revisit that initial judgment and to extend the time period if warranted by the public interest.[29] The initial judgment was more like a prediction or aspiration rather than a threat to kill the ERA upon late delivery of ratification.

Ginsburg was not saying that all the deadlines ever put in resolutions were invalid. But the language used in the ERA, like that in the Twenty-Fifth and Twenty-Sixth Amendments—passed by Congress in 1965 and 1971 in close temporal proximity to the drafting of the ERA—suggests only a soft deadline, one that can be renegotiated, changed, or ignored as appropriate. It was a promise to accept the amendment as valid if it did get ratified within seven years. If p (ratified within seven years) then q (amendment is valid). But any student of logic can tell you that if "not p" (not ratified within seven years) then "not q" (amendment is invalid) is a logical fallacy. The time limit states a sufficient, but not necessary, condition of the amendment's validity. If that sufficient condition is not met, the amendment is not dead. The proposer of the time limit—Congress—must then decide, as a political question within its sole discretion, whether to accept late ratifications. Converting a sufficient condition into a necessary one would be a logical sleight of hand.

Ginsburg concluded, "Based on experience since 1972, I believe Congress not only has the authority, it has the responsibility to extend the deadline." At the time, she framed the enforcement of the seven-year time limit as a moral and political problem, not a legal requirement: "It would be the bitterest of ironies if the amendment were to become the first proposed amendment in this Nation's history to die because of a procedural time bar—a bar stipulated without exacting deliberation by Congress—ran out. No amendment to date has failed for that reason."[30]

What does it say about the United States as a nation, and the US Constitution as its fundamental law, if it permits a constitutional amendment guaranteeing sex equality to die because of a procedural time bar that men in a dangerously imbalanced Senate created? What does it say about the political system enforced by the American Constitution when ratification deadlines are achieved by powerful minorities in Congress, and allow powerful minorities in state legislatures to prevent debate and deliberation on the amendment that would recognize the rights of half of "we the people"—the half that was originally not included in rights? These were the questions at stake when all the congresswomen in the House of Representatives united across political parties to change the deadline in 1978. The toothpick who toppled a monument, the mom who did not want to be one of the boys, the impeacher who needed a constitutional amendment to become included in "We the People"—these congresswomen who drove the extension of the ERA deadline were calling out game-playing and abuses of power all around them, and pushing for better processes in a democracy. Could they make a democracy that wasn't about horse-trading and bullying? Could they foster debate about the ERA in the states and make the Constitution take care of neglected problems?

Barbara Jordan was considered for the Supreme Court when Ruth Bader Ginsburg was nominated. But Jordan was struggling with health complications which took her life in 1996. Margaret Heckler had a long career in government after Congress, but she died in 2018 at age 87 without living to see Virginia finally ratify the ERA.

But the stakes of the questions they raised intensified in 2020 when the ERA attained the 38 ratifications required by Article V. To answer them, Congress and the people it represents need to consider why these states continued to ratify the ERA, decades after the deadline. Whether the ERA should be legitimized by accepting late ratifications depends on whether the ERA is still needed in the twenty-first century, and what it could do if it is added to the Constitution. Recent ratifiers made the twenty-first century case for why the ERA should stay alive, even though many of its 1970s champions are no longer with us.

PART IV

PERSISTENCE

10

The Resurrectors

IN 1977, WHILE PHYLLIS SCHLAFLY was planning the biggest STOP-ERA rally in history,[1] stirring up fears of women in the military and gay marriage, Pat Spearman became a commissioned officer in the US Army. She was stationed at Fort McClellan, Alabama, before serving in South Korea and Panama. She was one of seven women in her Military Officer Basic Leadership course, and the only African American woman.[2] While she was serving in Panama, a senior officer propositioned her sexually and regularly came knocking on the door of her hotel room.[3] A hotel maid helped her avoid the harasser by giving her access to the service elevator. The previous year in Virginia, she was chased by a group of white men in a pickup truck who taunted her with epithets and threats of violence, from which she protected herself by jumping into a ditch and belly-crawling for half a mile.[4] As a lesbian, she spent her military career in fear of being discharged. Spearman came out of the closet in 2009 while she fought to repeal Don't Ask Don't Tell. But before that, she was married to a man and became an ordained minister and a mother. In 2012, she was elected to the Nevada Senate.

Pat Spearman gave new life to the Equal Rights Amendment by leading the Nevada legislature to ratify it in 2017, forty years after the last state ratification. "It's never too late to support equality for all," she declared. "Never."[5] By then, most of the women who carried the ERA through Congress in the 1970s had passed away. But in Nevada, women of different generations, ages, colors, and political parties resurrected the ERA and updated its meaning for the twenty-first century.

The idea that equality knows no time limits was written into the preamble of Nevada's ERA ratification bill. It explained that even though Congress imposed a seven-year time limit on ratification, Congress's extension of the deadline in 1978 was evidence that "a time limit in a resolving clause may be disregarded if it is not part of the proposed amendment." Nevada would deliver a late ratification on the understanding that Congress could then decide whether to accept it. Under the Supreme Court precedent of *Coleman v. Miller*, Congress retains the power to decide whether an amendment is valid because ratifications were made within a reasonable period of time, even after the deadline. To aid in that decision, the Nevada legislature found "that the proposed amendment is meaningful and needed as part of the Constitution of the United States and that the present political, social, and economic conditions demonstrate that constitutional equality for women and men continues to be a timely issue in the United States."[6]

Would Nevada's overdue ratification be merely symbolic? Spearman made the case for the power of constitutional symbols by invoking other instances where deep commitment and fundamental values are manifested in perpetuity: "I would ask every person who is married or partnered to look at their left hand. There is a ring there. That, too, is a symbol. In churches, there are usually crosses. That is a symbol. Symbols are not just symbols. They are powerful because they point to what we believe in and what we hold dear."[7] The ERA was needed to make sex equality sacred in the American legal and political system.

At the beginning of 2017, the equal status of women seemed up for grabs. Donald Trump had just been inaugurated as president of the United States, in spite of—or perhaps because of—his demeaning boasts about his power to grab women's genitals at will. His remarks about women were widely regarded as disrespectful and misogynistic. With no political experience whatsoever, he managed to defeat the woman who was anticipated to become the first woman president. Despite Hillary Clinton's experience as a senator and secretary of state and her victory in the popular vote, the electoral system set up by our Constitution made Trump president. His election motivated millions of Americans across the country—and allies across the world—to participate in women's marches on the day after his inauguration. The Women's March on Washington, drawing half a million people, was the largest single-day protest in American history. The Unity Principles distributed by the march's organizers called for, among other things, an Equal Rights Amendment for the US Constitution.[8]

Equality, as Pat Spearman sometimes puts it, should not be debatable. In committee hearings, when asked why the ERA was needed for Nevadans, Spearman replied, "because we, as Nevadans, are better than inequality."[9]

But this born-again ERA went beyond big moral statements and unshakeable symbols. It was also about getting things done. The ERA's champions include women with a range of experiences and skills in the Nevada legislature. Besides Spearman—a lieutenant turned reverend—there was a prosecutor, a labor organizer, a university administrator, a regional Girl Scouts CEO. They had concrete plans and bills that went hand-in-hand with the ERA ratification. They wanted to solve real problems: unequal pay, lack of support for working mothers, violence against women, and more.

The Nevada Senate's hour of debate on ratifying the ERA opened with a speech by Spearman, who with several of her female colleagues in the Senate wore white suits that day, paying homage to the suffragists who wore white when they paraded and picketed the White House. Spearman borrowed the words of Justice Ruth Bader Ginsburg:

> This is what ratifying the ERA will do: In the words of Supreme Court Justice Ruth Bader Ginsburg, who wrote in the *Harvard Women's Law Journal*, and I quote, "With the Equal Rights Amendment, we may expect Congress and the state legislatures to undertake in earnest systematically and pervasively the law revision so long deferred and in the event of legislative default the courts will have an unassailable basis for applying the bedrock principle: All men and women are created equal."[10]

Ginsburg's description of the ERA's function in that 1978 article restated the vision articulated by Congresswomen Martha Griffiths and Patsy Mink during the 1971 hearings and floor debates in the House.[11]

These congresswomen envisioned Congress and the state legislatures in the driver's seat of implementing the ERA, by reviewing existing laws for consistency with the principle of equal rights. Courts and judges could also review legislation, but would take the backseat. The goal of the ERA was to open all public servants' eyes to inequalities that needed to be reduced and eliminated. This could not be done by court decisions alone. Much of the heavy lifting would come from the adoption of new laws and public policies. Patsy Mink said that further federal and state legislation would accompany the adoption of the ERA, to "eliminate situations which are discriminatory in effect."[12] Congress's role was clear in Section 2 of the ERA, which gives Congress the power to enforce equal rights. And the role of the state legislatures, while not made explicit in Section 2, was implicit in Section 3, which delays the effective date of the ERA by two years after ratification.

The purpose of such a delay, according to Martha Griffiths, was to give state legislatures the opportunity to repeal unequal laws and replace them with equal ones.[13] This idea was not invented by Griffiths—it was also mentioned in a 1945 statement submitted to the Senate judiciary subcommittee by the Industrial Women's League for Women's Equality.[14] Ruth Bader Ginsburg made the centrality of Congress and state legislatures to enforcing the ERA very clear in the 1978 *Harvard Women's Law Journal* article that Spearman quoted in the Nevada Senate's opening ratification debate of 2017. The ERA "would impel federal and state legislatures to undertake long overdue statutory reform," Ginsburg wrote. "The Equal Rights Amendment gives our legislators a two-year period to update laws now lagging behind social change."[15]

Spearman was standing on the shoulders of Ginsburg, who was standing on the shoulders of Griffiths and Mink, who were standing on the shoulders of the women who instigated, reformed, and broadened the ERA in the generation before. In addition to bringing Justice Ginsburg's words into the rationale of Nevada's twenty-first century ratification, Spearman also revived Shirley Chisholm's remarks made on the House floor when the ERA was debated on Griffiths's discharge petition. Spearman quoted Chisholm's observation that "Legal discrimination between the sexes is, in almost every instance, founded on outmoded views of society and the pre-scientific beliefs about psychology and physiology."[16]

Spearman's focus on the central role of Congress and the state legislatures in enforcing the ERA gives meaning to the claim—often made by activists who are not lawyers—that the ERA will end unequal pay. This claim has been the source of much confusion. Phyllis Schlafly wrote in her reports and newsletters that the ERA would do nothing about unequal pay,[17] because the amendment only prohibited sex discrimination "by the United States or by any State," and not by private companies that were underpaying women. Schlafly correctly read the ERA's text, but she misread and misinterpreted its legislative history, which Pat Spearman brought back into the conversation. The ERA was not intended to make the fact of women's eighty-two cents to the man's dollar unconstitutional instantly in the way that the Thirteenth Amendment made slavery unconstitutional. The ERA was intended to move lawmakers to do something about pay inequity.

In her testimony at the Nevada Assembly, Spearman spoke to pay inequity:

> We continue to see evidence of the need for passage of the ERA every day. Pay equity, or should I say pay inequity, is still a significant concern. Women earn 80 percent of what men earn. African American women earn 68 percent of what men earn. Latinas earn 60 percent of what their male counterparts earn. . . . This body even considered legislation last session to require paycheck fairness with tangible consequences for companies perpetuating economic discrimination based on gender.[18]

In Spearman's formulation, the ERA is needed when pay inequity persists and the legislature is considering legislation on paycheck fairness, because the ERA provides a strong political boost to the legislative agenda for women's equality.

Spearman amplified these points when she brought her testimony to Washington. Because of Nevada's resurrection of the ERA, and the Illinois ratification that followed in 2018, the House Judiciary Committee's Subcommittee on the Constitution, Civil Rights, and Civil Liberties held a hearing on the ERA on April 30, 2019—the first in over thirty years. The hearing was on the proposal in Congress to remove the time limit. But Spearman—believing that there should never be a time limit on equality—focused on equality. She highlighted pay inequity and the lack of paid leave and affordable childcare, without which women could not join the labor force and achieve equal pay.[19]

Spearman linked the problem of pay inequity to the unequal challenges that women face when they are working mothers. This has been her way of responding to ERA opponents who worry that the ERA will weaken the family. "I challenge them to look at the inequity in pay and the number of women heads of household in this country. If they are concerned about the strength and viability of the family, then I say give your passionate political voice and unwavering support for pay equity."[20] She has been a champion of paid parental leave proposals and many different efforts to address unequal pay.

Spearman also put the spotlight on sexual harassment. In the congressional hearing, she said, "We have clearly heard the voices of women that sexual harassment in the work place happens frequently and often silently."[21] In Nevada, the governor had just formed a task force on sexual harassment and discrimination law, working with the legislature to review possible legislation. On all these issues—equal pay, parental leave, childcare, and sexual harassment—there is a problem that the constitutional amendment helps to address, not by legal invalidation of governmental action, but by political validation of new legislative action.

Nevada state senator Nicole Cannizzaro also connected the ERA to problems facing working mothers and sexual assault victims. Cannizzaro grew up in Las Vegas as the daughter of a waitress and a bartender working shifts in the city's restaurants, hotels, and casinos. As a child, Cannizzaro's father picked her up from school on his way to work and dropped her off at the café near the courthouse where her mother was finishing her shift. There she would do her homework, fascinated by the lawyers coming in and out of the café in their suits. Her own parents had always worn uniforms to work. Cannizzaro decided she would become a lawyer one day. Years later, she went to law school and became a prosecutor who handled sexual assault cases.[22]

When her moment came to speak about the ERA on the Nevada Senate floor, Cannizzaro stood up in her suit—a crisp white suit to honor the suffragists' legacy—to tell the stories of three generations of Nevada women and the hurdles they faced as they went to school, worked, and raised their children. "When we have young women who struggle to make the decision about having children or keeping their career because they're afraid their bosses will think that they aren't interested . . . we deny women equal rights," she said. "When the first question we ask rape victims is what were they wearing and how many drinks did they have, or are you really sure that you weren't leading him on, we deny women equal rights."[23]

The Nevada ratification of the ERA was bipartisan. State senator Heidi Gansert, a Republican, reminded her colleagues of the history of ERA ratification in Nevada. She praised Sue Wagner, a former Republican state senator who led the ratification effort in Nevada in 1975, albeit unsuccessfully, and whose seat she now held. Senator Gansert pointed out that Nevada was a leader in nondiscrimination. An 1887 nondiscrimination law equalized teachers' salaries, and a 1961 law established the Nevada Equal Rights Commission. It was exciting that the Nevada legislature at that moment had a high percentage of women, 40 percent. As a university leader who worked in fields with very few women, such as engineering, Gansert was proud that "women are stepping up and stepping forward."[24]

By invoking Nevada's previous efforts at ratification and the high percentage of women currently in office, Gansert gestured at a history of failure that unwittingly produced eventual success.[25] In 1973 and 1975, the Nevada Assembly voted to ratify the ERA, but the Senate rejected it. In 1977, the Senate approved it by one vote, 11–10, but only because the lieutenant governor, an ERA supporter, cast a tie-breaking vote. Under Nevada Senate rules, a constitutional majority of the body—eleven votes—was required to pass the resolution, and the lieutenant governor was only entitled to vote if the twenty-member Senate reached a tie. Two men who opposed the ERA tried to prevent the tie to prevent the pro-ERA lieutenant governor from casting a vote. So those two senators abstained, with the plan of producing a 10–8 vote.

But then, a pro-ERA senator pointed to a little-known parliamentary rule—Senate Rule 30—which provided that anyone who was present had to be counted as an "aye" or "nay." Abstentions were not allowed and would thus be counted as "nay" votes. Once the two abstentions were counted as "nays," there was a 10–10 tie, which triggered the lieutenant governor's opportunity to cast the tiebreaking vote. With his vote, ERA ratification got eleven votes, the constitutional majority, in the Nevada Senate. But this victory, emerging after much bickering about parliamentary rules and procedure, sent divided signals to the assembly, which voted against ERA ratification.

Then, the Nevada Assembly decided later in 1977 to put ERA ratification up for an advisory referendum by the voters. Proponents were against a referendum, predicting that well-funded and well-organized Mormon groups had the phone-banking resources to mobilize a disproportionately large number of voters to oppose the ERA at the polls. But the referendum was held. Two-thirds of the Nevadans who voted in that election rejected the ERA. The referendum was challenged in litigation as contrary to Article V of the US Constitution, which assigns the job of ratifying amendments to state legislatures. The Nevada Supreme Court upheld the referendum because it was clearly designed as an advisory referendum that did not bind the legislature.[26] Nonetheless, even though the referendum against the ERA was produced by a voter turnout skewed to represent a Mormon phone-banking network rather than the popular will of Nevadans, legislators continued to point to the referendum for years as evidence of popular disapproval of the ERA, justifying their inaction on ERA ratification until the deadline passed.

But in all the years that Nevada legislators maneuvered parliamentary rules and exercised committee discretion to stop it from being ratified, the ERA changed Nevada without being ratified. Nevada legislators began to do voluntarily what Martha Griffiths believed they would be required by the ERA to do in the two-year period between ratification and effective date, as stipulated in the ERA's Section 3. Nevada began to review its own laws, checking for any sex discrimination. Even the opponents of the ERA sponsored legislation to reduce women's disadvantage, including a new law on equal pay. By the end of the 1975 session, even though Sue Wagner did not succeed in getting the ERA ratified, she and her colleagues passed a law prohibiting discrimination against credit applicants on the basis of sex, repealed language in the Nevada Constitution barring women from holding certain offices, equalized the responsibility of parents for minor children, and eradicated sex-based presumptions about entitlements to alimony in divorce, to name a few. The legislature also authorized a study of Nevada laws to better identify and analyze those that might discriminate on account of sex.[27] Without winning the symbolic trophy at the end of the battle, ERA proponents took home the real prize.

Over forty years later, as of 2017, Nevada was one of the nation's leaders for the representation of women in legislatures. The ERA ratification that Nevada completed in 2017 was accomplished by women across generations. State senators Joyce Woodhouse, age seventy-three, and Yvanna Cancela, age thirty, both spoke up for the ERA. Senator Woodhouse remembered working in the legislature forty years before as an educator, only to be told by one of the legislators that she needed to be home having babies. "If only he could see now how far we have come in serving our families, our communities, our state, and our nation," she remarked.[28]

Yvanna Cancela—who began her political career as an organizer of immigrant workers—stood proud to be the youngest member of the Nevada Senate, a beneficiary of those who battled for the ERA in the past. Now, she was doing her part to make sure that future generations could see women's gains across the generations on paper: "I am the youngest woman in this body. . . . I stand in support of this measure not only because I recognize that I stand on the shoulders of countless women who have both made their voices heard and sat in this body and supported this measure before but for young women and little girls everywhere who can see on paper that equality is real."[29] State senator Julia Ratti added, "I have been utterly touched by the number of women of all ages who have reached out to me to say this means something to them."[30]

The voices and vision of women legislators drove the twenty-first century ratification in Nevada. They united behind the Equal Rights Amendment because it would complete a transgenerational struggle by women and contribute significant political momentum to solving pay inequity, harassment, the hardships of working mothers, and barriers to women in leadership. Pat Spearman then brought these voices and these women's vision of the ERA to Washington, helping to shape Congress's understanding of what was at stake in removing the ERA deadline.

In Nevada and in all the other states that have considered a twenty-first century ratification, the ERA has met opposition. In Nevada, Republican senator Michael Roberson began by remembering his personal experience as a child of campaigning with his mother for ERA ratification in Kansas in the 1970s.[31] But as a state senator with the power to vote on ratification, Roberson appeared to have outgrown the ERA. He cited several prominent liberal law professors—Reva Siegel, David Strauss, and Cass Sunstein—to say that the United States already has a "de-facto ERA." Roberson noted that the Supreme Court began to strike down sex discrimination under the Equal Protection Clause in the 1970s while the ERA was pending.[32] The Equal Protection Clause already banned sex discrimination in the law. So what would a separate ERA do? It would have to find something else to do, in order to avoid being redundant. Roberson's conclusion was that the ERA would therefore morph into a constitutional guarantee of the unfettered right to choose an abortion—including "partial birth" and third trimester abortions on demand. And, since he opposed the unfettered right to abortion on demand, he would vote against ratifying the ERA.

Roberson was the last speaker before a vote was taken. He did not persuade the majority—the Nevada Senate voted 13–8 in favor of ERA ratification. The proponents did not respond to Roberson's comments before voting, so they did not affirm or deny the ERA's connection to abortion rights. Abortion was not a focus of proponents' arguments for why the ERA is needed now. It remains an open question on which supporters of the ERA might have different answers. The ERA may open up a new constitutional path for reproductive rights or reproductive justice, but the contours of that path have yet to be defined.

The ERA proponents' central issues—the persistence of economic inequality stemming from the burdens of motherhood, the persistence of sexual violence—are related to reproductive justice. A recent study by the Guttmacher Institute indicates that a leading reason why women get abortions in the United States is the inability to afford a child. Everything that Pat Spearman said about the need for childcare and paid parental leave in order to boost women's wages is directly relevant to adopting public policies that will enable women to choose motherhood. The law can ensure that pregnant women have healthy pregnancies by requiring employers to accommodate their needs on the job. Preventing fetal harm and unwanted miscarriages through such measures is pro-life. As Reva Siegel, the professor cited by Senator Roberson, has observed, prohibiting abortion is not the only—or even most effective—way to be a pro-life state.[33] Often, policies that make motherhood economically viable, safe, and humane go a long way to protect unborn life and living children alike.

In the legislative session that achieved Nevada's ERA ratification, the women lawmakers who backed the ERA went straight to work on adopting these policies. State senator Nicole Cannizzaro sponsored the Pregnant Workers' Fairness Act, which was signed into law by the governor in June 2017. That law requires employers to provide reasonable accommodations to employees for a condition relating to pregnancy, childbirth, or related medical conditions.[34]

State senator Julia Ratti concurrently sponsored the Nursing Mothers Accommodation Act, which was passed unanimously by both houses and signed by the governor in June 2017. That law requires employers to provide nursing mothers with a child under the age of one with a reasonable break time to express breast milk as well as a place to express breast milk other than a bathroom.[35] Led by Senator Cannizzaro, several of the women who spoke up in favor of the ERA also successfully sponsored a domestic violence bill that requires employers to provide leave to employees who are victims of domestic violence.[36]

In Nevada, the ratification of the ERA nourished the politics necessary to spawn new laws advancing real equality for women.

It empowered lawmakers with the legitimacy and confidence to respond boldly to unequal pay, the #MeToo movement, and the plight of working mothers. In the 1970s, the steps towards ratification were attempted repeatedly without success, but even the unfinished ERA made a difference: it brought political awareness and pressure to the need for new legislation for equality. Since 2017, ERA ratification has unleashed a flurry of legislation supporting working mothers, domestic violence victims, wage equality, and more. In the next election, Nevada voters elected even more women, making Nevada the first and only state in the United States with a female majority in its legislature. Making history, Nicole Cannizzaro became the Nevada Senate's first-ever woman majority leader.

In July 2019, Pat Spearman addressed a crowd at the annual conference of the National Organization for Women (NOW) about the recent surges in misogyny, racism, bigotry, and homophobia in America. She was sharing the stage with Jennifer McClellan and Hala Ayala, the Virginia legislators who would carry the 2020 ERA ratification bill in their state.

"We need a storm to wash away all the 'isms that divide us and threaten the principles of democracy," she announced. "We are the storm." Pretty soon, everyone in the room was repeating it, louder and louder. "We are the storm. We are the storm. WE ARE THE STORM."[37]

And soon enough, they were.

11

The Rectifiers

ILLINOIS WAS THE MOST CONTESTED battleground for ERA ratification from 1972 to 1982. Illinois was Betty Friedan's home state, where she was born and raised before she went on to become the bestselling author of *The Feminist Mystique*, which motivated millions of women across America to join the movement for equal rights and liberation from domestic life. Illinois was also the longtime home and headquarters of Phyllis Schlafly and her STOP-ERA movement, which mobilized millions of women across America to reject the ERA in the name of stay-at-home mothers. The Illinois legislature considered the ERA many times throughout the 1970s. ERA activists would go on hunger strike and spill animal blood in the halls of the statehouse, while the ladies of STOP-ERA would treat legislators to freshly baked bread and pies. The Illinois House of Representatives finally ratified the ERA by one vote on May 30, 2018, the very day that a grand jury indicted Harvey Weinstein of sexual assault in the case that came to define the nation's #MeToo era. Illinois confronted its own #MeToo moment that year, and the ratification of the ERA that day was one response.

When state senator Heather Steans proposed ERA ratification anew in 2018, she put it this way: "Illinois is a place where the Equal Rights [Amendment] died back in the late seventies and early eighties. We're rectifying a wrong."[1]

Shortly after Harvey Weinstein's accusers went public, an Illinois group calling itself the Women Who Make Illinois Run published an open letter: "Every industry has its own version of the casting couch. Illinois politics is no exception." Signed by 300 women, the letter declared that "Misogyny is alive and well in this industry." It went into the details: Male legislators asking female staffers out to dinner under the guise of offering mentorship, then proceeding to romanticize the encounter. Male political candidates groping their female fundraising consultants and then refusing to pay them after the advances were rebuked. County chairmen asking much younger female staffers up to their hotel rooms for a "nightcap" after a campaign fundraiser. And colleagues who witness this behavior and ignore it because it's "just how men talk."[2] The Women Who Make Illinois Run demanded "#NoMore in Illinois." "With each act of aggression, a woman internalizes the idea that she's not enough," they wrote. "That the only way to get ahead is to endure this type of dehumanizing behavior, with a smile no less." In the long run, it was not a sustainable way to live. Ultimately, this was bad for democracy in Illinois: it drove talented women out of their careers as public servants and deprived the state of their contributions.

When Heather Steans said that Illinois was rectifying a wrong by ratifying the ERA, she did not mention Phyllis Schlafly or the STOP-ERA movement. But she did talk about the power of women marching in recent memory. "[W]omen . . . around the country have been marching, demonstrating, expressing their concerns . . . that laws and policies may undermine our rights. I think voting to ratify the ERA helps give voice to these women and say that we're with you, we hear you, and we agree."[3] For months leading up to her introduction of ERA ratification in the Illinois Senate, Steans served on the Senate Task Force on Sexual

Discrimination Awareness and Prevention, which was created by legislation she sponsored in November 2017. The task force was a direct response to the national #MeToo movement and the Women Who Make Illinois Run's open letter.[4] It had been meeting monthly to hear from victims of sexual harassment and to consider proposed legislation, regulation, and best practices to improve the state's response to sexual discrimination and harassment.

At the same time that the #MeToo task force was created, Heather Steans also worked to create a bipartisan Senate Women's Caucus, along with Senators Kimberly Lightford and Toi Hutchinson. Women in the Illinois Senate had been meeting informally to talk policy for years, but as the spotlight was now on sexual harassment and misconduct in the statehouse, they decided to establish a formal institution to support each other's leadership.[5] In April 2018, Senator Lightford announced that the first measure to gain the backing of the newly formed Senate Women's Caucus was the Equal Rights Amendment.[6] Lightford has been a senator since 1998 and became the first African Amerian woman majority leader in 2019 as well as chair of the Illinois Legislative Black Caucus. She and Hutchinson joined Steans as Senate cosponsors of the ERA.

The Illinois House of Representatives also created its own task force with the same function.[7] Barbara Flynn Currie chaired the House's Task Force on Sexual Discrimination and Harassment. Currie was the House majority leader and longest-serving woman in the Illinois legislature. A legislator since 1979, she had participated in the contentious ERA ratification votes as an ERA proponent.[8] The House's task force included that chamber's most vocal advocates on women's issues, including Mary Flowers and Rita Mayfield, who had successfully sponsored Illinois's Pregnant Worker Accommodation Act in 2014.[9] It also included two rising African American stars in the House of Representatives—Litesa Wallace and Juliana Stratton—who were then running against each other for the Democratic nomination for lieutenant governor of Illinois. Stratton went on to win that primary and the general election. As her running mate, J. B. Pritzker, became the governor of

Illinois in 2019, Stratton was inaugurated as Illinois's first African American lieutenant governor. Flowers and Stratton cosponsored Currie's resolution creating the task force to address the issues raised by the #MeToo moment.

On the day that the Women Who Make Illinois Run published their open letter, Litesa Wallace and her gubernatorial running mate, Daniel Biss, reacted immediately by calling for legislation mandating sexual harassment training for everyone working in the statehouse. "We have the power to change this culture, and to set up our systems to support women—and with that power comes a responsibility to act. That's why raising awareness isn't enough," Wallace said. "We owe it to all the women who have shared their experiences, and to all those who haven't come forward, to build systems set up to prevent sexual harassment."[10] Soon thereafter, Wallace spoke publicly, in *Teen Vogue*, about her own experience. "I've been an Illinois state representative for three years, and I was a legislative staffer for the three years prior. I've experienced firsthand the pervasive culture of unchecked sexual harassment that disempowers and silences women, especially women of color."[11]

Over a decade before Hollywood celebrities made MeToo into a hashtag, there was already a MeToo movement started by African American activist Tarana Burke to empower black women who survived sexual assault, in homes and in working-class jobs.[12] The original MeToo movement focused on overcoming these women's powerlessness through collective action. The working women's MeToo movement focused on reversing the poverty that makes women of color easy targets of sexual abuse. Women of color are particularly prone to sexual harassment because of their disproportionate representation in low-wage work.

Even though women make up only half of all workers, they constitute nearly 60 percent of those making less than $11 per hour, and nearly 70 percent of those making less than $10 per hour. Black women and Latinas are overrepresented in the low-wage workforce: Black women make up 13 percent of women in the overall workforce but 18 percent of women in the low-wage workforce; Latinas make up 15 percent of the workforce and 24 percent of women in the low-wage workforce. Low wages sustain the economy of sexual harassment. Many low-wage women workers work in service and hospitality jobs, in hotels and restaurants.[13] In low-wage service jobs, women rely on tips rather than their wages to make a living. Women are generally overrepresented in this workforce; around 67 percent of all tipped workers are women. Tipped female wage workers are especially susceptible to sexual harassment. Because they are not guaranteed a living base wage, women put up with daily sexual harassment from customers and management because they might not get any tips if they don't.[14] If they are mothers, tips make the difference between feeding or not feeding their children. That is how abusive sexual behavior by men becomes a regular feature of working women's economic subsistence.

By 2018, the #MeToo movements came to a boiling point in Illinois. In March that year, a staffer sued the campaign of Michael Madigan, the long-serving speaker of the Illinois House of Representatives, accusing his top aide of sexual harassment and complaining of conduct mirroring what was described by the Women Who Make Illinois Run.[15] Sexual harassment and sexual assault were technically against the law, but the law had failed so many women in so many industries for so long. It was time to dig deeper for solutions. Would it make a difference to enact a constitutional amendment simply declaring equality of rights under the law as a permanent and foundational principle—never to be abridged because of a person's sex? Were women not respected because they did not have the ERA, or did women not have the ERA because they were not respected? The #MeToo moment pointed to the ERA as an obviously necessary—but by no means sufficient—step in the quest for durable legal and cultural change. Many members of the House Task Force on Sexual Discrimination and Harassment cosponsored the ERA ratification resolution, including its chair, Barbara Flynn Currie, as well as Litesa Wallace and Juliana Stratton.

For long-serving Illinois lawmakers like Currie, the ERA had a particular meaning as a signpost for women's equality because of its history within the Illinois legislature. The ERA's death, flagged by Senator Steans in 2018, was not singlehandedly caused by Phyllis Schlafly and the breadmaking ladies of STOP-ERA, as legend would have it. The ERA died in Illinois in the 1970s because men who exerted power in the state legislature adopted procedural rules to prevent constitutional change that would give women more power. Both houses of the Illinois legislature require a three-fifths supermajority vote to ratify a constitutional amendment. Women in the legislature, including Currie, tried to change that rule from 1973 to 1981.[16] But they were outnumbered by men who retained the power to change it. They chose not to.

Within two months of Congress's adoption of the ERA in March 1972, the Illinois Senate voted to ratify the ERA. Ratification received thirty "yes" votes and twenty-one "no" votes, making up a "constitutional majority" of the fifty-nine members of the Senate.[17] A constitutional majority is a majority of the Senate's total membership, not just a majority of those present and voting. Less than a year later, in a new session of the legislature, the Illinois House of Representatives also voted on an ERA ratification resolution, led by Goudyloch "Giddy" Dyer, a Republican who got her political start with the League of Women Voters. There, ERA ratification got ninety-five votes in favor and seventy-two votes against. The ERA received a constitutional majority of that chamber—which would be eighty-nine votes or more. Then, in the same legislative session, the Senate voted by a constitutional majority again—thirty-two votes in favor of the ERA, with efforts led by newly elected Democratic senator Dawn Clark Netsch, the first woman to become a professor at Northwestern University School of Law. As a law professor, Netsch spent her decades in Illinois politics as an independent Democrat, always critical of, and standing outside of, the Democratic Party's political machine. In almost every other state, the majority votes by both houses of the state legislature would have been enough for that state to ratify the ERA.

But not in Illinois. Illinois had adopted a new constitution in 1970 that imposed a higher bar for votes by its legislature to ratify any federal constitutional amendment. Article XIV, Section 4 of the 1970 constitution provided that the state legislature could not vote on ratifying any federal constitutional amendment until after the next election following Congress's adoption of the amendment. The same constitutional provision required federal constitutional amendments to be ratified by each chamber by a three-fifths majority vote, not a simple majority of those present and voting, and not a constitutional majority.

Under this provision of the Illinois constitution, the Illinois Senate's constitutional majority vote in May 1972 to ratify the ERA was invalid on two counts: it was taken before elections for a new legislative session, and the "yes" vote did not get the three-fifths support that appeared necessary. As for the votes that took place after the election in the new legislative session, ERA ratification got only a constitutional majority, not three-fifths of the vote in the House or the Senate. So, even though the majorities of both houses of the Illinois legislature voted to ratify the ERA, and even though the same set of events would have produced a valid ratification in most other states, the opponents of the ERA insisted that Illinois had not ratified the amendment.

The ERA's sponsors in each house—Giddy Dyer and Dawn Netsch—decided to litigate. They filed lawsuits against the speaker of the House of Representatives and the president of the Senate, arguing that the Illinois Constitution's rules about ratifying federal constitutional amendments were illegal. They argued that Article V of the US Constitution did not allow state constitutions to make it harder to ratify federal amendments. Article V says that an amendment proposed by Congress becomes valid "when ratified" by three-fourths of the states. Therefore, the state constitution could not require the state legislature to wait until the next election to ratify an amendment, nor could it require the state legislature to obtain a three-fifths majority to ratify.

The judges agreed with Giddy Dyer and Dawn Netsch on these constitutional points.[18] The opinion was written by John Paul Stevens, then a judge on the US Court of Appeals for the

Seventh Circuit, who shortly after this decision became a justice of the US Supreme Court. Then-Judge Stevens held that Article V of the US Constitution gave state legislatures the power to ratify amendments—which meant that state legislatures, not state constitutions or the people who made them, could decide their process and requirements for ratifying a federal amendment. The House of Representatives had adopted a rule mirroring the state constitutional provision requiring a three-fifths vote for constitutional amendments. The Senate—led by Dawn Netsch—had adopted a rule requiring a constitutional majority—not three-fifths—to ratify a constitutional amendment. Judge Stevens concluded that, even though it violated the US Constitution if the *Illinois state constitution* required a three-fifths vote to ratify a federal constitutional amendment, each chamber of the Illinois legislature was free to operate using a three-fifths rule as long as they didn't put that requirement in the state constitution.

That meant that the Senate's "yes" vote on ERA ratification was valid because it was consistent with the Senate's own rule requiring a constitutional majority. But it also meant that the House's rule requiring three-fifths was also valid, and by that rule, the House's vote to ratify the ERA came up short, because it attained a constitutional majority, not three-fifths. The court agreed with Netsch's excellently reasoned argument that the Illinois Constitution violated the US Constitution, but still gave ERA opponents in the legislature the green light to use a three-fifths rule to apply to future efforts to ratify the ERA.

Which is exactly what both chambers of the Illinois legislature did after that.

This procedural rule raised the bar on the ERA. It made Phyllis Schlafly's job a lot easier. A three-fifths rule requires the proponents of ratification to persuade the skeptics. If there is confusion or disagreement about what the amendment means and what it will accomplish, a three-fifths rule requires a consensus across competing visions. All Phyllis Schlafly needed to do was stir up some confusion or doubt in a few men—not even a majority. She and the ladies of STOP-ERA handed them home-baked goods and told them that the ERA would kill American family life in the home, as they went in to vote on ratification. Five days before the extended deadline expired in 1982, ERA ratification won a constitutional majority in both houses—103–72 in the House and 31–27 in the Senate—but not three-fifths. Years later, as a seasoned politician, Dawn Netsch said that she believed that Illinois ratification could have changed the game nationally. It could have encouraged other unratified states, like Florida, to come through.[19] But the procedural rule stopped the ERA in Illinois.

In 2018, both houses of the Illinois General Assembly ratified the ERA by three-fifths of the vote. In the Senate, there was no debate after Senator Steans presented the resolution, with forty-two votes in favor and thirteen votes against. That's several votes more than the thirty-six required to pass the three-fifths threshold. The ERA's passage by three-fifths in the Senate was not surprising—it had ratified the ERA by 39–11 in 2014 upon Steans's sponsorship of the bill.[20] But in the House of Representatives in 2018, the ERA passed 72–45. With seventy-one votes required to make three-fifths in the House, Illinois ratification barely squeaked by.

The three-fifths majority was almost lost because of two main concerns by "no" voters. As in Nevada, abortion rights came up in the Illinois House debates, with some Republicans alleging that the ERA would expand abortion rights, particularly taxpayer funding of abortions.[21] But Illinois ERA ratification had the sponsorship of pro-life Republican Steven Andersson, who has been vocal nationally about why pro-life Republicans should support the ERA. Andersson has argued that even if the ERA protects access to some abortions, particularly those that are medically necessary, this does not amount to an ERA that leads to the funding of all abortions on demand, as some opponents claim.[22]

In the House, the ERA faced opposition from the left as well as the right. Democratic representatives Mary Flowers and Rita Mayfield, both African American, questioned whether the ERA would help women of color, poor women, and working mothers.

While these objections almost stopped ERA ratification in Illinois, the proponents' efforts to persuade these skeptics improved the ERA that emerged from Illinois in 2018.

Representative Flowers raised doubts about Alice Paul, who is widely credited with authoring the ERA. "Alice Paul, she was a very proud racist woman,"[23] Flowers remarked. This image of Paul was not false—she did require the African American sororities and groups to march at the back of the Suffrage Parade of 1913. Mary Church Terrell, who worked with both Susan B. Anthony and Alice Paul on suffrage, believed that Paul would have sacrificed the African American women's vote if she could win the vote for white women by doing so. The racist sins of white suffragists are wrongs that had yet to be rectified, and Flowers could not support an amendment that is widely viewed as Alice Paul's legacy.

Extending that legacy, according to Flowers, would "put wealthy women against poor working women." Flowers was channeling the arguments of Florence Kelley almost a century before, or Myra Wolfgang half a century back: "Because, see, the wealthy women don't have to worry about lifting heavy bags and heavy boxes. They don't have to worry about having babysitters. They don't have to worry about their rights being violated."[24] What would it take to make equality work for poor women who have to go to work every day? Flowers did not see answers in the ERA. Furthermore, she would not support an ERA that would destroy affirmative action, one that "takes away the judges' ability to rule favorably toward the benefits of a woman because it requires same treatment."[25] Rita Mayfield also expressed concern that the bill "does not in any way, shape or form benefit a woman of color." "Why in the world would I vote for a Bill that would take away my rights? I am a mother."

At the same time, two other African American Democrats in the House—Litesa Wallace and Juliana Stratton—voted in favor of the ERA, after giving powerful floor speeches sympathetic to Flowers's concerns. Wallace began her speech with the story of her family and her experience as a working single mother:

I'm the daughter of a man who was born on a plantation. I'm the granddaughter of a woman who left the south to come to Chicago for opportunity but never found it because of her race and her gender. A woman who raised her children in Ida B. Wells's housing project, who had children with a man who was the janitor at Evanston High School, who was the daughter of a woman who died after childbirth. I stand here a single mother who has survived damn near anything you can think of.[26]

Many aspects of Wallace's personal story touched the concerns raised by Flowers and Mayfield.

Wallace then zeroed in on childcare, an issue that was important to her constituents. The working poor could not afford it. Mothers would work in order to support their children, but not make enough to pay for babysitters, as Mary Flowers pointed out. But if they worked and did not get a babysitter, they could get in trouble with the law. This was an issue that had affected her grandmother's generation, but had not been solved.

I go so hard on the child care issue because my grandmother worked on the north side of Chicago to take care of white women's children and had to leave her own children at home to raise themselves. And I go so hard about child care because when my mother found herself single, she worked the graveyard shift at the post office and I stayed home alone with my little sister and had DCFS [Department of Children and Family Services] found out we would have been taken.[27]

Wallace then criticized the very institution in which they were sitting, saying, "we refuse to recognize intersectionality, not just in this debate but in damn near every debate that occurs in this body."[28]

But unlike Flowers and Mayfield, Wallace acknowledged the opportunity presented by the ERA. "Today is extremely important and extremely historic . . . women who present to the world like me have been asking for centuries, ain't I a woman? And we continue to hear a resounding 'no' to that question almost every day."[29] She asked her colleagues to "continue to think about these things . . . and do some serious soul searching . . . particularly the things that were outlined by Leader Flowers."[30] Wallace voted "yes" on ERA ratification.

Representative Juliana Stratton spoke more positively about the ERA, while acknowledging sympathy with the concerns about its responsiveness to women of color raised by her colleagues. "The Equal Rights Amendment, once ratified, will help all people," she said.[31] Responding to the women whose stories made #MeToo ubiquitous in the moment leading up to this historic ERA ratification, Stratton connected the ERA to the work that had been facing the Illinois House's Task Force on Sexual Discrimination and Harassment, on which she had been serving for several months. The ERA would help domestic violence victims enforce orders of protection against abusive spouses. It would give Congress a constitutional basis for legislation targeting gender violence, and protecting its victims. It would help women vulnerable to violence in the custody of law enforcement.[32]

Stratton responded indirectly to Rita Mayfield's assertion that the ERA would do nothing for black women by connecting the present debate about the ERA to past controversies about women in the military. Showcasing how far we've come since the 1970s, Stratton said the ERA would increase women's opportunities in the military. She emphasized the importance of these opportunities to African American women in particular. African American women enlisted in the military at significantly higher rates than white or Hispanic women,[33] and therefore, she believed, would benefit from the ERA's effect on the military.

She was also confident that the ERA would reduce unequal pay. The amendment would reshape the pay practices of the state as employer, which would have immediate practical consequences for teachers and government workers. "Passage of the ERA should prompt all government employers to examine their pay and promotion practices to make sure that they are equal and to evaluate their protections for pregnant employees as well,"[34] she noted.

Stratton's reference to "protections for pregnant employees" was a partial response to Flowers' concerns about protecting women workers in physically demanding jobs. It is also a partial response to Republicans' concerns about whether the ERA will sufficiently protect unborn life. Protecting pregnant workers, promoting prenatal health, and reducing maternal mortality are all ways of protecting unborn life through means other than banning abortion.

Stratton also noted that "the ERA would not abolish all sex-based distinctions under the law."[35] Stratton was promoting an ERA that was compatible with affirmative action. On the substantive outcome—whether affirmative action should be permitted under the ERA—Stratton seemed to agree with Flowers. Flowers had expressed concern that the ERA would undermine measures to help women—particularly poor or working-class women of color.

Finally Stratton, like Senator Nicole Cannizzaro in Nevada, acknowledged the multigenerational struggle by ordinary women—mothers, grandmothers, daughters—for equal rights, and included her own African American foremothers and daughters in that struggle:

> As I make these comments, I do so standing on the shoulders of my mother, Velma Wiggins, my grandmother, Velma Slaughter, and my great grandmother, Anna Capshaw. None of whom lived to see this historical vote but left a legacy that I should value all people as equal and spend my days working for the same. And standing on my shoulders are Tyler, Cassidy, Ryan, and McKenzie and my hope is that their rights are also protected under the United States Constitution as being equal to those of their male counterparts.[36]

In the spirit of inclusion, Stratton, while remembering the ladies, did not forget about the men and the boys: "But also for all of the men and the boys who also stand for and are being raised to value justice and equality for all, we can and must act for them as well."[37]

In her closing comment, she spoke obliquely to Flowers and Mayfield again, saying, "as a black woman in particular, . . . I have experienced discrimination. Not just from being a woman in America but also from being a woman of color." But this was not a reason to reject the ERA. Quite the contrary. "I truly do believe that our Constitution, that living, breathing document that guides us and sets forth the ideals of this country, must reflect what we hope to be and serve as our compass."[38]

Illinois's ratification story, like the longer story of the Equal Rights Amendment, included dissenting feminists. They brought attention to some of the racial dynamics of suffrage's past. In chapter 4, we encountered Mary Church Terrell, one of the cofounders of the National Association of Colored Women, who marched in 1913 with her sorority in the back of Alice Paul's suffrage parade. But Ida B. Wells, another founder of the NACW, refused to march in the back and simply joined the procession of white Illinois women in that parade.[39] For over a century, African American women have taken different strategies in their fight for equality, from Mary Church Terrell and Ida Wells, to Shirley Chisholm and Barbara Jordan, to Pat Spearman, Mary Flowers, Rita Mayfield, Litesa Wallace, and Juliana Stratton.

In the Illinois House of Representatives, the rule requiring a three-fifths majority to ratify a constitutional amendment meant that ERA proponents could not ignore their colleagues' doubts about the ERA. They had to try to find common ground with the skeptics. Every vote mattered, and the ERA came very close to failing again, as it had so many times from 1972 to 1982. Litesa Wallace and Juliana Stratton tried to persuade Mary Flowers and Rita Mayfield—and any others who shared their skepticism—that the ERA would respond to the needs of working women of color. Even though they did not ultimately win Flowers's and Mayfield's votes, they did win a version of the ERA that they had remade on the House floor into an amendment that responded to the needs of working women of color.

Before and after the ERA vote, Mary Flowers and Rita Mayfield have worked to legislate the same things—like fairness for pregnant workers—that the Nevada ratifiers achieved. ERA sponsors in the Illinois Senate, including Toi Hutchinson and Kimberly Lightford, have worked with Flowers and Mayfield to enact legislation protecting pregnant women and mothers. After the ERA vote, they worked with colleagues who sponsored the ERA in the Senate and the House towards the successful adoption of legislation creating a task force on infant and maternal mortality among African Americans.[40] They continue to join forces with ERA sponsors on proposals for paid family leave, mental health services for pregnant and postpartum women, coverage of doula services for childbirth, and the right to evidence-based medical care in pregnancy and childbirth. Raising the minimum wage—which can make a major difference to the vulnerability of low-wage workers of color to harassment on the job—has also been a priority. These women are carrying on Florence Kelley's legacy of pushing the Equal Rights Amendment to make law responsive to women's needs, especially those of poor working women and mothers. Their objections to the ERA helped shape the pro-ERA positions taken by Litesa Wallace and Juliana Stratton. With political ambition and a strong sense of history, Wallace and Stratton turned intersectionality and the needs of working-class mothers into reasons to support the ERA rather than to oppose it.

Legislation to address the concerns of the MeToo movements have also moved ahead since the ERA was ratified. On the same day that the Illinois House voted to ratify the ERA, both houses of the legislature passed legislation sponsored by Barbara Flynn Currie and Heather Steans emerging from the work of the Task Forces on Sexual Discrimination and Harassment. The legislation strengthened the enforcement of antidiscrimination law by creating full-time commissioners on the Illinois Human Rights Commission. It also created a panel to address the backlog of cases, extended the time for filing a claim, and created online publication requirements for the Commission's opinions.[41]

In the next legislative session, dozens of legislators from both political parties sponsored and passed legislation requiring sexual harassment training for all state officials, employees, and lobbyists, and putting a reporting and investigation system in place. The law also prohibits employers from requiring their employees to sign nondisclosure or arbitration agreements related to harassment or discrimination. But the MeToo legislation goes beyond the concerns of state and professional employees—it addresses the needs of low-wage working women by focusing on tipped employees in the bar and restaurant industry. The state is now required to provide harassment training to all employers for free online, and a supplemental training for bars and restaurants, responding to the special vulnerabilities of tipped workers.[42] Among the legislation's many sponsors were Heather Steans and Rita Mayfield.

There are wrongs of gender injustice that the ERA won't rectify overnight. The women lawmakers of Illinois did not agree on whether the ERA could help eventually. Their disagreement almost killed the ERA, but in the end, the ERA that emerged from Illinois was better suited for the twenty-first century than it had ever been.

12
The History Makers

IN THE SUMMER OF 1996, Jennifer, a high school student in Petersburg, Virginia, listened to the words of Justice Ruth Bader Ginsburg quoted on the television news. Justice Ginsburg had just announced the Supreme Court's landmark decision ending the tradition of state-supported all-male education at the Virginia Military Institute (VMI). While Virginia "serves the state's sons, it makes no provision whatever for her daughters. That is not equal protection," she said. [1] In a 7–1 decision for the Supreme Court, Justice Ginsburg declared that sex classifications could not be used "to create or perpetuate the legal, social, and economic inferiority of women."[2] Women and men could be treated differently only to compensate women for economic disabilities they have suffered, to promote their access to equal employment opportunity, or to advance the development of the talent and capacities of our nation's people.[3] VMI's long tradition of excluding women was therefore no longer legal.

The state of Virginia would have to change.

That's when it dawned on Jennifer. "I can go to VMI," she announced, only to be ridiculed by a male classmate. He decided to enroll with her at VMI, just to watch her fail. He bet her a dollar that she would never graduate. Jennifer graduated from VMI in 2003, but never collected the dollar from her classmate. He had dropped out himself.[4]

Jennifer went on to become Delegate Jennifer Carroll Foy, the chief patron of the Virginia House of Delegates' 2020 resolution to ratify the Equal Rights Amendment. On January 15, 2020, when she presented the ERA to the House floor, she invoked Justice Ginsburg in *United States v. Virginia*. She quoted from Abigail Adams's letter to her husband John, telling him to "remember the ladies" when writing the new laws for the emerging nation. She recited parts of Shirley Chisholm's 1970 ERA speech in Congress. The words of these women from three different historical moments pointed to one conclusion: it was "time for Virginia to finally be on the right side of history."[5]

ERA ratification had failed several times in Virginia in the 1970s. Legal experts said during those battles that the ERA would require VMI to educate women.[6] ERA opponents resisted the integration of women into traditionally male turfs, and VMI was not the only bastion of male power in Virginia. The Virginia General Assembly was essentially a men's club, too. Until 1980, there was not a single woman in the Virginia Senate.[7] It was only after the ERA deadline lapsed in 1982 that the first African American woman was elected to either one of Virginia's legislative chambers. When Congress sent the ERA to states for ratification in 1972, the Virginia General Assembly had only 3 women out of 140. But on the day that both houses of the Virginia General Assembly voted to ratify the ERA, there were forty-one women making law in the Virginia capitol, with the first woman Speaker of the House of Delegates presiding over the proceedings.

On the other side of the Capitol building, state senator Mamie Locke, a chief patron of the ERA ratification bill in the Senate, had more to say about getting to the right side of history. "There's no time limit on equal rights," she began. Then she invoked Barbara Jordan, the congresswoman who played a crucial role in extending the ERA deadline. Locke recited the "We the People" speech that Jordan gave during Nixon's impeachment hearings.[8] Senator Locke, like Delegate Carroll Foy and Nevada senator Spearman, brought the words of the ERA's foremothers into their own justifications for ratifying the ERA. They are finishing the work begun by those who extended the fight. They are retelling history to make history.

Virginia state senator Jennifer McClellan, the other chief patron of the ERA ratification bill in the Senate, dug deeper into the wrong side of Virginia's history. Her own great-grandfather was born to former slaves on a plantation after emancipation, and was deprived of his right to vote. Women were brought to Virginia in 1619, to "make wives to the inhabitants," and they were deprived of rights to vote, hold public office, or hold property. Her own female ancestors were slaves, legally defined as property, with no rights. "We have come a long way, but we still have a long way to go," she said.[9] Over a hundred constitutions around the world had equal rights amendments, but American women had not achieved equality in the boardrooms or in the highest offices in the states or in the country because of years of discrimination that they had to overcome. That day, McClellan was wearing a replica of Alice Paul's jailhouse door pin, one of which Mary Church Terrell had accepted from Paul for her participation in suffrage pickets at the White House. McClellan is a member of Delta Sigma Theta,[10] the African American sorority that Terrell founded and led to march in the historic suffrage parade organized by Paul.

Jenn McClellan had her political start in the Virginia House of Delegates in 2006. When she became pregnant in 2010, she was only the second pregnant legislator in Virginia's history—the first was Jill Vogel in 2008,[11] a Republican senator who voted for ERA ratification. When McClellan was pregnant, many people assumed that she would not seek reelection, and she wondered why the same assumption was never made about her colleague, a male delegate who was expecting to become a father at roughly the same time.[12] But McClellan got reelected, and a few years later, she was elected to Virginia's upper chamber, the Senate. While she was campaign-ing for the Senate, Jennifer Carroll Foy campaigned in her first election for the House of Delegates, successfully, while pregnant with twins. Even before they introduced ERA ratification bills that finally succeeded, Jenn and Jennifer changed Virginia politics: They made it normal for expectant mothers to run for office and win.

On the day that both chambers voted to ratify the ERA, preg-nant Delegate Kelly Convirs-Fowler stood up and directly con-nected the ERA to this cultural shift. The mother of two daughters, ages ten and seven, said, "Most people already know, but in case you can't tell, I am pregnant. My husband and I are expecting our third in April." She spoke of her experience of trying to hide her first pregnancy when she applied for a job as a third grade teacher: "I was really concerned that they wouldn't hire me if they knew that I would be taking six weeks off when I gave birth."[13]

She described the road of working parenthood as bumpy and challenging. Like Jenn McClellan, she too has been asked on the campaign trail how she could serve as a legislator and have a baby. "Although David and I have always tried to split our parental duties 50/50, society honestly expects more from me when it comes to our children," she observed. That would sometimes interfere with their efforts at egalitarian parenting. "When the kids have been sick and he calls out of work he's often questioned as to why he has to stay home and why can't his wife stay home with the sick children." The ERA would be a constitutional recognition of the value of gender-equal parenting. "I'm extremely grateful for a partner who recognizes our equal duties, and I am ready for our constitution to recognize it as well," she concluded. By talking about childcare and the struggle to implement equal roles for women and men within the family, Convirs-Fowler highlighted problems that concerned the ERA's champions, from Crystal Eastman in the 1920s to Bella Abzug in the 1970s, and which have yet to find satisfactory solu-tions in the twenty-first century.

Virginia's ratification of the ERA also drew out new twen-ty-first-century meanings of sex equality: the equal rights of people of all sexes and genders, beyond male and female. This idea is in the text of the ERA, which guarantees "equality of rights" unabridged "on account of sex," even though the ERA began as a response to discrimination against women. Danica Roem, Virginia's first transgender delegate, stood up in support of the ERA, wearing her mother's bicentennial ERA necklace from 1976. Roem spoke of her experiences as a transgender person—being compared to predators and pedophiles, for instance. She campaigned for her seat in the House of Delegates with the Equal Rights Amendment on her platform. "To single someone out based on sexual orientation and gender identity is to inherently single them out on account of sex,"[14] she said. Roem noted that she and her conservative mother disagreed on politics more than they agreed. But they agreed that the ERA should be part of the Constitution.

Roem highlighted the multigenerational and bipartisan efforts that had carried the Virginia lawmakers to this historic moment. Delegate Kaye Kory also talked about how her passion for the ERA dated back to an earlier moment when she met "the author of Title IX"—presumably Patsy Mink. Talking with her about how hard she worked for Title IX and the ERA, Kory became a believer in the ERA and spent years advocating for it. Like Carroll Foy and Locke and McClellan, Kory also acknowledged the forgotten foremothers of women's equality whose torch she was carrying.

Delegate Vivian Watts held up a picture of herself with her daughter, forty-four years earlier, on the mall of Washington, marching for the Equal Rights Amendment. "I speak from that generation; I speak with the same sash that I wore in this picture," she said, making visible the purple, gold, and white suffragist sash she was wearing. In those days, she remembered—responding to her pregnant colleague—"It wasn't whether or not the teacher would have been pregnant. No woman that was married could teach high school."[15] Those exclusions were no longer in effect, so why was the ERA still needed? She praised the progress that had been made, but said that these positive changes "can be erased tomorrow." She noted that the legislature now had forty-one women—mostly younger and more recently elected than she. With these numbers, it was now finally possible to make "the statement of equality," and to make sure it would not be erased.

While most of the vocal proponents of the ERA were Democrats, Virginia, like Nevada and Illinois, had key Republican supporters as well. In 2019, the ratification bill that had been passed by a healthy majority of the Senate had a Republican chief co-patron, Glen Sturtevant. (He lost his 2019 reelection bid to Democratic ERA supporter Ghazala Hashmi, the first Muslim woman ever to be elected to the Virginia Senate.) When the ERA was reintroduced in 2020, Republican Jen Kiggans spoke to support it in the Senate. Kiggans had been a naval officer and nurse practitioner before joining the Virginia Senate. She said, "I believe it's the right thing to do and the right side of history to be on. I support equality for all races, all genders—equality is the message I think we should leave to our daughters."

Kiggans acknowledged, however, that because of the ratification deadline, "this vote may be purely symbolic." Agreeing with some of the ERA's opponents, Kiggans said that she never needed a constitutional amendment to achieve her life goals. But she was swayed by Ronald Reagan, who supported ERA ratification as governor of California in 1972, and described the ERA's commitment to equality between women and men as "morally unassailable." Kiggans made clear that she was "a defender of life at all stages" and "an advocate for recognition of physiological birth gender differences in sports and privacy matters." Therefore, her support for the ERA did not amount to support for abortion and transgender rights. In both chambers, ERA opponents had raised these issues—the ratification deadline, abortion rights, and transgender rights—as reasons to vote against the amendment. But Kiggans recognized that the pursuit of equal rights was larger than the ERA, and that the ERA was an important statement of principle rather than a specific position on policies and pronouns. Like the pro-life Republicans who supported the ERA in Illinois, Kiggans voted for it on the understanding that its meaning with regard to abortion and transgender rights was not fixed in advance.

That day, the House of Delegates voted first; 59–41 in favor of ratification. Less than an hour later, the Senate followed, 28–12 for the ERA.

If this vote had taken place under the Illinois three-fifths rule, the ratification resolution would have failed because the House of Delegates' vote to ratify the ERA was one vote shy of three-fifths. But Virginia just requires a constitutional majority. Once each chamber approved the other's ratification resolution in crossover votes two weeks later, it was official: Virginia had made history by becoming the thirty-eighth state to ratify the ERA. Although legal and political fights about the deadline loomed ahead, there was no denying that women had scaled a major peak in a long quest for constitutional equality.

Virginia's ratification produced an unprecedented situation in American constitutional history. It is the only instance of a constitutional amendment reaching the three-fourths threshold for state ratifications after a congressionally imposed deadline has lapsed. It is the only proposed amendment that was drafted in one generation, adopted in another generation, and fully ratified in yet another generation. If it is not added to the Constitution, it will be the only constitutional amendment that met the requirements spelled out in Article V—adoption by two-thirds of Congress and ratification by three-fourths of the states—that has not been added to the Constitution based on deadlines or rescissions that the Constitution does not mention. Even if the ERA is not formally added to the Constitution, there is no question that the thirty-eighth ratification, delivered by Virginia, carries tremendous political force and historical significance that, over time, could make a difference to constitutional interpretation.

Virginia's history-making moment is all the more remarkable in light of the state's many failed attempts to ratify the ERA, year after year, from 1972 to 1982 and from 2011 to 2020, even during moments when a majority of Virginians and their legislators supported the ERA. Virginia, after all, is a state that did not ratify the Nineteenth Amendment before 1920—it finally came around and ratified women's suffrage in 1952, after a generation of women had already exercised their constitutional right to vote. For years, procedural rules and maneuvers in a predominantly male legislature prevented the ERA from being debated and considered in earnest. In Congress, during the 1978 floor debates about the extension of the ratification deadline, Congresswoman Margaret Heckler explicitly pointed to Virginia as an example of a legislature where a few men who controlled committees were preventing the ERA from reaching the floor for a vote, despite growing popular support.[16]

In Virginia, it is not automatic that a constitutional amendment adopted by Congress gets a debate or a vote by the entire state legislature. The Privileges and Elections (P&E) Committee of each chamber acts as gatekeeper. When the ERA was sent to the states for ratification in 1972, the House of Delegates' P&E Committee was chaired by a vocal opponent of the ERA. The P&E Committee had long been considered a prestigious committee to sit on, and most of the men who were then members had been on it since 1965. They regarded their record of keeping legislation off the floor as a measure of their job performance.[17]

The P&E Committees of the two legislative chambers held hearings on the ERA in 1973. Phyllis Schlafly flew to Virginia to testify, and 800 women made appearances in these hearings, on both sides of the debate. Then the House of Delegates P&E Committee voted 13–2[18] to "pass by indefinitely," which means that there is no further action on that bill during that legislative session. In other words, it goes to the legislative graveyard. The Senate committee did not vote, but instead created a task force on the ERA to investigate and report on what the ERA would do. Meanwhile, the seven-year ratification clock was ticking.

In 1974, the committee voted again, 12–8, not to take further action. In 1975, the Senate P&E Committee decided to take the lead and voted the ERA out to the Senate floor by a vote of 6–5. But one of the committee members was absent when the committee took this vote. So when the ERA reached the Senate floor, the majority voted—by one vote—to refer the ERA back to the committee, out of respect to the man who had been absent from the committee meeting. Back in committee, the men quibbled about whether to have a state referendum on the ERA, and decided to take no further action. And the seven-year ratification clock continued to tick.

In 1976, an ERA proponent in the Senate tried to get the ERA to the floor by way of a discharge motion. That was how Martha Griffiths had gotten the ball rolling on the ERA in Congress in 1970. But in Virginia, even the proponents of the ERA frowned upon the discharge motion. They did not want to disturb the committee system. They were now half-way to the seven-year ratification deadline.

In 1977, ERA proponents proposed to change the parliamentary rules of the House of Delegates. Because of the importance of federal constitutional amendments, they proposed that amendments to the US Constitution be sent automatically to the floor for a vote within twenty days of the P&E Committee receiving it. That motion failed, 62–36. Virginia's legislature opted to preserve its traditional committee system. That year, the discharge motion succeeded in the Senate and the ERA reached the floor. But there, the ERA got twenty votes out of forty, one vote shy of the constitutional majority. One ERA proponent who had sponsored the ratification resolution in previous years switched sides at the last minute. He was running for lieutenant governor, and his "no" vote on the ERA led to donations from conservative backers. Congress extended the ratification deadline in 1978, giving states until 1982.

After that, the ERA continued to be held up by both chambers' committees, year after year. In 1980, the ERA made it back to the floor of the Senate. Again, it got only twenty votes. One pro-ERA senator changed his vote at the last minute. Another senator refused to vote, citing a Senate rule that prohibits voting by a senator who has a "conflict of interest."[19] In 2020, state senator Dick Saslaw remembered being in the room during that episode in 1980—he recalled that the "conflict of interest" referenced by his colleague was that he was married to a woman and therefore could not vote fairly about the ERA.[20] A survey as early as 1977 suggests that while men holding committee power frequently stopped the ERA from being voted on by all the representatives in the legislature, 59 percent of Virginians supported the ERA, with higher rates of support from African Americans (69 percent) and manual and semiskilled laborers (80 percent).[21]

Rules of parliamentary procedure, which assign a powerful gatekeeping function to one committee, enabled ERA opponents to block the path to ratification for years. Since 2011, the ERA resolution was passed by the Virginia Senate six times with a bipartisan majority. In 2019, the vote was 26–14, with a Republican chief patron on the resolution. Despite sufficient bipartisan support for ratification in the House of Delegates to produce the majority to pass it if it reached a floor vote, the resolution did not get out of committee in 2019.

After the Virginia Senate voted to ratify the ERA in January 2019, four members of the House of Delegates' six-person P&E Subcommittee No. 1 voted against all the ERA ratification resolutions.[22] This subcommittee vote prevented the ERA from reaching the floor of the House of Delegates. For Delegate Hala Ayala, an ERA patron, it seemed undemocratic to allow four committee members to prevent the full body of the House of Delegates from voting on a matter as important as the ratification of a federal constitutional amendment.

Ayala was one of the first Latinas elected to the Virginia legislature in 2017,[23] a former PTA president, and a single working mother of two. She identifies herself as "an outspoken advocate for women and families."[24] Ayala proposed to change the House of Delegates' rule to allow the full body to vote by a majority on whether to consider a federal constitutional amendment on the floor, regardless of whether that amendment had been reported out by a House committee.[25] In response to Ayala's proposal, Todd Gilbert, the Republican House majority leader and vocal ERA opponent, responded with a blocking resolution that would require motions like Ayala's to receive a two-thirds majority vote instead of a simple majority to prevail.[26]

Perhaps Ayala was trying to stand on Martha Griffiths's shoulders—to make what was effectively the same as Griffiths's discharge petition in 1970, which was the key to getting the ERA out of the House Judiciary Committee. One wonders, then, why a rules change was needed. Couldn't Ayala simply get signatures on a discharge petition to discharge the Privileges and Elections Committee of its control over the ERA ratification resolution?

In the House of Delegates, discharge petitions are already available under its own rules for bills, but not for resolutions. The ratification of a federal constitutional amendment is not really legislation, which is what bills propose. So ratifications are mere resolutions, and the discharge petition procedure is not available. Another solution was fashioned: Delegate Marcus Simon proposed a simple amendment to the discharge petition rule that would make discharge petitions available for resolutions as well as bills.[27] Ayala's proposed rule change obtained fifty votes, just one vote short of the constitutional majority—fifty-one votes— required for a rules change. Simon's proposal obtained forty-nine votes, coming up two votes short. Although there were three Republicans who said they would vote for ERA ratification if it came to the floor of the House of Delegates, not all of them were willing to go the extra step of approving a more general change to longstanding parliamentary procedures. As a result of the procedural rules, four Republican legislators were able to use their power on a subcommittee to send the ERA ratification to the legislative graveyard in Virginia's 2019 session.

But the women who championed the ERA did not let the committee system and its legislative graveyard stop them. If they didn't have the votes to change the rules, they would just have to get the voters to change the legislature. On November 5, 2019, they did.

Every single seat in the Virginia legislature was on the ballot that day. After the ERA failed in Virginia months before the election, women across the state made the ERA an issue in the 2019 election campaigns. Virginia voters flipped the legislature from Republican to Democrat, electing record numbers of women to both houses of the Virginia General Assembly. The first Muslim-American woman legislator was seated. With a new majority, Eileen Filler-Corn became the first woman and first Jew to become the speaker of the House. It is the speaker of the House who appoints the members of the Privileges and Elections Committee. Another first was Charniele Herring, the first African American woman House majority leader. Louise Lucas, an African American woman who has served in the Virginia Senate since 1992, became the president pro tempore of the Senate.

In her January 2020 floor speech in support of the ERA, almost a year after her ordeal with attempting the rules change, Hala Ayala could not help shouting out these amazing firsts that the historic election of 2019 had produced. She began her story with Sarah Lee Fain and Helen Henderson, the first women to be elected to the House of Delegates in 1923, and Yvonne Bond Miller, the first African American woman, elected in 1983. Ayala was proud to stand on the shoulders of these women who, with Shirley Chisholm, "have ensured that I have a seat at the table, versus being on the menu."[28] In 2020, women made up 29.3 percent of the Virginia legislature—so close to the one-third threshold that Pauli Murray suggested in 1970 as the proportion that might overcome a dangerous imbalance of power. It was notably higher than the percentage of women in Congress, which reached only 23.7 percent, even after the "Pink Wave" of 2018 swept record numbers of women into national office.

Virginia women managed to get elected in record numbers, along with a new legislative majority that was certain to ratify the ERA, without having an ERA to help them. Did that mean that the ERA was no longer needed? Some of the opponents of the ERA thought so. Delegate John J. McGuire III said, "I got to tell you, Madam Speaker, I'm very proud of you—you didn't need the ERA to be the Speaker," and proceeded to vote against the ERA, claiming that it was outdated, expired, and harmful to women. Some of the men in the House of Delegates did not seem happy with the new dynamic in the room. One man tried to make procedural objections to delay the bill, suggesting that a minor amendment to the resolution to make its preamble conform to that of the Senate's ERA resolution showed that ERA proponents were scurrying around and making new, bad protocol moving forward.[29] Another man tried to refer the ERA back to committee, claiming insufficient time to consider this minor amendment, instead of voting on it that day.[30] He challenged Delegate Jennifer Carroll Foy about the evidentiary basis of the preamble's claim, based on polls, that 80 percent of Virginians favored the ERA.[31] And when some audience members cheered after Delegate Carroll Foy's speech, he said that Madam Speaker was not doing her job and violating a parliamentary rule, "Rule 53," which required the Speaker of the House to "preserve order and decorum in the chamber at all times."[32]

But their parliamentary maneuvers did not stop the ERA this time. The women who had been working for years to get the ERA ratified knew that they had the votes they needed to make history.

And so they did.

They did not have the words of the ERA in the written Constitution of the United States to get them to this point, but they harnessed the power of the unwritten ERA that was generated by generations of women in constitution-making who came before them. The Virginia women who carried the ERA to ratification did not stop there. They proposed more laws to make equal rights real for women, and for people of all genders. They passed the Pregnant Worker Fairness Act, which was adopted by both chambers with strong bipartisan support.[33] That law requires employers to provide reasonable accommodations to expectant moms on the job. They passed a reproductive healthcare bill to repeal mandatory ultrasound, twenty-four-hour waiting periods, and hospital-grade medical standards for abortions.[34] That law removed barriers to women's reproductive freedom that are not justified by medical evidence. They passed the Virginia Values Act, which made pregnancy, childbirth, lactation, sexual orientation, and gender identity protected classes in the law that bans discrimination in housing, employment, and public accommodations.[35] And they introduced a bill to provide paid family leave for all parents regardless of sex, which would guarantee twelve weeks of leave at 80 percent pay.[36]

With *United States v. Virginia,* the Constitution made Virginia change for women in 1996. A generation later, Virginia changed the Constitution for women across the United States. Virginia was the birthplace of Thomas Jefferson, who wrote, "all men are created equal," and James Madison, the principal framer of the constitution that began with, "We the People, to form a more perfect Union." At long last, Virginia women completed ratification of the Equal Rights Amendment to that constitution. They led their state to make the Union more perfect for the twenty-first century.

Epilogue
The Unstoppables

WHAT'S NEXT FOR THE ERA?

Virginia's ratification created an unprecedented situation in American constitutional history. Never has an amendment been adopted by two-thirds of Congress, ratified by three-fourths of the states, as Article V prescribes, and stopped from becoming part of the Constitution because of a time limit. By getting this far in the centennial year of women's right to vote, the ERA has thrust the nation into uncharted constitutional waters, where we face some profound choices.

Phyllis Schlafly's hero and ERA opponent Barry Goldwater once said, "We must decide what sort of people we are and what sort of world we want—now and for our children."[1] He was not talking directly about the ERA, but he was absolutely right in one respect: American people and the lawmakers we elect make choices every day about who we are, and what kind of world we want to make for our children to inherit. These fundamental questions are at stake when deciding what to do about the ERA and its time limit.

The National Archives and Records Administration rejected Virginia's ratification and refused to publish the ERA as the

Twenty-Eighth Amendment to the US Constitution. The National Archivist was just following the instructions of the Trump Administration.[2] The week before the Virginia legislature's historic vote to ratify the ERA, the Department of Justice Office of Legal Counsel (OLC) published a legal opinion explaining the Trump Administration's position on the ERA.[3] The opinion said that the ERA expired in 1979, and could not be ratified or revived after that date. Trump's OLC said that Congress could not even remove the deadline.

The National Archivist is primarily a recordkeeper. A law adopted by Congress tells the National Archives and Records Administration to publish amendments in the Constitution once it receives notice that a proposed amendment has been adopted according to the provisions of the Constitution.[4] But it's not the Archivist's act of publishing that causes a proposed amendment to become part of the Constitution. The ERA becomes part of the Constitution if and when the Constitution's process for amending it has been followed by Congress and the states.

Some ERA proponents believe that the ERA became part of the Constitution on the day that Virginia ratified it. Some ERA opponents believe that the ERA cannot be made part of the Constitution by counting the late ratifications, no matter what Congress tries to do with the deadline. Both sides have sued the National Archivist, demanding a court decision on these matters.[5] Virginia, Nevada, and Illinois want a court order requiring the National Archivist to publish the ERA immediately and recognize it as the Twenty-Eighth Amendment. Alabama, Louisiana, South Dakota, Nebraska, and Tennessee—states that never ratified the ERA and states that ratified but then tried to rescind their ratifications—are demanding a court order to stop the Archivist from adding the ERA to the Constitution. These lawsuits raise two big questions: Is the seven-year ratification deadline a legitimate and binding part of the Constitution's amendment process? What is the legal effect of the states' attempts to rescind their ratifications?

The text of the Constitution, the history and practice of amending the Constitution, and the relevant Supreme Court decisions all point to one answer to both questions: It's up to Congress.

The House of Representatives voted 232–183 in February 2020 in favor of recognizing the ERA as part of the Constitution "whenever ratified" by three-fourths of the states.[6] The House passed the deadline removal resolution again in March 2021. Since three-fourths of the states have ratified as of January 2020, the House resolution would make the ERA part of the Constitution immediately. A parallel bipartisan resolution was introduced in the Senate by Senator Lisa Murkowski, a Republican from Alaska, and Senator Ben Cardin, a Democrat from Maryland.[7]

The Constitution does not mention deadlines in Article V, the only provision that addresses amendment procedures. Article V says:

> The Congress, whenever two thirds of both Houses shall deem it necessary, shall propose Amendments to this Constitution, or, on the Application of the Legislatures of two thirds of the several States, shall call a Convention for proposing Amendments, which, in either Case, shall be valid to all Intents and Purposes, as Part of this Constitution, when ratified by the Legislatures of three fourths of the several States, or by Conventions in three fourths thereof, as the one or the other Mode of Ratification may be proposed by the Congress; Provided that no Amendment which may be made prior to the Year One thousand eight hundred and eight shall in any Manner affect the first and fourth Clauses in the Ninth Section of the first Article; and that no State, without its Consent, shall be deprived of its equal Suffrage in the Senate.

Article V only requires that an amendment garner a two-thirds supermajority of each house of the legislature, after which it must then be ratified by the legislatures of three-fourths of all the states. Nearly all twenty-seven amendments have been ratified in this manner.[8]

Seven-year deadlines became a somewhat routine part of the constitutional amendment process in the twentieth century with the Prohibition Amendment, and the Supreme Court affirmed that such time limits were within Congress's power to propose amendments.[9] But time limits are not a necessary part of the constitutional amendment process. In fact, the last amendment that was added to the Constitution took 203 years to ratify.

In 1992, the Twenty-Seventh Amendment to the United States Constitution was ratified by the thirty-eighth state, centuries after Congress adopted it in 1789. Written by Founding Father (and slaveholder) James Madison, that amendment reads, "No law, varying the compensation for the services of the Senators and Representatives, shall take effect, until an election of Representatives shall have intervened." Although it was sent to the states for ratification in 1789 along with the original bill of rights that became the first ten amendments, the Madison amendment, as it has come to be known, was only ratified by seven states before the end of the eighteenth century. Nonetheless, the process of ratification picked up again starting in 1982, when the public debate about the ERA deadline inspired one young man to write letters to state legislators to persuade them to ratify the Madison amendment, which had no congressionally imposed time limit.[10]

It worked. After the thirty-eighth state ratification was completed in 1992, both houses of Congress adopted resolutions recognizing that the amendment had been validly ratified.[11] The legitimacy of the Twenty-Seventh Amendment was widely accepted; indeed, even after the Archivist certified it and Congress acknowledged its constitutional status, additional states continued to ratify the amendment, bringing the count to forty-six states as of 2016. The Twenty-Seventh Amendment, introduced in 1789 and ratified 203 years later in 1992, proved that Article V allows amendments to be ratified across generations. There is no constitutional problem with ratification beginning in one century and being completed in another. Congress is free to accept the ratifications of three-fourths of the states as long as the other constitutional requirements of Article V have been followed.

Almost every amendment that was proposed and adopted in the twentieth century after Prohibition had seven-year time limits on ratification. But there is one notable exception: the Nineteenth Amendment. Suffragists and their proponents in Congress rejected the seven-year time limit because they knew how long it had taken to advance women's quest for the vote without the vote. Suffrage proponents in Congress relied on a report written by Florence Kelley about the states' procedural rules, which could be gamed to delay their ratification of a federal constitutional amendment.[12] Small numbers of men in power could deploy the discretion they had over procedure to prevent consideration of women's suffrage—a political tactic that would allow suffrage to die without any one man taking the political heat for killing it.

Consider how often this very dynamic has delayed and stopped the Equal Rights Amendment in the last century—from Emanuel Celler keeping the ERA bottled up in the House Judiciary Committee for years until Martha Griffiths's discharge petition signed by the House majority forced it out, to Sam Ervin's crippling amendments that sent the ERA to the legislative graveyard in 1970, which led its proponents to include a seven-year deadline in the next go-around, to the three-fifths rule in Illinois and the committee system in the Virginia General Assembly. Men in power have let the constitutional rights of women die, time and time again, without owning up to what they've done.

Meanwhile, the Constitution's founding mothers—from Abigail Adams to Susan B. Anthony and Elizabeth Cady Stanton, from Alice Paul and Crystal Eastman to Shirley Chisholm and Patsy Mink—did not live to see the next milestone of the constitutional amendment they championed. Will the twenty-first century ratifiers of the ERA in Nevada, Illinois, and Virginia live to see the Equal Rights Amendment added to the Constitution and accepted by the American people as legitimate? Or will we all be dead by the time that the US Constitution officially enshrines the principle of gender equality?

For amendments that expand who is included as full and equal citizens in "We the People," time limits can be oppressive and undemocratic. Yet, enforcing the seven-year deadline on ERA ratification is another way of letting it die without publicly opposing equal rights for women. It gives the appearance of playing by the rules of the game, with the unfortunate outcome that women can't win this time. Maybe next time? Go back to square one, and start over. Women's collective political work across generations is conveniently ignored.

But the seven-year time limit is not a legal rule that ties Congress's hands. Congress can choose to keep the ERA alive. Remember the words that Congress used in 1971 when it proposed the ERA: "the following article is proposed as an amendment to the Constitution of the United States, which shall be valid to all intents and purposes as part of the Constitution when ratified by the legislatures of three-fourths of the several States within seven years from the date of its submission by the Congress." The time limit was worded differently from the deadlines in the Eighteenth, Twentieth, Twenty-First, and Twenty-Second Amendments, which said that the amendments would be "inoperative unless" ratified within seven years, and the deadlines in the Twenty-Third and Twenty-Fourth Amendments, which said the amendments would be valid "only if" ratified within seven years. "Inoperative unless" and "only if" "ratified within seven years" were poison pills. "When ratified" "within seven years" is a goal. This milder language simply encouraged the states to get their ratifications in quickly without threatening them. Only in a fairy tale does "Be home by midnight" mean that one's vehicle will turn into a pumpkin upon a post-midnight return.

Congress can choose to clear up any confusion about the meaning of "when ratified" "within seven years" in the ERA resolution. It can do so by declaring, once and for all, that the ERA is valid "whenever ratified" by three-fourths of the states, effectively removing the seven-year time limit and recognizing the thirty-eight ratifications that have occurred as sufficient to add the ERA to the Constitution.[13]

But why should it?

To empower mothers and families. With record numbers of women elected to Congress, the House voted twice, in 2020 and 2021, to accept the ERA as legitimate by removing the deadline. The House Judiciary Committee Report acknowledged that the ERA could provide a basis for Congress to engage in affirmative efforts to support gender equality both at home and in the workplace.[14] At the House Judiciary Committee's markup hearing, Congresswoman Pramila Jayapal highlighted the persistence of pay gaps between women and men, which were more pronounced for women of color. The ERA could strengthen constitutional protection for parents in many ways, including with respect to discrimination based on pregnancy, childbirth, and caregiving responsibilities. "A vote for the ERA is a vote for families," she declared.[15] The need for a constitutional boost for women and families was laid bare after the COVID-19 pandemic shut down schools and daycares, leaving working mothers to shoulder the burdens.

To fix the democratic process. Congresswoman Jayapal is one of the faces of a changing Congress that is beginning to represent the diversity of twenty-first century America: she is an immigrant from India who was an activist for women's rights before she was elected to Congress in 2016. Unlike the all-male House Judiciary Committee that kept the ERA off the floor throughout the 1960s, the House Judiciary Committee that sent the ERA deadline removal to the floor included thirteen women out of the forty-one members, including Jayapal. Noting the presence of women on the committee, after years of being left out, Congresswoman Sheila Jackson Lee said, "That evidences the crux of the ERA." Formerly a judge, Jackson Lee is an African American woman from Texas representing Barbara Jordan's congressional district. Channeling her legacy, Congresswoman Jackson Lee believed that by removing the ERA deadline, "We are fixing process."[16]

Because it's shameful not to. The House floor debates on removing the ERA deadline unified Jayapal and Jackson Lee with Congresswomen Jackie Speier and Carolyn Maloney, who had persistently introduced ERA bills year after year for over a decade, and Speaker of the House Nancy Pelosi. Pelosi read the ERA's first sentence, "Equality of rights under the law shall not be denied or abridged by the United States or by any State on account of sex," and asked, "How can you have a problem with that?" Pelosi said it was a shameful reality that the ERA was still not enshrined in the US Constitution, one hundred years after women obtained the right to vote. She pointed to the 62 percent of pregnant women and new mothers who were in the workforce; yet the law allowed them to be placed on unpaid leave or forced out of their jobs. The law also allowed sexual harassment and assault to go unchecked too often. All these dynamics led to women's underrepresentation at the decision-making table. The ERA would bring justice for families, by increasing paychecks for mothers. "The ERA will strengthen America. It's not just about women, it's about America," Pelosi concluded.[17]

Because legislators, not judges, can make equality real. It was in the twenty-first century, not sooner, that Nancy Pelosi became the first woman Speaker of the House, and by 2020, she led a House that included the all-time highest number of women representatives—102. A new crop of younger women responding to Trump and the era of #MeToo were elected to the House in 2018, weeks after Brett Kavanaugh's contentious appointment to the Supreme Court amid credible sexual assault allegations, a quarter century after Clarence Thomas was appointed, also amid credible sexual harassment allegations. On the very day that many of these women took the floor of the House to support the ERA and the removal of its deadline, a subcommittee of the House Judiciary Committee heard testimony by a woman lawyer about her experiences of demeaning misogynistic harassment at the hands of the man for whom she worked as a law clerk—a federal appeals court judge who was lionized by liberals as a judicial hero.[18]

Because real equality can lift up everyone neglected by "We the People." It was time for the ERA to change America, to deliver on its promise of democracy for all. Representative Rashida Tlaib, the first Muslim woman ever to be elected to Congress in 2018, stood up to speak for an America that had already changed, and would be helped by the ERA to keep moving towards greater inclusion. "I want you all to know this is about women of color, women with disabilities, transgender women, immigrant women. These women are affected by issues of unequal pay, sexual violence, lack of access for healthcare, and poverty, so much of what we're doing here in trying to promote women's equality is about gender, racial, economic justice." The vision of women's equality had broadened so much because of the generations of women of color who improved the ERA over time. Tlaib then warned, "Know this: A 'no' vote today is condoning the oppression of women in America."[19]

The renewed efforts to stop the ERA may be based on a deadline rather than open misogyny, but the legislators who are sticking to the deadline are making a political and moral choice. They have the power to lift the deadline. If they use that power to block the ERA's path rather than to open it up, they suffer from willful blindness to one hundred years of women's work as constitution-makers, which improved America and remade the ERA towards greater inclusion. How should we judge that choice?

Congress was faced with a choice with similar moral stakes in 1868, when it had to decide whether to add the Fourteenth Amendment to the US Constitution, even though two states, Ohio and New Jersey, had voted to rescind their ratifications.[20] Article V says nothing about rescissions, just as it says nothing about deadlines. When Article V says nothing, the decision-maker with power—whether it's Congress or a judge—has to do the right thing.[21] Congress rejected the rescissions of the Fourteenth Amendment in 1868 to enshrine the guarantees of equal protection, due process, and the rights and privileges of citizenship in the Constitution. That was a necessary step (though by no means sufficient) toward the recognition of formerly enslaved African Americans as full persons and equal citizens. The Fourteenth Amendment did not produce racial equality quickly enough, but it was a crucial constitutional building block of the more humane future that eventually emerged with the civil rights movement. The history of rescissions of the Fourteenth Amendment should motivate a similar approach to Congress's discretionary decision on whether to ignore the ERA's deadline and rescissions.

★ ★ ★

IT BOILS DOWN TO whether or not the ERA is worth fighting for.[22] Some opponents say that the ERA is no longer necessary because much of what the ERA was intended to achieve has already been written into law—or achieved through judicial rulings like *United States v. Virginia*. In practice, the ERA might operate similarly to the Fourteenth Amendment, which evolved to combat some forms of gender discrimination. But those transformations would not have occurred without the political force of the ERA, even before its ratification was complete.

It's time to give credit to the generations of women who triggered that constitutional change by pushing for the ERA. In the early 1970s, the Supreme Court began to respond to the equal rights advocates' century-old plea to their brethren to get their feet off women's necks. The brilliant advocacy of the late Justice Ruth Bader Ginsburg was crucial. Supreme Court justices recognized Congress's passage of the ERA as they invalidated laws that discriminated on account of sex. The ERA also spawned Title IX in 1972, which opened many doors of educational opportunity to women, led by Congresswoman Patsy Mink, who also fought relentlessly for the ERA on the House floor months before. In 1978, Congresswoman Liz Holtzman led Congress to extend the deadline on ERA ratification. The Congresswomen's Caucus that she cofounded with Republican ERA champion Margaret Heckler rallied behind the Pregnancy Discrimination Act to support working mothers-to-be, and Congress passed it in the same month that it extended the ERA deadline. Even when the ERA was not officially part of the Constitution, it was a force that expanded women's rights by fueling transformative work by judges, lawyers, and legislators that would never have occurred otherwise. Adding it to the Constitution now would be an honest acknowledgment of the tremendous contributions by women to change the Constitution for the better.

The force empowered women lawmakers in Nevada, Illinois, and Virginia to ratify the ERA, standing on the shoulders of their predecessors to unite across differences of race and political party. State senator Pat Spearman valiantly led Nevada's resurrection of the ERA. In Illinois, state senator Heather Steans developed institutional responses to the #MeToo movement's challenges to the Illinois political machine and organized a new bipartisan women's caucus to get behind ERA ratification. In Virginia, Delegate Jennifer Carroll Foy brought her legislature to the right side of history after graduating from Virginia Military Institute, which she attended only because the US Supreme Court ordered it to admit women in a landmark decision authored by Justice Ruth Bader Ginsburg. These women have also been at the forefront of legislation in their states to promote real equality for women.

The Fourteenth Amendment moved towards realizing women's equal status as citizens, but that evolution is still incomplete.[23] The lawmakers who have led twenty-first century ERA ratification in the states and the deadline removal in Congress are proposing and enacting new laws. They are meeting the unmet needs of working mothers and gender non-conforming people, curbing the abuses of power manifested in sexual harassment and violence, and providing access to reproductive justice, including policies that actually enable women to choose motherhood as well as abortion in appropriate circumstances.

The recent ERA ratifications are pushing state and federal lawmakers to make equality real for women, in all their diversity. From strengthening protections against gender-based discrimination, to pregnant worker fairness legislation, to more robust equal pay laws, to new public policy solutions to sexual harassment and gender violence, these legislative agendas are legitimized politically by the ERA. Once enacted, if such legislation is challenged in court, the ERA could provide a constitutional shield.[24] The ERA is giving political legitimacy to the humane and large-scale redefinition of "We the People," and the public policies necessary to implement it. This is what democracy looks like.

Whether through the deadline or through misinformation about what the ERA will do, efforts to stop the ERA will continue. The ERA has been stopped many times, but it can be *unstopped*. The truth is that the ERA was never fully stopped when it got sent to its many legislative graveyards, and when it fell three states short of ratification. Through the women who wrote it, adopted it, fought for it, litigated for its core principles, and ratified it, the ERA has been a vital force shaping the law since 1970, even without being a formal and legitimate amendment published in the National Archivist's official copy of the Constitution. The ERA gave birth to the Fourteenth Amendment's commitment to sex equality. It nourished the laws that raised women's status, to the point where women attained just enough power to get the ERA fully ratified.

Despite disappointments and deaths along the way, the generations of women who made the ERA did not stop believing in the Constitution. They followed its rules for changing it. They continued the work left unfinished by the generation of women who came before them, all while birthing and raising the next generation of this nation. Yet, the female framers' hopes for securing the blessings of liberty to working mothers and mothers-to-be have yet to be fulfilled. That's why the ERA still matters, even though it has taken so long. In fact, it matters *because* motherhood and fights about motherhood took time, and slowed down the path that brought women closer than ever to enshrining equality in the Constitution.

We the Women are persisting, to secure the blessings of democracy, for our posterity.

Acknowledgments

THIS BOOK WOULD NOT EXIST without my literary agent, Karen Gantz, who encouraged me to bring my scholarly research on women in constitution-making to a broader audience and readership. She has been a fierce advocate for this project, and very committed to moving things forward at every stage.

At Skyhorse, my editors Caroline Russomanno and Rebecca Shoenthal brought talent and kindness to the making of this book, which improved it immeasurably.

I had not given much thought to the ERA until the American Bar Association invited me to be a panelist for their Law Day program in May 2013 on "Constitutional Equality for Women?" and set me on the path to writing this book. Before then, I had spent a decade researching recent constitutional sex equality amendments in European countries in my scholarly writing. Women in European countries were constitution-makers, not only after World War I and World War II, but also within my adult life, amending their countries' constitutions to empower women and address the gender inequalities that persisted for our generation. It was only after the ABA panel that I began to take the ERA seriously as a potential site of anything similar.

I began to have serious conversations about the ERA with a global and comparative lens when I wrote my scholarly article, "An Equal Rights Amendment for the Twenty-First Century: Bringing Global Constitutionalism Home," which was published in the *Yale Journal of Law and Feminism* in 2017. I was a law professor at Cardozo Law School and a visiting professor at Columbia when I wrote that article. I was lucky to get feedback on drafts of that project as well as other articles that addressed the ERA and global constitutionalism. I am grateful to audiences at workshops or panels at the law schools of Cardozo, Columbia, Chicago-Kent, Boston College, University of Cincinnati, and Humboldt University in Berlin. The University of Akron invited me to be their keynote speaker for Constitution Day in 2017, where I spoke on "The Constitution of Mothers," which helped me develop the themes of this book. There are many law professor colleagues who read and/or commented on these scholarly projects, which shaped the questions I was asking about the ERA and laid the foundations for this book. They include Cynthia Bowman, Jessica Bulman-Pozen, Mathilde Cohen, Erin Delaney, Rosalind Dixon, Liz Emens, David Fontana, Jamal Greene, Stéphanie Hennette-Vauchez, Vicki Jackson, Olatunde Johnson, Jeremy Kessler, David Law, Ruth Rubio-Marin, Serena Mayeri, Ralf Michaels, Russell Miller, Henry Monaghan, Douglas NeJaime, Giovanni Piccirilli, Reva Siegel, Nicholas Stephanopoulos, Gila Stopler, Susan Sturm, Tracy Thomas, Mila Versteeg, Robin West, and Joan Williams.

I owe a special debt of gratitude to the Robert H. Smith Center for the Constitution at James Madison's Montpelier, where I first presented my work on the ERA and related work on motherhood in comparative constitutional law. The Comparative Constitutional Law Scholars roundtable has provided a rigorous and generous environment to develop the ideas in this book, and I have especially enjoyed returning to Montpelier to teach the seminar for high school educators on gender and the Constitution.

Between the time I started writing about the ERA and completion of this book, I moved from Cardozo Law School, where

I was a law professor for thirteen years, to the CUNY Graduate Center, where I joined a sociology department and serve as dean for master's programs. Dean Melanie Leslie at Cardozo supported my research at every stage, and my colleagues there, especially Kate Shaw, Michelle Adams, Alex Reinert, Ekow Yankah, and Michel Rosenfeld, were excellent interlocuters as I considered a book project on the ERA. Alex Stein—now Justice Alex Stein at the Israeli Supreme Court—provided feedback and encouragement as I developed the book project.

At the Graduate Center, provosts Joy Connolly and Julia Wrigley provided a warm environment as I found my feet in an arts and sciences faculty and a public university administration. My new colleagues in sociology, especially Lynn Chancer, have been wonderful to talk to about some of the ideas. Philosopher Nick Pappas and historian Sarah Covington read my law journal article on the ERA and provided useful reactions from the perspective of disciplines outside of law. That was very helpful as I embarked on writing a book about the ERA for nonlawyers.

At the Graduate Center, the Futures Initiative generously supported my course, "Mothers in Law," which helped me think about the mother as lawmaker and the lawmaker as mother, a theme that I explore in this book. The students in that course provided a great discussion of an early draft excerpt of the manuscript. Kelley Akhiemokhali pointed me to aspects of Pauli Murray's biography that I had not previously noticed, and Aimee Maddalena's research on Florence Kelley and maternal mortality helped me focus on that issue. Sara McDougall, my co-instructor for the course, patiently read several early drafts of the manuscript. Sara—a medieval historian of motherhood—was the perfect teaching partner as I was completing this book.

Audiences at Harvard Law School, Berkeley Law, University of Texas School of Law, Fordham Law School, Association of American Law Schools, the University of Richmond ERA Convention, the Graduate Center, and NYU Law School's Birnbaum Women's Leadership Project provided valuable feedback on earlier drafts of this book. I am especially grateful to Jill Lepore, Vicki Jackson, Michael Klarman, Jeannie Suk Gersen (who happens to be my sister, see below), Sarah Song, Josh Cohen, Richard Albert, Elizabeth Sepper, Jed Shugerman, Saul Cornell, Steven Calabresi, and Paula Monopoli for exchanges during these occasions. The audience of the workshop on Virginia ratification at the NOW conference in July 2019, which I conducted with Senator Jennifer McClellan, provided useful questions that helped direct my research.

I am grateful to Louise Melling, Katherine Grainger, and Fatima Goss Graves for all the discussions of the ERA as the situation evolved in the final stages of this manuscript. Louise graciously read the whole manuscript and discussed it with my class at the Graduate Center.

Thank you to Bettina Hager, Carol Jenkins, Jessica Neuwirth, and Linda Coberly for inviting me to participate on the ERA Coalition's Legal Task Force.

I am grateful to Jennifer McClellan, Jennifer Carroll Foy, Hala Ayala, Pat Spearman, and Steven Andersson for coming to academic conferences to share your ratification (and attempted ratification) stories. I've learned so much from listening to you.

I am grateful to Liz Holtzman for her brilliance and political sensibility in our many conversations about the goals and challenges of putting equality in a constitution.

Kirsten Swinth and Debbie Dinner read several early draft chapters and provided invaluable feedback. Our writing group has been one of the highlights of writing this book.

My research assistant Andrew Dunn has brought off-the-charts competence, efficiency, and brilliance to every task associated with this book.

I am deeply grateful to Reva Siegel, who has been an amazing mentor, friend, and sounding board for everything in this book. Her advice, her eyes, and her ears have sharpened my thinking about the ERA and pointed me intellectually and politically in the right direction.

The Constitution's preamble says we should secure the blessings of liberty for "our Posterity," so it is fitting for me to end by expressing my deepest gratitude to my family for securing the blessings of liberty for me. I dedicate the book to my mother and my sisters, who are all unstoppable in different ways. I'm also grateful to my dad for being graciously outnumbered but not overwhelmed by us.

My greatest debt by far is to my outstanding husband Youngjae Lee, who has remained calm and loving while doing the lion's share of absolutely everything at home, so that I could finish this book. Our sons, Emile and Niccolo, have an instinctive passion for equality that I hope will make the world better than they found it some day. I love you all more than you know.

Notes

Chapter 1: The Pioneers

1. Abigail Adams to John Adams, Braintree, 31 March 1776, in *Charles Francis Adams, Familiar Letters of John Adams and His Wife Abigail Adams During the Revolution with a Memoir of Mrs. Adams* (New York: Hurd and Houghton, 1876), 149.

2. I have argued that the continuation of the political order past the lifetime of constitution-makers is a general concern in constitution-making, which must have concerned the Founding Fathers. See Julie C. Suk, "The Constitution of Mothers: Gender Equality and Social Reproduction in the United States and the World," *ConLawNOW* 9 (2018), 23 (Constitution Day 2017 keynote address at the University of Akron).

3. Eleanor Flexner, *Century of Struggle: The Woman's Rights Movement in the United States* (Cambridge: Harvard University Press, 1959, revised edition 1975), 7.

4. See Carol Faulkner, *Lucretia Mott's Heresy: Abolition and Women's Rights in Nineteenth-Century America* (Philadelphia: University of Pennsylvania Press, 2013), chapter 6. Note that African American women were also organizing through other channels, including churches, for both the abolition of slavery and women's emancipation. See Martha S. Jones, *The Woman Question in African American Culture, 1830–1900* (Chapel Hill: University of North Carolina Press, 2007).

5. See generally Tracy A. Thomas, *Elizabeth Cady Stanton and the Feminist Foundations of Family Law* (New York: NYU Press, 2016); Lori D. Ginzberg, *Elizabeth Cady Stanton: An American Life* (New York: Hill and Wang, 2009).

6. Elizabeth Cady Stanton. "Declaration of Sentiments," *Report of the Woman's Rights Convention, Held at Seneca Falls, New York, July 19 and 20, 1848.* (Rochester, NY: The North Star office of Frederick Douglass, 1848), available at https://www.loc.gov/exhibitions/women-fight-for-the-vote/about-this-exhibition/seneca-falls-and-building-a-movement-1776-1890/seneca-falls-and-the-start-of-annual-conventions/declaration-of-sentiments/.

7. Flexner, *Century of Struggle*, 72.

8. See Ellen Carol DuBois, *Suffrage: Women's Long Battle for the Vote* (New York: Simon & Schuster, 2020).

9. See Lisa Tetrault, *The Myth of Seneca Falls: Memory and the Women's Suffrage Movement, 1848–1898* (Chapel Hill: University of North Carolina Press, 2014), 6.

10. US Constitution, Amendment XIV, Section 2.

11. *Bradwell v. State of Illinois*, 83 US 130 (1873).

12. *Bradwell v. State of Illinois*, 141 (Justice Bradley, concurring).

13. *Bradwell v. State of Illinois*, 141 (Justice Bradley, concurring).

14. Prohibiting the Several States from Disfranchising United States Citizens on Account of Sex, Hearing Before the Senate Committee on Privileges and Elections, 45th Cong. 5 (1878) (Statement of Mrs. Elizabeth Cady Stanton).

15. Arguments of the Woman Suffrage Delegates, Hearing Before the Senate Committee on the Judiciary, 46th Cong. (1880) (Statement of Susan B. Anthony), reprinted in Woman Suffrage Reports and Hearings, Senate Document No. 1035, 62nd Cong. 35 (1918) ("1880 Senate Suffrage Hearing").

16. Flexner, *Century of Struggle*, 140–55.

17. Susan Ware, *Why They Marched: Untold Stories of the Women Who Fought for the Right to Vote* (Cambridge: Harvard University Press, 2019), 21.

18. 1880 Senate Suffrage Hearing, 36.

19. The history of floor votes is provided on a Senate website on the Woman Suffrage Centennial. United States Senate, Woman Suffrage Centennial, Timeline: The Senate and the Nineteenth Amendment,

available at https://www.senate.gov/artandhistory/history/People/Women /Nineteenth_Amendment_Vertical_Timeline.htm.

20. See US House of Representatives, "Women Must Be Empowered": The US House of Representatives and the Nineteenth Amendment, May 2019, available at https://history.house.gov/Exhibition-and -Publications/WIC/Women-in-Congress/ at 10.

21. See DuBois, *Suffrage*, 223.

22. Extending the Right of Suffrage to Women, Hearings on H. J. Res. 200 Before the House Committee on Woman Suffrage, 65th Cong. 252 (1918) (Statement of Carrie Chapman Catt) ("1918 House Woman Suffrage Hearings").

23. 1918 House Woman Suffrage Hearings, 10 (Statement of Dr. Anna Howard Shaw).

24. Flexner, *Century of Struggle*, 336.

25. 1918 House Woman Suffrage Hearings, 36 (Statement of Carrie Chapman Catt).

26. 1918 House Woman Suffrage Hearings, 32.

27. 56 Congressional Record 807–08 (1918).

28. 56 Congressional Record, 808–09.

29. 1918 House Woman Suffrage Hearings, 154–58 (reprinting Mary Beard & Florence Kelley, "Why Women Demand a Federal Suffrage Amendment—Difficulties in Amending State Constitutions—A Study of the Constitutions of the Non-Suffrage States").

30. Carrie Chapman Catt and Nettie Rogers Shuler, *Woman Suffrage and Politics: The Inner Story of the Suffrage Movement* (New York: Charles Scribner's Sons, 1923), 107–08.

Chapter 2: The Instigators

1. See J. D. Zahniser and Amelia Fry, *Alice Paul: Claiming Power* (Oxford: Oxford University Press, 2019); Aileen Kraditor, *The Ideas of the Woman's Suffrage Movement, 1890–1920* (New York: Columbia University Press, 1965), chapter 8; Christine A. Lunardini, *From Equal Suffrage to Equal Rights: Alice Paul and the National Woman's Party, 1910–1928* (New York: NYU Press, 1986); Ware, *Why They Marched*, chapters 17–19. Inez Milholland, whose image during the suffrage parade has become an icon of the suffrage movement, died at the age of 30 in 1916, having collapsed after giving a suffrage speech during a tightly scheduled national tour. For more about Inez

Milholland, see Linda J. Lumsden, *Inez: The Life and Times of Inez Milholland* (Bloomington: Indiana University Press, 2004).

2. National Photo Co., "National Woman's Party activists watch Alice Paul sew a star onto the NWP Ratification Flag, representing another state's ratification of the Nineteenth Amendment, Circa 1919–1920," Library of Congress, https://www.loc.gov/resource/mnwp.160073.

3. Crystal Eastman, "Now We Can Begin." *The Liberator,* December 1920, reprinted in Blanche Wiesen Cook (ed.), *Crystal Eastman on Women and Revolution* (Oxford: Oxford University Press, 1978), 52–57.

4. See Amy Aronson, *Crystal Eastman: A Revolutionary Life* (Oxford: Oxford University Press, 2020), 234–35 n.64.

5. See June Sochen, *The New Woman* (New York: Quadrangle Books, 1972). Village feminists' ideas largely came from Charlotte Perkins Gilman's work in *Women and Economics: A Study of the Economic Relation Between Men and Women as a Factor in Social Evolution* (1898) (New York: Prometheus Books, 1994). See also Judith Schwartz, *Radical Feminists of Heterodoxy: Greenwich Village, 1912–1940* (Norwich, VT: New Victoria Publishers, 1986).

6. See "Women Urge Amendment," *New York Times,* April 13, 1914. Yale law professor Reva Siegel cites this evidence that the first proposal for an Equal Rights Amendment was made in 1914 by the Feminist Alliance, with Crystal Eastman's involvement, even before she and Alice Paul began to draft the ERA that was introduced in Congress after the Nineteenth Amendment. See Reva B. Siegel, "The Nineteenth Amendment and the Democratization of the Family," *Yale Law Journal Forum* (January 20, 2020), 467.

7. See John Fabian Witt, *Patriots and Cosmopolitans: Hidden Histories of American Law* (Cambridge: Harvard University Press, 2007), 160.

8. Eastman, "Now We Can Begin," 54.

9. Crystal Eastman, Letter, "The Equal Rights Amendment," *The New Republic,* November 19, 1924.

10. H. J. Res. 75, 68th Cong. (1923).

11. Equal Rights Amendment to the Constitution, Hearing on H.J. Res. 75 Before the House Committee on the Judiciary, 68th Cong. 34, 36 (1925) ("1925 House Judiciary Committee ERA Hearing") (Statement of Mrs. Mary Murray, President of the Women's League of the Rapid Transit Co.).

12. Aronson, *Crystal Eastman*, 234.

13. Married Women's Independent Nationality Act, 42 Stat. 1021 (1921).

14. See Jill Norgren, *Stories from Trailblazing Women Lawyers* (New York: NYU Press, 2019), 15.

15. Kathanne W. Greene, "Burnita Shelton Matthews: Feminist, Suffragist, and Judicial Pioneer," Mississippi History Now, http://mshistorynow.mdah.state.ms.us/articles/417/burnita-shelton-matthews-suffragist-feminist-judicial-pioneer.

16. See Linda Greenhouse, "Burnita S. Matthews Dies at 93, First Woman on U.S. Trial Courts," *New York Times*, April 28, 1988.

17. 1925 House Judiciary Committee ERA Hearing, 12 (Statement of Burnita Matthews).

18. 1925 House Judiciary Committee ERA Hearing, 6 (Statement of Mabel Vernon, executive secretary of the National Woman's Party).

19. A leaflet titled "Equal Rights by National Amendment," reprinted from the National Woman's Party publication *Equal Rights*, was included in the National Woman's Party's submissions at congressional hearings in 1929 and 1931. See Equal Rights Amendment, Hearing on S.J. Res. 64 Before a Subcommittee of the Senate Committee on the Judiciary, 70th Cong. 34 (1929) ("1929 Senate Judiciary Subcommittee ERA Hearing") and Equal Rights, Hearing on S.J. Res. 52 Before a Subcommittee of the Senate Committee on the Judiciary, 71st Cong. 32 (1931) ("1931 Senate Judiciary Subcommittee ERA Hearing"). In 1932, the National Woman's Party's submissions noted that "some of the newer postwar constitutions of Europe have in a single sentence established the principle of equality without regard to race, nationality, religion, rank, or sex." See Equal Rights Amendment to the Constitution, Hearing on H. J. Res. 197 Before the House Judiciary Committee, 72nd Cong. 65 (1932) ("1932 House Judiciary Committee ERA Hearing").

20. See Amy E. Butler, *Two Paths to Equality: Alice Paul and Ethel M. Smith in the ERA Debate, 1921–1929* (Albany: State University of New York Press, 2002).

21. See Nancy Woloch, *A Class by Herself: Protective Laws for Women Workers, 1890s–1990s,* (Princeton: Princeton University Press, 2015), 86.

22. Woloch, *A Class by Herself*, 87.

23. *Lochner v. New York*, 198 US 45 (1905).

24. See Jamal Greene, "The Anticanon," *Harvard Law Review* 125(2011): 379–475.

25. For example, *West Coast Hotel v. Parrish*, 300 US 379 (1937). The Court also began to reverse its earlier jurisprudence holding federal labor laws unconstitutional under the Commerce Clause. See *Carter v. Carter Coal Company*, 298 US 238 (1936); *United States v. Darby*, 312 US 100 (1941).

26. *Muller v. Oregon*, 208 US 412, 421 (1908).

27. *Muller v. Oregon*, 422 (emphasis added).

28. *Adkins v. Children's Hospital*, 261 US 525, 553 (1923).

29. See Vivien Hart, *Bound by Our Constitution: Women, Workers, and the Minimum Wage* (Princeton: Princeton University Press, 1994), 132.

30. Woloch, *A Class by Herself*, 116.

31. 1925 House Judiciary Committee ERA Hearing, 31 (Written Statement of Burnita Matthews).

32. See Nancy F. Cott, "Feminist Politics in the 1920s: The National Woman's Party." *Journal of American History* 71 (1984): 43–68; Nancy F. Cott, *The Grounding of Modern Feminism* (New Haven: Yale University Press, 1987).

33. Crystal Eastman, "Equality or Protection." *Equal Rights*, March 15, 1924, reprinted in Cook, *Crystal Eastman on Women and Revolution*, 156, 159.

34. Crystal Eastman, *Work-Accidents and the Law* (New York: Charities Publication Committee, 1910). See also Siegel, "The Nineteenth Amendment and the Democratization of the Family," 466.

35. "First Woman Named as House Chairman," *Washington Post*, December 14, 1923.

36. Greenhouse, "Burnita S. Matthews Dies at 93" (quoting a 1985 interview in *The Third Branch*, a newsletter published by the federal court system).

Chapter 3: The Reformers

1. See Hart, *Bound by Our Constitution*, 132. For an account of the split between Florence Kelley and the National Woman's Party, see William O'Neill, *Everyone Was Brave: A History of Feminism in America* (Chicago: Quadrangle Books, 1969), 275–90.

2. See Kathryn Kish Sklar, *Florence Kelley and the Nation's Work: The Rise of Women's Political Culture* (New Haven: Yale University Press, 1995), 80.

3. See Josephine Goldmark, *Impatient Crusader: Florence Kelley's Life Story* (Urbana: University of Illinois Press, 1953), 36–65.

4. See Woloch, *A Class by Herself*, chapter 3.

5. For an account of the contrasting approaches to sociological data underlying Alice Paul's ERA and Florence Kelley's opposition to it, see Joan G. Zimmerman, "The Jurisprudence of Equality: The Women's Minimum Wage, the First Equal Rights Amendment, and *Adkins v. Children's Hospital*, 1905–1923," *Journal of American History* 78 (1991): 188–225.

6. See Kathryn Kish Sklar, "Why Were Most Politically Active Women Opposed to the ERA in the 1920s?" in Joan Hoff-Wilson, *Rights of Passage: The Past and Future of the ERA* (Bloomington: Indiana University Press, 1986): 25–38.

7. See Stanley Lemons, *The Woman Citizen: Social Feminism in the 1920s* (Charlottesville: University of Virginia Press, 1973), 154.

8. See Janet Zollinger Giele, *Two Paths to Women's Equality: Temperance, Suffrage, and the Origins of Modern Feminism* (New York: Twayne Publishers, 1995).

9. See Jan Doolittle Wilson, *The Women's Joint Congressional Committee and the Politics of Maternalism, 1920–30* (Urbana: University of Illinois Press, 2007), 44.

10. Pub. L. 67–97. 42 Stat. 224 (1921).

11. See *Massachusetts v. Mellon*, 262 US 447 (1923).

12. See Lemons, *The Woman Citizen*, 162.

13. See Lemons, *The Woman Citizen*, 19. Emma Wold, an attorney who served as legislative secretary of the National Woman's Party, repeated this argument in 1929 hearings before a subcommittee of the Senate Judiciary Committee. 1929 Senate Judiciary Subcommittee ERA Hearing, 11 (Statement of Miss Emma Wold).

14. See Goldmark, *Impatient Crusader*.

15. 1929 Senate Judiciary Subcommittee ERA Hearing, 56–57 (Statement of Florence Kelley).

16. 1925 House Judiciary Committee ERA Hearing, 72 (Statement of Florence Kelley).

17. 1929 Senate Judiciary Subcommittee ERA Hearing, 56.

18. Dorothy Kenyon represented Gwendolyn Hoyt in *Hoyt v. Florida*, in an unsuccessful challenge to a Florida law exempting women from jury service. *Hoyt v. Florida*, 368 US 57 (1961).

19. 1929 Senate Judiciary Subcommittee ERA Hearing, 42 (Statement of Dorothy Kenyon).

20. 1931 Senate Judiciary Subcommittee ERA Hearing, 51 (Statement of Mrs. B. Marconnier).

21. Florence Kelley expressed these views in letters to her close associates. See Hart, *Bound by Our Constitution*, 131–32. See Kathryn Kish Sklar, *The Selected Letters of Florence Kelley, 1869–1931* (Urbana: University of Illinois Press, 2009), 312, 314. In letters to Julia Lathrop and James Haight within a month of *Adkins*, Kelley compared *Adkins* to *Dred Scott* and explicitly said that women judges were needed in the federal courts.

22. For a history of these fifty-fifty rules, see Jo Freeman, *A Room at a Time: How Women Entered Party Politics* (New York: Rowman and Littlefield Publishers, 2000), 110.

23. Emily Newell Blair, "Women in the Political Parties," *Annals of American Political and Social Science* 143 (May 1929): 217, 223. See Kristi Andersen, *After Suffrage: Women in Partisan and Electoral Politics before the New Deal* (Chicago: University of Chicago Press, 1996), 90.

24. In re *Cavellier*, 159 Misc. 212 (NY 1936).

25. 1929 Senate Judiciary Subcommittee ERA Hearing, 64. See also 1932 House Judiciary Committee ERA Hearing 43–44 (featuring identical text).

26. See Serena Mayeri, "Constitutional Choices: Legal Feminism and the Historical Dynamics of Change," *California Law Review* 92 (2004): 755, 798.

27. See Joan Williams, "The Misguided Push for an Equal Rights Amendment," *New York Times*, January 16, 2020, https://www.nytimes.com/2020/01/16/opinion/sunday/equal-rights-amendment.html.

Chapter 4: The Globalizers

1. U.N. Charter, Preamble, https://www.un.org/en/sections/un-charter/preamble/index.html.

2. *Plessy v. Ferguson*, 163 US 537 (1896).

3. *Brown v. Board of Education*, 347 US 483 (1954).

4. Mary Church Terrell, *A Colored Woman in a White World* (Washington, DC: Ransdell, Inc., 1940) (unpaginated introduction).

5. See Kimberlé Crenshaw, "Demarginalizing the Intersection of Race and Sex: A Black Feminist Critique of Antidiscrimination Doctrine, Feminist Theory, and Antiracist Politics," *University of Chicago Legal Forum* 1 (1989): 139–167. For an account of Mary Church Terrell as a public intellectual see Brittney Cooper, *Beyond Respectability: The Intellectual Thought of Race Women* (Urbana: University of Illinois Press, 2017), chapter 2.

6. Ware, *Why They Marched*, 103, 175.

7. Equal Rights Amendment to the Constitution and Commission on the Legal Status of Women, Hearings Before Subcommittee No. 1 of the House Committee on the Judiciary, 80th Cong. 39 (1948) ("1948 House Judiciary Subcommittee ERA Hearings") (Statement of Mrs. Mary Church Terrell, founder and first president, National Association of Colored Women). See also Equal Rights Amendment, Hearing on S.J. Res. 61 Before a Subcommittee of the Senate Judiciary Committee, 79th Cong. 50 (1945) ("1945 Senate Judiciary Subcommittee ERA Hearing").

8. The Japanese Constitution of 1946 was similar in structure and rights to many postwar European constitutions. Article 14 declared that "All of the people are equal under the law" and explicitly declared that there shall be no discrimination "because of race, creed, sex, social status, or family origin." Article 24 declared that husbands and wives had equal rights in marriage. The Japanese Constitution of 1946 is available at https://www.constituteproject.org/constitution/Japan_1946.

9. Terrell, *A Colored Woman*, 98.

10. Terrell, *A Colored Woman*, 197.

11. For an English-language reproduction of Mary Church Terrell's 1904 speech in Berlin, see "Mary Church Terrell Speaks in Berlin," *Social Justice Feminists in the United States and Germany*, edited by Kathryn Kish Sklar, Anja Schuler, & Susan Strasser (Ithaca: Cornell University Press, 1998), 114–123.

12. See May Wright Sewall, *The International Council of Women: from 1899 to 1904* (1910). One American historian identifies Helene Lange as "the leading German feminist between 1890 and 1914" who

"more than any other single individual held together the coalition of conservative and progressive women activists during the first decade of the twentieth century." Lange was an admirer of American feminist Elizabeth Cady Stanton. See Sklar, *Social Justice Feminists*, 24–25.

13. Helene Lange and Gertrud Bäumer, *Handbuch der Frauenbewegung* (*Handbook of the Women's Movement*) (Berlin: S. W. Moeser, 1901).

14. See Richard J. Evans, *The Feminist Movement in Germany, 1894–1933* (London: Sage Publications, 1976), 154.

15. 1925 House Judiciary Committee ERA Hearing 6 (Statement of Mabel Vernon, executive secretary of the National Woman's Party). The debate about the German Constitution between ERA proponents and opponents in the 1920s and 1930s is discussed in chapter 3.

16. The word "grundsätzlich" is translated here as "basically," but the League of Women Voters translated it as "fundamentally," and others have translated it as "in principle."

17. The Weimar Constitution of 1919 is available in English translation at https://www.zum.de/psm/weimar/weimar_vve.php. I discuss these provisions in Julie C. Suk, "Gender Equality and the Protection of Motherhood in Global Constitutionalism," *Law & Ethics of Human Rights* 12 (2018): 151–180.

18. See Robert G. Moeller, *Protecting Motherhood: Women and the Family in the Politics of Postwar West Germany* (Berkeley: University of California Press, 1993) and Susanne Baer, "The Basic Law at 60—Equality and Difference: A Proposal for the Guest List to the Birthday Party," *German Law Journal* 11 (2010).

19. J.O.A.N. (Official Journal of the French National Assembly), No. 83 of 1946, at 3332. 2d Session on August 27, 1946 (Statement of Gilberte Roca).

20. J.O.A.N. (Official Journal of the French National Assembly), No. 83 of 1946, at 3332.

21. J.O.A.N. (Official Journal of the French National Assembly), No. 83 of 1946, at 3332.

22. Commissione per la costituzione (Commission for the Constitution), September 13, 1946, at 2105 (Italy). For an account of the women in the Italian constituent assembly, see Molly Tambor, *The Lost Wave: Women and Democracy in Postwar Italy* (Oxford: Oxford University Press, 2014), chapter 2.

23. For an account of the evolution of the ERA between World War I and World War II, see Susan D. Becker, *The Origins of the Equal Rights Amendment: American Feminism Between the Wars* (Westport, CT: Greenwood Press, 1981). Gwendolyn Mink (incidentally, the daughter of Congresswoman Patsy Mink, who advocated for the ERA in the 1970s) has also published an excellent study of social policies affecting mothers between the two wars. See Gwendolyn Mink, *The Wages of Motherhood: Inequality in the Welfare State, 1917–1942* (Ithaca: Cornell University Press, 1995). For an account of the women's movement between the two wars, see Lois Scharf & Joan M. Jenson (Editors), *Decades of Discontent: The Women's Movement, 1920–1940* (Boston, MA: Northeastern University Press, 1987).

24. 1945 Senate Judiciary Subcommittee ERA Hearing, 120 (Statement of Anna Lord Straus, President of the National League of Women Voters).

25. See 92 Congressional Record 9405 (1946).

26. See 1948 House Judiciary Subcommittee ERA Hearings, 90–218 (Statements of various witnesses, including several representatives of labor organizations).

27. 1948 House Judiciary Subcommittee ERA Hearings, 7 (Statement of Katharine St. George).

28. 96 Congressional Record 870 (1950).

29. 96 Congressional Record, 872.

30. 99 Congressional Record 8974 (1953).

31. 1948 House Judiciary Subcommittee Hearings, 75 (Statement of Margaret Chase Smith).

Chapter 5: The Framers

1. See Emily George, *Martha W. Griffiths* (New York: University Press of America, 1982), 4–5.

2. See Rules of the House of Representatives, § 891, Rule XV, clause 2, available at https://www.govinfo.gov/content/pkg/HMAN-115/pdf/HMAN-115-pg685.pdf.

3. 116 Congressional Record 27,999 (1970).

4. A thorough analysis of the ERA's legal impact is found in a *Yale Law Journal* article written by Professor Thomas Emerson of Yale Law School, and three of his students. Legal scholars regard this article as the informal legislative history of the ERA. It was cited by many ERA

proponents throughout the floor debates in 1970–72. See Barbara A. Brown, Thomas I. Emerson, Gail Falk, & Ann E. Freedman, "The Equal Rights Amendment: A Constitutional Basis for Equal Rights for Women," *Yale Law Journal* 80 (1971): 871–985. Another scholarly source frequently cited in Congress was Leo Kanowitz, *Women and the Law: The Unfinished Revolution* (Albuquerque: University of New Mexico Press, 1969).

5. 116 Congressional Record, 28,003.

6. 116 Congressional Record, 28,003.

7. President's Task Force on Women's Rights and Responsibilities, *A Matter of Simple Justice* (April 1970); Citizens Advisory Council on the Status of Women, *The Proposed Equal Rights Amendment to the United States Constitution: A Memorandum* (1970).

8. 116 Congressional Record, 28,003.

9. 116 Congressional Record, 28,004.

10. 116 Congressional Record, 28,020.

11. 116 Congressional Record, 28,020.

12. The "Equal Rights" Amendment, Hearings on S.J. Res. 61 Before the Subcommittee on Constitutional Amendments of the Senate Committee on the Judiciary, 91st Cong. 42 (1970) ("May 1970 Senate Judiciary Subcommittee ERA Hearings") (Statement of Margaret Heckler) (reprinted at 116 Congressional Record, 28,030).

13. 116 Congressional Record, 28,019.

14. For a scholarly treatment of the dynamics caused by the Senate filibuster, see Catherine Fisk and Erwin Chemerinsky, "The Filibuster," *Stanford Law Review* 49 (1997): 181–254.

15. 1948 House Judiciary Subcommittee ERA Hearings, 75 (Statement of Margaret Chase Smith).

16. About the filibuster of the Civil Rights Act, see Charles W. Whalen & Barbara Whalen, *The Longest Debate: A Legislative History of the 1964 Civil Rights Act* (Cabin John, MD: Seven Locks Press, 1985) and Clay Risen, *The Bill of the Century: The Epic Battle for the Civil Rights Act* (New York: Bloomsbury Press, 2014).

17. For a biographical account of Bayh's leadership on constitutional amendments during this era, see Robert Blaemire, *Birch Bayh: Making a Difference* (Bloomington: Indiana University Press, 2019).

18. 116 Congressional Record, 35,947.

19. 116 Congressional Record, 35,947.

20. 116 Congressional Record, 35,959.
21. *Hoyt v. Florida*, 368 US 57, 62 (1961). Dorothy Kenyon filed an amicus brief unsuccessfully arguing that the jury law violated the Fourteenth Amendment.
22. 116 Congressional Record, 36,312.
23. 116 Congressional Record, 36,478–36,479.
24. 116 Congressional Record, 36,278.
25. Equal Rights for Men and Women 1971, Hearings on H.J. Res. 35, 208 and Related Bills and H.R. 916 and Related Bills Before Subcommittee No. 4 of the House Committee on the Judiciary, 92nd Cong. 41 ("1971 House Judiciary Subcommittee ERA Hearings") (Statement of Martha Griffiths).
26. 1971 House Judiciary Subcommittee ERA Hearings, 41 (Statement of Martha Griffiths).

Chapter 6: The Mothers

1. Biographical material about Patsy Mink can be found in "Gwendolyn Mink Oral History Interview," Office of the Historian, US House of Representatives, March 14, 2016; Kimberly Bassford, *Patsy Mink: Ahead of the Majority* (Honolulu: Making Waves Films, 2008); and "Patsy Mink: Ahead of the Majority and Ahead of Her Time," March 22, 2019, Densho Blog, https://densho.org/patsy-mink/.
2. See Shirley Chisholm, *Unbought and Unbossed* (New York: Houghton Mifflin Harcourt, 1970); Shirley Chisholm, *The Good Fight* (New York: Harper & Row Publishers, 1973); Shola Lynch, *Chisholm '72: Unbought and Unbossed* (documentary film) (Sundance, 2004).
3. 115 Congressional Record 13,380 (1969).
4. 115 Congressional Record, 13,380.
5. S. Rep. No. 72–689 (1972), 6.
6. 116 Congressional Record, 28,028.
7. May 1970 Senate Judiciary Subcommittee ERA Hearings, 318 (Statement of Myra Wolfgang).
8. Equal Rights 1970, Hearings on S. J. Res. 61 and S. J. Res. 231 Before the Senate Committee on the Judiciary 31 (1970) ("September 1970 Senate Judiciary Committee ERA Hearings") (Statement of Myra Wolfgang).
9. See *Phillips v. Martin Marietta*, 416 F.2d 1257 (5th Cir. 1969) (per curiam order denying rehearing en banc); 411 F.2d (5th Cir. 1969)

(affirming district court's judgment in favor of the employer). The US Supreme Court eventually vacated and remanded the Fifth Circuit's decision a year after the Carswell hearings, 400 US 542 (1971). Historian Kirsten Swinth discusses the case as attempting to establish "the right to bear children." See Kirsten Swinth, *Feminism's Forgotten Fight: The Unfinished Struggle for Work and Family* (Cambridge: Harvard University Press, 2018), chapter 7.

10. George Harold Carswell, Hearings on the Nomination of George Harold Carswell of Florida to be Associate Justice of the Supreme Court of the United States Before the Senate Committee on the Judiciary, 91st Cong. 81–88 (1970) (Statement of Patsy Mink).

11. Betty Friedan founded the National Organization of Women in 1966, after her 1963 bestseller, *The Feminine Mystique* (New York: W.W. Norton & Co., 1963), drew public attention to women's dissatisfaction with their traditional roles and status in society.

12. Betty Friedan, *"It Changed My Life." Writings on the Women's Movement* (Cambridge: Harvard University Press, 1998), 181.

13. Linda Charlton, "Women's Liberation Unit Gives Details of Its Nationwide Protest," *New York Times*, August 19, 1970, at 43.

14. See Bonnie Dow, *Watching Women's Liberation, 1970: Feminism's Pivotal Year on the Network News* (Urbana: University of Illinois Press, 2014), chapter 2. To situate the strike in the context of the 1970s women's movement, see Jo Freeman, *The Politics of Women's Liberation: A Case Study of an Emerging Social Movement and its Relation to the Policy Process* (New York: David McKay Company, Inc., 1975).

15. Linda Charlton, "Women March Down Fifth in Equality Drive," *New York Times*, August 27, 1970, at 1, 30.

16. Linda Charlton, "Women March Down Fifth in Equality Drive."

17. Judy Syfers, "I Want a Wife," *Ms. Magazine, New York Magazine,* December 1971. (Originally delivered as a speech at San Francisco Women's Strike for Equality, August 26, 1970).

18. Comprehensive Preschool Education and Child Day-Care Act of 1969, Hearings on H. R. 13520 Before the Select Subcommittee on Education, of the House Committee on Education and Labor, 91st Cong. 792 (1970) ("1970 Comprehensive Preschool Hearings") (Statement of Shirley Chisholm).

19. 1970 Comprehensive Preschool Hearings, 793.

20. 1970 Comprehensive Preschool Hearings, 794.

21. 20 USC §§ 1681–1688.

22. Discrimination Against Women, Hearings on Section 804 of H. R. 16098 Before the Special Subcommittee on Education of the House Committee on Education and Labor, Part I, 91st Cong. 434 (1971) ("1971 Title IX Hearings") (Statement of Patsy Mink).

23. 116 Congressional Record, 28,029.

24. 116 Congressional Record, 28,029.

25. 116 Congressional Record, 28,029.

26. H. R. Rep. No. 92–359 (1971), 1.

27. H. R. Rep. No. 92–359, at 2.

28. 117 Congressional Record 35,314 (1971).

29. 117 Congressional Record, 35,318.

30. To analogize to other constitutional amendments, Title VII can be seen as a "super-statute" that enforces the Equal Protection Clause of the Fourteenth Amendment and the Voting Rights Act enforces the Fifteenth Amendment.

31. 1971 House Judiciary Subcommittee ERA Hearings, 521 (Statement of Patsy Mink).

32. 117 Congressional Record, 35,319.

33. S. Rep. No. 72–689, at 7.

34. 117 Congressional Record, 35,323.

35. 116 Congressional Record, 28,004.

36. 117 Congressional Record, 35,799.

37. 117 Congressional Record, 35,799.

38. For a biographical account of Bella Abzug's politics, see Leandra Ruth Zarnow, *Battling Bella: The Protest Politics of Bella Abzug* (Cambridge: Harvard University Press, 2019).

39. 117 Congressional Record, 35,799.

40. Bella Abzug later wrote a book taking up the themes of women and inequality that animated her contributions while she was a member of Congress. See Bella Abzug and Mim Kelber, *Gender Gap: Bella Abzug's Guide to Political Power for American Women* (New York: Houghton Mifflin Company, 1984).

41. 117 Congressional Record, 35,789.

42. S. Rep. No. 72–689, at 12.

43. 117 Congressional Record, 35,324.

44. 117 Congressional Record, 35,320.

45. See Donald G. Mathews and Jane Sherron DeHart, *Sex, Gender, and the Politics of the ERA* (Oxford: Oxford University Press, 1990), 53.

Chapter 7: The Breadmakers

1. Phyllis Schlafly, *A Choice Not an Echo* (Regnery Publishing, 2014) (Pere Marquette Press, 1964).
2. 118 Congressional Record 8452 (1972).
3. 118 Congressional Record, 9315, 9317, 9524, 9529, 9531.
4. 116 Congressional Record, 36,271.
5. 116 Congressional Record, 35,935.
6. 116 Congressional Record, 35,935.
7. See Carol Felsenthal, *The Sweetheart of the Silent Majority: The Biography of Phyllis Schlafly* (Garden City, NY: Doubleday), 203–04.
8. Felsenthal, *Sweetheart*, 240.
9. See Mathews and DeHart, *Sex, Gender, and the Politics of the ERA*, 50.
10. Phyllis Schlafly, "What's Wrong with Equal Rights for Women?" *The Phyllis Schlafly Report*, February 1972.
11. 118 Congressional Record, 9084.
12. 118 Congressional Record, 9596–97.
13. Mitch McConnell, *The Long Game: A Memoir* (New York: Sentinel, 2016), 33–35.
14. 117 Congressional Record, 35,808.
15. Phyllis Schlafly, *The Power of the Positive Woman* (New York: Crown Pub, 1977), 79.
16. See Marjorie Spruill, *Divided We Stand: The Battle Over Women's Rights and Family Values that Polarized American Politics* (New York: Bloomsbury Publishing, 2017), 95.
17. See Mathews and DeHart, *Sex, Gender, and the Politics of the ERA*, 51.
18. Schlafly, *The Power of the Positive Woman*, 136.
19. See Spruill, *Divided We Stand*, 83.
20. The account of Phyllis Schlafly's STOP-ERA campaign in Illinois relies largely on Felsenthal, *Sweetheart*, 242–66. See also Donald T. Critchlow, *Phyllis Schlafly and Grassroots Conservatism: A Woman's Crusade* (Princeton: Princeton University Press, 2005), 212–242.
21. Schlafly, "What's Wrong with Equal Rights for Women?"
22. See Sylvia Hewlett, *A Lesser Life: The Myth of Women's Liberation in America* (New York: William Morrow & Co, 1986); Joan Williams,

Unbending Gender: Why Family and Work Conflict and What To Do About It (Oxford: Oxford University Press, 2000).

23. See Spruill, *Divided We Stand.*

24. National Women's Conference, National Plan of Action, November 18–21, 1977, at 14.

25. National Women's Conference, National Plan of Action, 7.

26. National Women's Conference, National Plan of Action, 5.

27. National Women's Conference, National Plan of Action, 15.

28. See Judy Klemesrud, "Equal Rights Plan and Abortion Are Opposed by 15,000 at Rally," *New York Times*, November 19, 1977.

29. Scholars published books in the aftermath about why the ERA failed. See Mary Frances Berry, *Why ERA Failed: Politics, Women's Rights, and the Amending Process of the Constitution* (Bloomington: Indiana University Press, 1986) and Jane J. Mansbridge, *Why We Lost the ERA* (Chicago: University of Chicago Press, 1986).

30. Pew Research Center, "They're Waiting Longer, but U.S. Women Today More Likely to Have Children Than a Decade Ago," January 18, 2018, https://www.pewsocialtrends.org/2018/01/18/theyre-waiting -longer-but-u-s-women-today-more-likely-to-have-children-than-a -decade-ago/.

31. *Geduldig v. Aiello*, 417 US 484 (1974).

32. Abraham Lincoln Presidential Library and Museum, Phyllis Schlafly Oral History, ERA Fight in Illinois, https://www2.illinois.gov/alplm /library/collections/OralHistory/illinoisstatecraft/era/Pages/Schlafly Phyllis.aspx.

Chapter 8: The Change Agents

1. Jessica Glenza and Alana Casanova-Burgess, "The U.S. air force gave her a choice: your baby or your job." *The Guardian*, December 13, 2019, https://www.theguardian.com/world/2019/dec/13/us-air -force-pregnancy-susan-struck-abortion-motherhood-america; Podcast, "Body of Law: Beyond Roe, No Way Are They Going to Do This to Struck," On the Media, WNYC, December 13, 2019, https://www.wnycstudios.org/podcasts/otm/episodes/on-the -media-body-law-beyond-roe.

2. 1971 House Judiciary Subcommittee ERA Hearings, 39–40 (Statement of Martha Griffiths).

3. *Struck v. Secretary of Defense*, 460 F.2d 1372, 1374 (9th Cir. 1971) (describing District Court's conclusions of law, and affirming).

4. 116 Congressional Record, 28,004.

5. Brief for the Petitioner, *Struck v. Secretary of Defense*, No 72–178, United States Supreme Court, filed December 4, 1972, 1972 WL 135840, 34. For a scholarly account of Ginsburg's brief in the Struck case, see Neil S. Siegel and Reva B. Siegel, "Struck by Stereotype: Ruth Bader Ginsburg on Pregnancy Discrimination as Sex Discrimination," *Duke Law Journal* 59 (2010): 771–798.

6. Brief for the Petitioner, *Struck v. Secretary of Defense*, 48.

7. Brief for the Petitioner, *Struck v. Secretary of Defense*, 30.

8. Jane Sherron DeHart, *Ruth Bader Ginsburg: A Life* (New York: Borzoi Books, Knopf, 2018), 51. A few years after her work on Captain Struck's case, Ginsburg also advocated on behalf of an African American woman who had been sterilized and therefore deprived of her opportunity to become a mother without her consent. See *Cox v. Stanton*, 529 F.2d 47 (1975).

9. See Irin Carmon and Shana Knizhnik, *Notorious RBG: The Life and Times of Ruth Bader Ginsburg* (New York: Dey St., 2015), 67.

10. DeHart, *Ruth Bader Ginsburg: A Life*, 55.

11. *Reed v. Reed*, 404 US 71 (1971).

12. *Reed v. Reed*, 73.

13. *Reed v. Reed*, 76.

14. 1971 House Judiciary Subcommittee ERA Hearings 36 (Statement of Martha Griffiths).

15. Brief for American Veterans Committee, Inc., and NOW Legal Defense and Education Fund as Amici Curiae Supporting Appellant, *Reed v. Reed*, 404 US 71 (1971) (No. 70–4).

16. See Brief for Appellant, *Reed v. Reed*, 404 US 71 (1971) (No. 70–4), 55.

17. See Brief for Appellant, *Reed v. Reed*, 55.

18. The cover page of the brief listed Pauli Murray and Dorothy Kenyon as authors of the brief. Ginsburg insisted on including their names, even though they had not drafted this particular brief, because of what she learned from the arguments they made in *White v. Crook*, 251 F. Supp. 401 (M.D. Ala. 1966) to challenge an all-white and all-male jury in Alabama. See Irin Carmon and Shana Knizhnik, *Notorious RBG*, 55.

19. Quoted in Serena Mayeri, "Constitutional Choices: Legal Feminism and the Historical Dynamics of Change," *California Law Review* 92 (2004): 755, 798 (Letters of Dorothy Kenyon to Rolland O'Hare and Betsy Nolan).

20. Mayeri, "Constitutional Choices," 794. See also Serena Mayeri, *Reasoning from Race: Feminism, Law, and the Civil Rights Revolution* (Cambridge: Harvard University Press, 2011).

21. Pauli Murray & Mary O. Eastwood, "Jane Crow and the Law: Sex Discrimination and Title VII," *George Washington Law Review* 34 (1965): 232–56.

22. See Rosalind Rosenberg, *Jane Crow: The Life of Pauli Murray* (New York: Oxford University Press, 2017), 77, 137 (detailing her rejection from the University of North Carolina Law School because she was black and Harvard Law School because she was a woman).

23. See Pauli Murray, *Song in a Weary Throat: Memoir of an American Pilgrimage* (New York: Liveright Publishing), 328–30.

24. *Frontiero v. Richardson*, 411 US 677 (1973).

25. For an account of Ginsburg's philosophy of gender stereotypes, and particularly the influence of Swedish law, culture, and policy on her thinking, see Cary Franklin, "The Anti-Stereotyping Principle in Constitutional Sex Discrimination Law," *New York University Law Review* 85 (2010): 83–173.

26. See *Frontiero v. Richardson*, 684.

27. See Brief for Appellant, *Reed v. Reed*, 21.

28. Oral Argument, *Frontiero v. Richardson*, 411 US 677 (1973) (No. 71-1694), January 17, 1973, https://www.oyez.org/cases/1972/71-1694. The origin of this quote is Sarah Grimké, *Letters on the Equality of the Sexes, and the Condition of Woman. Addressed to Mary S. Parker, President of the Boston Female Anti-Slavery Society* (Boston: Isaac Knapp, 1838), 10 (Letter II, "Woman Subject Only to God," July 17, 1837).

29. May 1970 Senate Judiciary Subcommittee ERA Hearings, 78 (Statement of Emma Goldman, Women's Liberation, Washington, DC, accompanied by Sarah Grimké, Angelina Grimké).

30. *Frontiero v. Richardson*, 686–87.

31. *Frontiero v. Richardson*, 687–88.

32. September 1970 Senate Judiciary Committee ERA Hearings, 427–33 (Statement of Pauli Murray). See also Pauli Murray, "The Negro Woman's Stake in the Equal Rights Amendment," *Harvard Civil Rights-Civil Liberties Law Review* 6 (1971): 253–59.

33. September 1970 Senate Judiciary Committee ERA Hearings, 428.

34. September 1970 Senate Judiciary Committee ERA Hearings, 432–33.

35. September 1970 Senate Judiciary Committee ERA Hearings, 432–33.

36. Subsequent Supreme Court decisions solidified the rule that sex discrimination was generally impermissible under the Equal Protection Clause. Ginsburg litigated some of these cases, and discussed them as she argued in favor of the ERA as "a clear statement of the nation's moral and legal commitment to a system in which women and men stand as full and equal individuals before the law" in a published scholarly lecture. See Ruth Bader Ginsburg, "Gender and the Constitution," *University of Cincinnati Law Review* 44 (1975):1, 27. In addition to *Reed* and *Frontiero*, these cases included *Stanley v. Illinois*, 405 US 675 (1972), *Weinberer v. Wiesenfeld*, 420 US 636 (1975), *Craig v. Boren*, 429 US 190 (1976) and *Taylor v. Louisiana*, 419 US 522 (1975).

37. *United States v. Virginia*, 518 US 515, 531 (1996).

38. *United States v. Virginia*, 531.

39. See Jeffrey Rosen, "The New Look of Liberalism on the Court," *New York Times Magazine*, October 5, 1997.

40. 1971 House Judiciary Subommittee ERA Hearings, 38 (Statement of Martha Griffiths).

41. 1971 House Judiciary Subcommittee ERA Hearings, 41.

42. See *Phillips v. Martin Marietta*, 400 US 542 (1971). Pauli Murray and Dorothy Kenyon filed an amicus brief on behalf of the plaintiff, a working mother, in this case.

43. *Gilbert v. General Electric*, 429 US 125 (1976).

44. Pregnancy Discrimination Act of 1978, Public Law 95–555, 92 Stat. 2076, 95th Congress, October 31, 1978, codified at 42 USC. § 2000e(k) (2012).

45. Discrimination on the Basis of Pregnancy, Hearings Before the Subcommittee on Labor of the Senate Committee on Human Resources, 95th Cong. 6 (1977) (Statement of Birch Bayh).

46. *McNeil et al. v. Yale University*, Complaint, Case 3:19-cv-00209 (US District Court, District of Connecticut), 82–83, at https://int.nyt.com/data/documenthelper/610-mcneil-et-al-v-yale/67b-c816e4054281d1543/optimized/full.pdf#page=1.

47. *J. A. Croson v. City of Richmond*, 488 US 469 (1989).

48. *Adarand Constructors v. Peña*, 515 US 200 (1995).

49. Justice Ginsburg has avoided using the language of "strict scrutiny" to describe the Court's approach to sex distinctions in the law. In *Frontiero*, only four justices favored the application of the same legal standard to scrutinize sex distinctions as was applied to race distinctions in the law. In the case of *Craig v. Boren*, 429 US 190 (1976), the Supreme Court opted for "intermediate scrutiny" for sex classifications, which is what Justice Ginsburg builds on in *United States v. Virginia*. Sex distinctions that perpetuate gender stereotypes are generally struck down, but not all sex distinctions are suspect under this standard. In 1987, the Supreme Court upheld a California law that required employers to guarantee maternity leave, albeit unpaid, to women only. It was argued that the law gave special treatment to women and was incompatible with federal employment discrimination law, which prohibits employers from discriminating because of sex. But the Supreme Court concluded that a maternity leave law was not pre-empted by federal sex discrimination law. See *California Federal Savings & Loan Association v. Guerra*, 479 US 272 (1987).

50. *United States v. Virginia*, 534.

51. Cal. Corp. Code § 301.3 (West 2019).

52. Hearing on S.B. 826 Before the Assembly Committee on Judiciary, 2018 Leg., Leg. Session 6–7. (Cal. 2018) (analysis prepared by Thomas Clark and Sandra Nakagawa).

53. *Meland v. Padilla*, Complaint, November 13, 2019 (US District Court, Eastern District of California), https://pacificlegal.org/wp-content/uploads/2019/11/Creighton-Meland-v.-Alex-Padilla-Secretary-of-State-of-California-Complaint.pdf.

54. This is discussed in chapter 6. As the ERA was being adopted, the Supreme Court had defined discrimination under Title VII of the Civil Rights Act to include policies that had a disparate impact on groups protected by the statute, including race and sex. See *Griggs v. Duke Power Company*, 401 US 424 (1971). However, the Supreme Court refused to recognize policies having a disparate impact on women or racial minorities as violations of the Fourteenth Amendment's Equal Protection Clause or the due process guarantee of the Fifth Amendment. See *Washington v. Davis*, 426 US 229 (1976) and *Personnel Administrator of Massachusetts v. Feeney*, 442 US 256 (1979). The broader definition of discrimination, which includes disparate impact, as articulated by the Supreme Court in 1971 in

Griggs, is the definition that appears operative in ERA discussions in Congress in 1970–72.

55. In both France and Germany, for instance, constitutional amendments adopted from the mid-1990s to 2008 authorize the government to take positive steps to promote equality for women and men. I discuss these provisions in detail in Julie C. Suk, "An Equal Rights Amendment for the Twenty-First Century: Bringing Global Constitutionalism Home." *Yale Journal of Law and Feminism* 28 (2017): 381, 412–14, 423–26.

56. See Women in National Parliaments, Inter-Parliamentary Union, https://data.ipu.org/women-ranking?month=10&year=2019.

57. *Sessions v. Morales-Santana*, 583 US (2017); 137 S.Ct. 1678 (2017). In 2001, the Supreme Court applied the reasoning of *United States v. Virginia* to uphold different citizenship rules for children born overseas to unmarried citizen fathers as compared to those born to unmarried citizen mothers. See *Nguyen v. INS*, 533 US 53 (2001).

58. *Sessions v. Morales-Santana*, 1698.

Chapter 9: The Game Changers

1. Elizabeth Holtzman, *Who Said It Would Be Easy? One Woman's Life in the Political Arena* (New York: Arcade, 1996).

2. It is noteworthy that both Patsy Mink and Bella Abzug gave up their House seats because they decided to run for the Senate, and they both lost in those Senate elections. Jeannette Rankin had done the same in 1918, and therefore did not return to the session of Congress that voted to adopt the 19th Amendment. Liz Holtzman also gave up her House seat to run for a Senate seat that she did not win.

3. *Holtzman v. Power*, 62 Misc. 2d 1020 (1970).

4. See Irwin Gertzog, *Congressional Women: Their Recruitment, Treatment, and Behavior* (New York: Praeger, 1984), 183.

5. Editorial, "ERA: Resistance in Richmond," *Washington Post*, February 14, 1978, A18.

6. 124 Congressional Record 26,201 (1978).

7. Equal Rights Amendment Extension: Hearings on H. J. Res. 38 Before the Subcommittee on Civil and Constitutional Rights of the House Committee on the Judiciary, 95th Cong. 4 (1977–78) ("House Judiciary Subcommittee ERA Extension Hearings").

8. See generally Mary Beth Rogers, *Barbara Jordan: American Hero* (New York: Bantam Books, 1998).

9. Debate on Articles of Impeachment, Hearings on H. Res. 803 Before the Committee on the Judiciary, 93rd Cong. 110–13 (1973–74) (Statement of Barbara Jordan).

10. In recent years, Holtzman has been a major commentator making the case for impeaching Donald Trump. See Elizabeth Holtzman, *The Case for Impeaching Trump* (New York: Skyhorse Publishing, 2019).

11. See Spruill, *Divided We Stand*.

12. National Women's Conference, National Plan of Action, 14.

13. *Coleman v. Miller*, 307 US 433, 454 (1939).

14. *Dillon v. Gloss*, 256 US 368, 376 (1921).

15. 124 Congressional Record, 26,198.

16. 124 Congressional Record, 26,200.

17. House Judiciary Subcommittee ERA Extension Hearings, 107 (Statement of Erwin Griswold).

18. House Judiciary Subcommittee ERA Extension Hearings, 239 (Statement of Barbara Jordan).

19. 124 Congressional Record, 26,215.

20. 124 Congressional Record, 26,215.

21. 124 Congressional Record, 26,215.

22. See Norgren, *Stories from Trailblazing Women Lawyers*, 91–92.

23. See Neil A. Lewis, "Patricia Wald, First Woman to Preside Over D.C. Appeals Court, Dies at 90," *New York Times*, January 12, 2019, https://www.nytimes.com/2019/01/12/obituaries/patricia-wald-dead.html.

24. Equal Rights Amendment Extension: Hearings on S. J. Res 134 Before the Subcommittee on the Constitution of the Senate Committee on the Judiciary, 95th Cong. 57 (1978) ("Senate Judiciary Subcommittee ERA Extension Hearings") (Statement of Patricia Wald).

25. Senate Judiciary Subcommittee ERA Extension Hearings, 57 (Statement of Patricia Wald).

26. Senate Judiciary Subcommittee ERA Extension Hearings, 262 (Statement of Ruth Bader Ginsburg).

27. House Judiciary Subcommittee ERA Extension Hearings, 128 (Statement of Ruth Bader Ginsburg).

28. House Judiciary Subcommittee ERA Extension Hearings, 128.

29. House Judiciary Subcommittee ERA Extension Hearings, 128.

30. Senate Judiciary Subcommittee ERA Extension Hearings, 264 (Statement of Ruth Bader Ginsburg).

Chapter 10: The Resurrectors

1. See Judy Klemesrud, "Equal Rights Plan and Abortion Are Opposed by 15,000 at Rally," *New York Times*, November 19, 1977.
2. See Pat Spearman, "Remembering the progress and pain of women's military service," *The Hill*, May 27, 2019, https://thehill.com /opinion/national-security/445646-remembering-the-progress -and-pain-of-womens-military-service.
3. See Soni Brown, "How Pat Spearman went from the pulpit to the polls," *The Nevada Independent*, May 20, 2018, https://thenevadaindependent. com/article/how-pat-spearman-went-from-the-pulpit-to-the-polls.
4. Pat Spearman, Panel Remarks, Panel on "Recent Ratifiers," Conference on A New Era for the Equal Rights Amendment, University of Richmond School of Law, October 26, 2019, https://urcapture.hosted.panopto.com/Panopto/Pages/Viewer. aspx?id=45c0b3f5-53fd-4636-ba5a-aaf2001bc88b.
5. Feminist Majority Foundation, "Nevada Becomes 36th State to Ratify the ERA," *Feminist Newswire*, March 20, 2017, https://feminist .org/blog/index.php/2017/03/20/nevada-becomes-36th-state -to-ratify-the-era/.
6. Nevada State Assembly, SJR 2, 79th Sess. Amendment No. 50, March 22, 2017.
7. Nevada Assembly Committee on Legislative Operations and Elections, Meeting Minutes, 79th Session, March 7, 2017, 9, https: //www.leg.state.nv.us/Session/79th2017/Minutes/Assembly/LOE/ Final/428.pdf ("Nevada Assembly Committee, March 7, 2017").
8. J. Bob Alotta et al. Women's March on Washington, Guiding Vision and Definition of Principles, 4 (Jan. 12, 2017), https://www.womens march.com/principles.
9. Alotta et al.
10. See Nevada Legislature, Senate Floor Session, March 1, 2017, https: //nvleg.granicus.com/MediaPlayer.php?view_id=29&clip_id=6871. ("Nevada Senate Floor Session, March 1, 2017"). The citation for now-Justice Ginsburg's article is Ruth Bader Ginsburg, "The Equal Rights Amendment is the Way," *Harvard Women's Law Journal* 1 (1978): 19, 26. The article was based on remarks that she delivered

at the Judicial Conference of the Second Circuit on September 11, 1976.

11. 117 Congressional Record, 35,295–35,296, 35,318–35,319, 35,799.

12. 1971 House Judiciary Subcommittee ERA Hearings, 521–22 (Statement of Patsy T. Mink).

13. 1971 House Judiciary Subcommittee ERA Hearings, 44 (Statement of Martha W. Griffiths).

14. 1945 Senate Judiciary Subcommittee ERA Hearing, 47 (Statement of Mrs. Kathryne B. Withrow, Industrial Women's League for Equality).

15. See Ginsburg, "The Equal Rights Amendment Is the Way," 21, 23.

16. See Nevada Assembly Committee, March 7, 2017, at 5.

17. See Phyllis Schlafly, "How the ERA Would Change Federal Laws," *The Phyllis Schlafly Report*, Vol. 15, No. 4, Section 2 (1981). Schlafly decried "phony arguments made by the ERAers about the job discrimination and '59¢.'" She wrote, "This is what changes ERA will bring in employment," followed by an empty rectangle. The article was a criticism of a report authored by Ruth Bader Ginsburg, "Sex Bias in the United States Code," which catalogued 800 laws that discriminated on account of sex. See US Commission on Civil Rights, Report, *Sex Bias in the US Code* (April 1977).

18. Nevada Assembly Committee, March 7, 2017, at 4.

19. Equal Rights Amendment, Hearing on H. J. Res. 79 Before the Subcommittee on the Constitution, Civil Rights, and Civil Liberties of the House Committee on the Judiciary, 116th Cong. (2019), (Spearman Testimony) https://judiciary.house.gov/legislation/hearings/equal-rights-amendment.

20. Nevada Assembly Committee, March 7, 2017, at 6.

21. Nevada Assembly Committee, March 7, 2017, at 6.

22. Megan Messerly, "Working class roots, experience as criminal prosecutor led Nicole Cannizzaro to top role in Senate," *The Nevada Independent*, March 24, 2019, https://thenevadaindependent.com/article/working-class-roots-experience-as-criminal-prosecutor-led-nicole-cannizzaro-to-top-role-in-senate.

23. Nevada Senate Floor Session, March 1, 2017.

24. Nevada Senate Floor Session, March 1, 2017.

25. The history of Nevada's ratification fight is excellently detailed in an unpublished doctoral dissertation. See Caryl Batt Dzeidziak, "The Gendering of Nevada Politics: The ERA Ratification

Campaign, 1973–1981," University of Nevada, Las Vegas, PhD in History, https://digitalscholarship.unlv.edu/cgi/viewcontent. cgi?article=1672&context=thesesdissertations.

26. See *Kimble v. Swackhamer*, 94 Nev. 600 (1978).

27. See Dennis Myers, "Equality: How the Failed Equal Rights Amendment changed Nevada," *Reno News & Review*, March 13, 2017, https://www.newsreview.com/reno/equality/content?oid=23947283.

28. Nevada Senate Floor Session, March 1, 2017.

29. Nevada Senate Floor Session, March 1, 2017.

30. Nevada Senate Floor Session, March 1, 2017.

31. Nevada Senate Floor Session, March 1, 2017.

32. Roberson quoted Reva B. Siegel, "Constitutional Culture, Social Movement Conflict and Constitutional Change: The Case of the de facto ERA," *California Law Review* 94 (2006): 1323, 1332–1334, and explicitly mentioned David A. Strauss, "The Irrelevance of Constitutional Amendments," *Harvard Law Review* 114 (2001): 1457–1505, and Cass Sunstein, *The Second Bill of Rights* (New York: Basic Books, 2004).

33. Reva B. Siegel, "Prochoicelife: Asking Who Protects Life and How— and Why It Matters in Law and Politics," *Indiana Law Journal* 93 (2018): 207–232.

34. Pregnant Workers' Fairness Act, Senate Bill No. 253, 79th Sess. (Nevada 2017).

35. Nursing Mothers' Accommodation Act, Assembly Bill No. 113, 79th Sess. (Nevada 2017).

36. Domestic Violence Leave Law, Senate Bill No. 361, 79th Sess. (Nevada 2017).

37. Pat Spearman, Plenary IV Speech, National Organization for Women (NOW) Conference, Minneapolis, Minnesota, July 20, 2019. Video available at https://www.facebook.com/NationalNOW /videos/2957435661147620/.

Chapter 11: The Rectifiers

1. Illinois Senate, Regular Session, Senate Transcript, 100th General Assembly, April 11, 2018, at 26.

2. "Read the Full Open Letter on Sexual Harassment in Illinois Politics," *NBC Chicago*, October 24, 2017, https://www.nbcchicago.com/news /local/read-the-full-me-too-illinois-harassment-open-letter/26773/.

3. Illinois Senate, Regular Session, Senate Transcript, 100th General Assembly, April 11, 2018, at 26.

4. S. R. 1076, 100th General Assembly (2017). See also Senate Task Force on Sexual Discrimination and Harassment Awareness and Prevention, "Task Force Assessment 2018: Findings and Proposals for Addressing Sexual Harassment in Illinois," 100th General Assembly, 3, http://www.ilga.gov/reports/ReportsSubmitted/290RSGAEmail 638RSGAAttachSenate%20Sexual%20Discrimination%20and%20 Harassment%20Task%20Force%202018%20Final%20Report.pdf.

5. Jaclyn Driscoll, "Women's Caucus Created By State Senators," *NPR Illinois*, November 9, 2017, https://www.nprillinois.org/post /womens-caucus-created-state-senators#stream/0.

6. See "Senate Women's Caucus announces first bipartisan effort," Illinois Senate Democrats, April 11, 2018, http://illinoissenatedemocrats .com/caucus-news/feature-story-archive/6231-senate-women-s-caucus -announces-first-bipartisan-effort.

7. Illinois General Assembly, H.R. 0687, 100th General Assembly (2017).

8. See Abraham Lincoln Presidential Library and Museum, Barbara Flynn Currie Oral History, ERA Fight in Illinois, https://www2 .illinois.gov/alplm/library/collections/OralHistory/illinoisstatecraft /era/Pages/Currie,-Barbara-Flynn.aspx.

9. See Illinois General Assembly, H. B. 0008, 98th General Assembly, http://www.ilga.gov/legislation/BillStatus.asp?DocNum=8& GAID=12&DocTypeID=HB&SessionID=85&GA=98; enacted and codified at Illinois Human Rights Act, 775 ILCS 5/2–102 (2014).

10. See Natasha Korecki & Kristen East, "Biss calls for Springfield sexual harassment training," Illinois Playbook, *Politico*, October 24, 2017, https://www.politico.com/tipsheets/illinois-playbook/2017/10/24 /biss-calls-for-springfield-sexual-harassment-training-veto-session -showdown-rauner-is-top-dga-target-222956.

11. See Litesa Wallace, "Rep. Litesa Wallace Details Sexual Harassment of Black Women in Government," *Teen Vogue*, November 15, 2017, https://www.teenvogue.com/story/rep-litesa-wallace-details-sexual -harassment-of-black-women-in-government.

12. See Morgan Jerkins, "The way forward for MeToo, according to founder Tarana Burke," *Vox*, October 15, 2019, https://www.vox .com/identities/2019/10/15/20910298/tarana-burke-morgan-jerkins.

13. Sixty percent of food preparation and service workers, 70 percent of waitresses, 86 percent of hostesses, and 88 percent of maids and housekeepers are women. See Bureau of Labor Statistics, "Labor Force Statistics from the Current Population Survey, 2018," https://www.bls.gov/cps/cpsaat11.htm.

14. This is particularly acute in the restaurant industry. See Saru Jayaraman, *Behind the Kitchen Door* (Ithaca, NY: Cornell University Press, 2013). See Alana Samuels and Malcolm Burnley, "Low Wages, Sexual Harassment, and Unreliable Tips. This is Life in America's Booming Service Industry," *Time*, August 22, 2019, https://time.com/5658442/tipped-restaurant-workers-american-economy/.

15. See Complaint, *Hampton v. Democratic Party of Illinois and Friends of Michael Madigan*, Case: 1:18-cv-02069 (US District Court, Northern District of Illinois), March 21, 2018, https://news.wttw.com/sites/default/files/article/file-attachments/Complaint_3.21.18.01.pdf.

16. See Abraham Lincoln Presidential Library and Museum, Dawn Clark Netsch Oral History, ERA Fight in Illinois, https://www2.illinois.gov/alplm/library/collections/OralHistory/illinoisstatecraft/era/Pages/NetschDawnClark.aspx; Abraham Lincoln Presidential Library and Museum, Barbara Flynn Currie Oral History, ERA Fight in Illinois, https://www2.illinois.gov/alplm/library/collections/OralHistory/illinoisstatecraft/era/Pages/Currie,-Barbara-Flynn.aspx.

17. The history of the 1970s ratification efforts, in relation to the procedural rules, is taken from *Dyer v. Blair*, 390 F. Supp. 1291 (US District Court, Northern District of Illinois, 1975) and an oral history of Dawn Clark Netsch. See Abraham Lincoln Presidential Library and Museum, Dawn Clark Netsch Oral History, ERA Fight in Illinois, https://www2.illinois.gov/alplm/library/collections/OralHistory/illinoisstatecraft/era/Pages/NetschDawnClark.aspx.

18. *Dyer v. Blair*, 1308. The court cited the Supreme Court precedents of *Hawke v. Smith*, 253 U.S. 221 (1920), which held that the state legislatures could not delegate their ratification duties to the people by way of a popular referendum on the ratification of a federal constitutional amendment, and *Leser v. Garnett*, 258 U.S. 130 (1921), which held that the Nineteenth Amendment was valid despite a challenge suggesting that it violated Article V by overcoming the equal representation of the states in the Senate. Both of these cases supported

the conclusion that the Illinois state constitution could not validly change the ratification process detailed in the federal constitution.

19. Edward McClelland, "When Illinois Conservatives Blocked the ERA," *Chicago Magazine*, January 16, 2020, http://www.chicagomag.com/city-life/January-2020/Illinois-and-the-ERA/.

20. See Illinois General Assembly, Senate Joint Resolution SC 0075, 98th General Assembly (2014).

21. Illinois House of Representatives, Transcription Debate, 100th General Assembly, May 30, 2018, at 292 ("Illinois House, May 30, 2018") (Rep. Breen).

22. Illinois House, May 30, 2018, 295–96. In *Harris v. McRae*, 448 US 297 (1980), the US Supreme Court upheld the Hyde Amendment, which withheld federal funding for abortions under Medicaid, even those that were medically indicated, reasoning that the exclusion of abortion from medically necessary care was not an Equal Protection violation. By contrast, the state supreme courts of Connecticut and New Mexico relied on their states' Equal Rights Amendments, which explicitly prohibit sex discrimination, to reach the opposite conclusion in subsequent years. Those courts reasoned that coverage of all medically necessary procedures but not abortion was sex discrimination. These decisions did not, however, say that sex equality required unfettered access to funded abortions on demand. See *Doe v. Maher*, 40 Conn. Supp. 394 (1986); *New Mexico Right to Choose/NARAL v. Johnson*, 126 N.M. 788 (1998).

23. Illinois House, May 30, 2018, at 306.

24. Illinois House, May 30, 2018, at 307.

25. Illinois House, May 30, 2018, at 337.

26. Illinois House, May 30, 2018, at 315–16.

27. Illinois House, May 30, 2018, at 316.

28. Illinois House, May 30, 2018, at 317.

29. Illinois House, May 30, 2018, at 318.

30. Illinois House, May 30, 2018, at 319.

31. Illinois House, May 30, 2018, at 342.

32. Illinois House, May 30, 2018, at 342.

33. Illinois House, May 30, 2018, at 342.

34. Illinois House, May 30, 2018, at 343.

35. Illinois House, May 30, 2018, at 343.

36. Illinois House, May 30, 2018, at 343.

37. Illinois House, May 30, 2018, at 343.
38. Illinois House, May 30, 2018, at 343–44.
39. See Ware, *Why They Marched*, 103, 175. Note that the housing project that Litesa Wallace mentioned as the home where her grandmother raised her children as a single mother was named for Ida B. Wells.
40. Illinois General Assembly, House Bill 0001, 101st General Assembly (2019).
41. Illinois General Assembly, Senate Bill 20, 100th General Assembly (2018).
42. See Workplace Transparency Act, Public Act 101–0221, Illinois General Assembly Senate Bill 0075 (2019).

Chapter 12 The History Makers

1. Joan Biskupic, "Supreme Court Invalidates Exclusion of Women by VMI," *Washington Post*, June 27, 1996. Justice Ginsburg, in announcing the decision at the Supreme Court, summarized her opinion in *United States v. Virginia*, 518 US 515 (1996).
2. *United States v. Virginia*, 534.
3. *United States v. Virginia*, 533.
4. See Jennifer Carroll Foy '03, Virginia Military Institute, https://www.vmi.edu/admissions-and-aid/our-graduates/people/jennifer-carroll-foy-03.php. Carroll Foy shared this story on the floor of the House of Delegates in 2019 when she used a Point of Personal Privilege to advocate for the ERA, although the ERA had not been voted out of committee. Virginia House of Delegates, Regular Session, January 9, 2019 (Delegate Carroll Foy's Point of Personal Privilege). All videos of House of Delegates sessions are available, by date, at https://virginiageneralassembly.gov/house/chamber/chamberstream.php.
5. Virginia House of Delegates, Regular Session, January 15, 2020.
6. Megan Taylor Shockley, *Creating a Progressive Commonwealth: Women Activists, Feminism, and the Politics of Social Change in Virginia, 1970s–2000s* (Baton Rouge: Louisiana State University Press, 2018), chapter 2.
7. See National Conference of State Legislatures, First Women to Serve in State and Territorial Legislatures, https://www.ncsl.org/legislators-staff/legislators/womens-legislative-network/first-women-in-state-legislatures.aspx.

8. Virginia Senate, Regular Session, January 15, 2020. Locke paraphrased from Barbara Jordan's televised speech before the House Judiciary Committee in 1974 justifying the articles of impeachment against President Nixon. See Barbara Jordan Impeachment Speech, July 25, 1974, https://watergate.info/1974/07/25/barbara-jordan-speech-on-impeachment.html.
9. Virginia Senate, Regular Session, January 15, 2020.
10. About Jenn, Website, Jennifer McClellan, Virginia State Senate, http://www.jennifermcclellan.com/about.
11. Patrick Wilson. "Va. lawmaker announces she's pregnant with her third child," *Richmond Times-Dispatch*, October 2, 2019, https://www.richmond.com/news/virginia/va-lawmaker-announces-she-s-pregnant-with-her-third-child/article_4dfd80e1-15c5-5521-a77e-e57a-d00d1a40.html.
12. Jennifer McClellan, Plenary IV Speech, National Organization for Women (NOW) Conference, Minneapolis, Minnesota, July 20, 2019. Video available at https://www.facebook.com/NationalNOW/videos/2957435661147620/.
13. Virginia House of Delegates, Regular Session, January 15, 2020.
14. Virginia House of Delegates, Regular Session, January 15, 2020.
15. Virginia House of Delegates, Regular Session, January 15, 2020.
16. 124 Congressional Record, 26,201. Heckler included a *Washington Post* piece with her remarks.
17. See Shockley, *Creating a Progressive Commonwealth*, chapter 2.
18. The details of the committee votes are thoroughly recounted, relying largely on news articles from the period, in an unpublished master's thesis by Mary Bezbatchenko. See Mary Bezbatchenko, "Virginia and the Equal Rights Amendment," Master of History Thesis, Virginia Commonwealth University, 51–103, https://scholarscompass.vcu.edu/cgi/viewcontent.cgi?article=1747&context=etd.
19. Shockley, *Creating a Progressive Commonwealth*, chapter 2.
20. Virginia Senate, Regular Session, January 15, 2020.
21. Shockley, *Creating a Progressive Commonwealth*, chapter 2.
22. See Laura Vozzella, "Virginia House panel nixes ERA bills, in a blow for feminist groups," *Washington Post*, January 22, 2019, https://www.washingtonpost.com/local/virginia-politics/virginia-house-panel-nixes-era-bills-but-the-fight-goes-on/2019/01/22/2800ee98-1e51-11e9-8b59-0a28f2191131_story.html.

23. Fenit Nirappil, "In a changing Virginia suburb, a slate of diverse Democrats hopes to show path back to power," *Washington Post*, September 28, 2017, https://www.washingtonpost.com/local /virginia-politics/in-a-changing-va-suburb-a-diverse-democratic -slate-hopes-to-show-path-back-to-power/2017/09/28/a5756c70 -9962-11e7-82e4-f1076f6d6152_story.html.

24. See Hala Ayala's campaign website at https://www.ayalafordelegate .com/.

25. Virginia House of Delegates, Regular Session, February 21, 2019.

26. See Patricia Sullivan, "Inside the Virginia Capitol, a legislative duel over the ERA," *Washington Post*, February 14, 2019, https://www .washingtonpost.com/local/virginia-politics/inside-the-virginia -capitol-a-legislative-duel-over-the-era/2019/02/14/fc50c5e6-3081 -11e9-813a-0ab2f17e305b_story.html.

27. Virginia House of Delegates, Regular Session, Feb. 21, 2019, discussing Virginia House of Delegates, HR 280, Rules of the House of Delegates; voting requirement to discharge a committee from consideration of a resolution, February 13, 2019, available at http://lis .virginia.gov/cgi-bin/legp604.exe?191+sum+HR280.

28. Virginia House of Delegates, Regular Session, January 15, 2020.

29. Virginia House of Delegates, Regular Session, January 15, 2020. Remarks of Delegate Todd Gilbert, a Republican from Shenandoah.

30. Virginia House of Delegates, Regular Session, January 15, 2020. Remarks of Delegate Robert D. "Bobby" Orrock Sr., a Republican from Caroline.

31. Virginia House of Delegates, Regular Session, January 15, 2020. Remarks of Delegate Robert D. "Bobby" Orrock Sr., a Republican from Caroline.

32. Virginia House of Delegates, Regular Session, January 15, 2020. Remarks of Delegate Robert D. "Bobby" Orrock Sr., a Republican from Caroline.

33. H.B. 827, Pregnant Worker Fairness Act. S.B. 712, Virginia Human Rights Act; Discrimination on the Basis of Pregnancy, Virginia General Assembly, 2020 Session. These bills were chiefly sponsored by Delegate Jennifer Carroll Foy and Senator Jennifer McClellan, the chief patrons of ERA ratification in their respective chambers.

34. S.B. 733, Abortion; informed consent, regulations. Virginia General Assembly, 2020 Session. Senator McClellan was the chief Senate patron on this bill.

35. S.B. 868, Discrimination; prohibited in public accommodations, etc., causes of action. Virginia General Assembly, 2020 Session. Senator Jennifer McClellan was a chief co-patron of this bill.

36. H.B. 825 Paid family and medical leave program; Virginia Employment Commission to establish. Virginia General Assembly, 2020 Session. This bill was introduced by Delegate Jennifer Carroll Foy in the House of Delegates.

Epilogue: The Unstoppables

1. Barry Goldwater, Announcement of Presidential Candidacy, January 3, 1964, AP Archive, https://www.youtube.com/watch?v=lCN3Qnfy334.

2. Associated Press, "US Archives confirms it won't take steps to certify the ERA," *Richmond Times-Dispatch*, January 29, 2020, https://www.richmond.com/news/national-world/us-archives-confirms-it-won-t-take-steps-to-certify/article_bfc4f1f9-dc36-51fb-a59e-5b174a92725d.html.

3. Department of Justice, Slip Opinion, Ratification of the Equal Rights Amendment, Memorandum for the General Counsel, National Archives and Records Administration, Opinions of the Office of Legal Counsel, Vol. 44, January 6, 2020.

4. See 1 USC. § 106(b).

5. Complaint, Virginia, Nevada, & Illinois v. Ferriero, Case 1:20-cv-00242 (U.S. District Court, District of the District of Columbia), filed January 30, 2020. See Complaint, *Alabama, Louisiana & South Dakota v. Ferriero*, Case 7:19-cv-02032-LSC (U.S. District Court, Northern District of Alabama), December 17, 2019. Alabama, Louisiana, and South Dakota have voluntary dismissed their complaint in the Alabama federal court, and have joined as intervenors in Virginia's lawsuit against the Archivist. Meanwhile, a pro-ERA group, Equal Means Equal, has also sued the Archivist in a federal court in Boston. See Complaint, *Equal Means Equal et al. v. Ferriero*, Case 1:20-cv-10015 (U.S. District Court, District of Massachusetts), January 7, 2020. The plaintiffs voluntarily dismissed the lawsuit in Alabama, and instead moved to intervene in Virginia's lawsuit in DC, raising the same arguments.

6. H. J. Res. 79, 116th Cong. (2019).

7. S. J. Res. 6., 116th Cong. (2019). See Lisa Murkowski & Ben Cardin, "It's time to finally pass the Equal Rights Amendment," *Washington Post*, January 25, 2019, https://www.washingtonpost.com/opinions/its-time-to-finally-pass-the-equal-rights-amendment/2019/01/25/54b3626e-20d0-11e9-9145-3f74070bbdb9_story.html.

8. The Twenty-First Amendment, which repealed the earlier Eighteenth Amendment prohibiting the sale and manufacture of alcoholic beverages, went slightly differently. As prescribed by Congress consistent with Article V, the Repeal of Prohibition Amendment was ratified by state ratifying conventions in three-fourths of the states, rather than by the state legislatures. Article V authorizes amendments to be proposed by a convention for proposing amendments, if called by two-thirds of the states, but there has never been an Article V convention of this sort, despite some movements throughout history and in the present calling for one.

9. The congressional debates about the seven-year deadline on the Prohibition Amendment are found at 55 Congressional Record 5648–49 (1917).

10. See Matt Largey, "The Bad Grade That Changed the US Constitution," NPR, May 5, 2017, https://www.npr.org/2017/05/05/526900818/the-bad-grade-that-changed-the-u-s-constitution.

11. 138 Congressional Record 11,869 (1992) (Senate); 138 Congressional Record 12,052 (1992) (House).

12. 1918 House Woman Suffrage Hearings, 154–58 (reprinting Mary Beard & Florence Kelley, "Why Women Demand a Federal Suffrage Amendment—Difficulties in Amending State Constitutions—A Study of the Constitutions of the Non-Suffrage States").

13. This is what H. J. Res 79 says.

14. H. Rep. 116–387 (2020), 6.

15. Removing the deadline for the ratification of the equal rights amendment, Full Committee Markup of H. J. Res. 79, House Committee on the Judiciary, November 13, 2019 ("2019 Committee Markup") (Statement of Congresswoman Pramila Jayapal), https://judiciary.house.gov/legislation/markups/h-j-res-79-removing-deadline-ratification-equal-rights-amendment.

16. 2019 Committee Markup (Statement of Congresswoman Sheila Jackson Lee).

17. 166 Congressional Record H1137 (2020).
18. Protecting Federal Judiciary Employees from Sexual Harassment, Discrimination, and Other Workplace Misconduct, Hearings Before the Subcommittee on Courts, Intellectual Property, and the Internet of the House Committee on the Judiciary, February 13, 2020 (Testimony of Olivia Warren).
19. 166 Congressional Record, H1140.
20. The Supreme Court precedent is clear that the decision whether to accept rescissions is for Congress to make, not courts. *Coleman v. Miller* dicusses the history of the Fourteenth Amendment rescissions. For an account of the Article V irregularities of the Fourteenth Amendment's adoption and ratification, see Bruce Ackerman, *We the People: Transformations* (Cambridge: The Belknap Press of Harvard University, 1998).
21. Idaho brought a lawsuit seeking a court declaration that its rescission of the ERA was valid. A federal district court judge agreed with Idaho, and also concluded that Congress did not have power to extend the deadline. See *Idaho v. Freeman*, 529 F.Supp. 1107 (1981). The Supreme Court agreed to take the case initially, but after the 1982 deadline elapsed, the Supreme Court dismissed the case on the understanding that it was moot.
22. In 2014, Catharine MacKinnon, the feminist legal scholar who pioneered the law's recognition of sexual harassment, wrote in favor of a renewed ERA. See Catharine A MacKinnon, "Towards a Renewed Equal Rights Amendment: Now More than Ever," *Harvard Journal of Law and Gender* 37 (2014): 559–579. More recently, MacKinnon and critical race scholar Kimberlé Crenshaw have also proposed a new equality amendment for the Constitution that would go beyond the ERA by enshrining a substantive intersectional equality to overcome the limits of the Fourteenth Amendment for both race and sex equality. See Catharine A. MacKinnon & Kimberlé Crenshaw, "Reconstituting the Future: A New Equality Amendment," *Yale Law Journal Forum* 129 (2019), https://www.yalelawjournal.org/forum/reconstituting-the-future-the-equality-amendment.
23. ERA activists, including ERA Coalition co-president Jessica Neuwirth, often argue that the ERA is needed because it would require judges to change certain Fourteenth Amendment precedents with regard to women, including the Supreme Court's rejection of pregnancy

discrimination as a violation of the Equal Protection Clause, invalidation of the Violence Against Women Act, and hostility to disparate impact as a violation of Equal Protection. See Jessica Neuwirth, *Equal Means Equal: Why the Time for an Equal Rights Amendment is Now* (New York: The New Press, 2015). While the language of the ERA would not require judges to change any of the Supreme Court's Fourteenth Amendment precedents affecting women, the legislative history of the ERA as detailed in *We the Women* could point judges to new interpretive possibilities under the ERA, which would not be bound by Fourteenth Amendment precedent.

24. In 2000, the Supreme Court struck down the civil remedy provision in the Violence Against Women Act on the grounds that Congress did not have constitutional authority to enact it. See *United States v. Morrison*, 529 US 598 (2000). After that case was decided, the state of Nevada argued in litigation that Congress did not have constitutional authority to pass the Family and Medical Leave Act, which guarantees job-protected unpaid leave to employees to care for family members, including newborn infants, or to care for themselves when they have a serious health condition. The Supreme Court held that the Family and Medical Leave Act was constitutional under Congress's power to enforce the Fourteenth Amendment's Equal Protection Clause in *Nevada v Hibbs*, 538 US 721 (2003). However, more recently, the Supreme Court held that Congress lacked the power to require employers to provide medical leave under the Fourteenth Amendment's Equal Protection Clause, calling into question the constitutionality of federal laws to support pregnancy leave. See *Coleman v. Court of Appeals of Maryland*, 566 US 30 (2012). These decisions suggest the future possibility that litigants will attempt to challenge the constitutionality of federal laws protecting pregnant workers, on various legal theories. If a litigant were to challenge laws that promote equality for women, such as the Pregnant Worker Fairness Act, on similar grounds regarding lack of congressional authority, the ERA section 2 would provide support for the constitutionality of such laws and thus work as a constitutional shield.

Index

Abzug, Bella, 72, 73, 80, 85, 86, 91, 92, 161, 203, 210
Adams, Abigail, 9, 11, 12, 20, 159, 176
Adams, John, 9, 10
Adarand Constructors v. Peña, 110
Adkins v. Children's Hospital, 28, 29, 30, 32, 33, 37, 39, 40, 41, 194, 195, 196
American Civil Liberties Union, 22, 37, 42, 97, 98
Andersson, Steven, 150, 187
Anthony, Daniel R, Jr., 24
Anthony, Susan B., 13–17, 21, 24, 48, 49, 151, 176
Ayala, Hala, 141, 167–169, 187
bathrooms, unisex, 87, 90
"baby-ins," 72
Bäumer, Gertrud, 50
Bayh, Birch, 62–65, 84, 109
Biss, Daniel, 145, 215
Blackmun, Harry, 71
"blind man with a shotgun," 37, 39, 42, 105, 102

Bond Miller, Yvonne, 169
Bradwell v. State of Illinois, 104, 190
Bradwell, Myra, 13
Brandeis Brief, 33
Brandeis, Louis, 33
"bring a folding chair," 69, 113
Burke, Tarana, 145, 215
Burn, Harry, 18, 20
Cady Stanton, Elizabeth, 11–17, 121, 176, 190, 198
California corporate board law, 111
Cancela, Yvanna, 138
Cannizzaro, Nicole, 135, 140, 141, 154, 213
Cardin, Ben, 174, 222
Carroll Foy, Jennifer, 159–162, 170, 182, 187, 218, 220, 221
Carswell, George Harrold, 71, 81, 202
Catt, Carrie Chapman, 16–21, 48, 49, 191
Celler, Emanuel, 56, 58, 65, 114, 116, 176

Chisholm, Shirley, 69, 70, 73–75, 77, 81, 103, 112, 113, 115, 133, 155, 159, 169, 176, 201, 202

choice in occupation, 23, 60

Citizens' Advisory Council on the Status of Women, 58, 59, 200

Citizenship and Nationality Law, 24, 25

Civil Rights Act of 1964, 62, 68, 71, 84, 88, 200

Civil Rights Movement, 5, 57, 106, 180

Civil War, 13

Clinton, Hillary, 131

Coleman v. Miller, 118, 119, 130, 211, 223, 224

Comprehensive Child Development Act (1971), 75, 78, 93

Comprehensive Preschool Education and Child Day-Care Act (1969), 73, 75, 78, 93, 202, 203

Congress, composition, women, 103, 112, 115, 136, 141, 159, 168, 169, 179

Congress of the International Council of Women, 49, 197

Convirs-Fowler, Kelly, 161

Cook, Marlow, 62, 63, 77

Cooper, John Sherman, 88

Crenshaw, Kimberlé, 46, 197, 223

de-facto ERA, 139, 214

Declaration of Independence, 9–11, 14

Declaration of Sentiments, 11, 12, 14, 101, 190

list of grievances/proposed rights, 11, 12

Delta Kappa Epsilon, 110

Delta Sigma Theta, 46, 160

Dillon v. Gloss, 119, 120, 211

discharge petition, 58, 59, 61, 65, 70, 79, 133, 168, 176

discrimination against pregnant women and mothers, 5, 76, 98, 100, 108, 144, 156, 160, 162, 170, 220, 224

disparate impact on women, 78

Dred Scott v. Sandford, 27, 196

dual strategy for women's rights, 103, 106, 113

Dwyer, Florence, 59, 60, 62, 63, 71, 86

Dyer, Goudyloch "Giddy," 147, 148

Dyer v. Blair, 148–49

Eastman, Crystal, 22–26, 29, 30, 36, 37, 40–42, 52, 59, 70, 92, 93, 112, 161, 176, 192–194

equal education of boys and girls / liberation from traditional gender roles, 24, 72–75, 181

equal participation in trade and commerce, 12, 24, 73, 74

equal pay, 4, 6, 24, 53, 73, 134, 135, 137, 139, 154, 178, 180

Equal Pay Act of 1963, 59

Equal Rights Amendment (ERA), 1, 4, 12, 22–26, 29, 31, 33, 34, 36–38, 40, 47, 51, 54, 57, 58, 60, 61, 69, 70, 72, 73, 75, 77, 78, 83, 88, 92, 98, 102, 103, 105, 106, 108–110, 112, 125, 130–133, 138, 143, 144, 153, 155, 156, 159, 160, 162,

171, 176, 185, 193, 195–197, 199, 200, 210–214, 217, 219, 221, 222, 224
address lack of governmental action, 78–80, 98, 132–135, 178, 182
anticipated consequences, 1920s, 25
anticipated consequences, right to abortion, 139, 150, 163
arguments against, 37–42
congressional votes, 1970s, 58, 65, 67, 70
effects on bathrooms, 85–87, 90
effects on child support, 26, 54, 85–87, 89–92
effects on childcare, 72–75, 78, 81, 82, 92, 152
effects on labor protections, 26, 27, 29, 30, 33, 37–40, 42, 54, 70, 75, 77, 78, 86
effects on military service, 84, 87, 90, 104, 153
effects on rape laws, 85–87, 90
effects on same-sex marriage, 85, 87
effects on unequal pay, 92, 131, 133–135, 153, 178
failure, 55, 56, 62–67, 114, 136, 137, 141, 142, 147, 149, 150, 159, 164, 166, 167, 183
Hayden Rider, 55
House votes, 1960s, 60, 61
interpretations, role of congressional intent/legislative history, 62, 63, 75, 86, 88, 90, 113, 121, 133

interpretations, judicial, 37–42, 88, 151
Martha Griffith's political calculations / incorporation of 'minor technical changes', 65, 66, 80, 123
National Woman's Party position, 26, 27, 29, 30, 37
Phyllis Schlafly's arguments against, 84, 86, 88–91, 116, 133
ratification,
1970s, 58, 82
Illinois, 91, 142, 147; effects of state constitution on, 147–150, 155; objections from congresswomen of color, 150, 151
Nevada, 130, 138; vote, 136, 137; voter referendum, 137
next steps, 172
resulting controversies, 2, 4, 164, 172–176
sports analogies / games / politics of horse-trading, 116, 119–121, 125
time limit, 4, 63, 65, 66, 80, 114–121, 124–126, 130, 159, 163, 173, 175–177, 180; constitutionality of/ congressional authority over, 118, 119, 121, 122, 124, 130, 175, 177, 180; extensions, 92, 115–126; legal analysis based on language and location, 120–124, 177
Virginia, 4, 159, 163, 164; votes, 164, 166–168; delays due to parliamentary procedures, 116, 165–170

Sam Ervin's amendments, 63, 64, 65, 85, 87–90, 176
Senate vote, 1946, 54
Senate vote, 1950s, 55, 56
Two-year delay on effective date, 63, 65, 66, 80
vague language/difficulty interpreting, 37, 75
Wiggins Amendment, 76, 77, 79, 81, 82
women's exemptions from military draft, 63, 64, 76, 84, 87, 90, 104
working mothers, 24, 36–38, 40, 42, 47, 53, 54, 61, 70, 71, 73–75, 81, 82, 85, 86, 108, 131, 135, 151, 153
equal treatment vs. identical treatment, 37, 41, 59, 86, 87, 111
Ervin, Sam, 62–67, 76, 82, 84–90, 176
Fain, Sarah Lee, 169
Fair Labor Standards Act, 41
Federation of German Women's Organizations, 49, 50
Feminist Alliance, 22
Fenwick, Millicent, 122
fifty-fifty plans, 40
Filler-Corn, Eileen, 169
Flowers, Mary, 144, 145, 150–156
Flynn Currie, Barbara, 144–147, 156, 215, 216
"foment a rebellion," 9, 11, 12, 20, 100
foreign constitutions, 26, 40, 55, 197;
European, 26, 40, 55, 112, 184, 197;

France, 51, 52, 112, 210;
Germany, 51, 112, 198, 210;
Article 119, 50; Basic Law, 51
Italy, 51, 52, 112, 198
Japan, 47, 53, 197
"founding fathers," 3, 6, 10, 13, 61, 76, 189
"founding mothers," 2, 3, 42, 76, 92, 112, 176
freedom of contract, 27, 28, 37
French, Burton, 19
Friedan, Betty, 58, 72, 142, 202
Frontiero v. Richardson, 103–107, 207–209
Gansert, Heidi, 136
Geduldig v. Aiello, 108, 205
Gilbert v. General Electric, 108, 208
Ginsburg, Ruth Bader, 97–104
Goldman, Emma, 105, 207
Goldmark, Josephine, 33, 195
Goldwater, Barry, 62, 83, 172, 221
Grasso, Ella, 79
Green, Edith, 73, 74
Griffiths, Martha, 57, 58, 59, 61, 62, 64, 65–67, 70, 74, 76, 79, 80, 84, 92, 98, 101, 108, 123, 132, 133, 137, 166, 168, 176, 199, 201, 205, 206, 208, 213
Grimké, Angelina, 105, 207
Grimké, Sarah, 104, 105, 207
Griswold, Erwin, 100, 101, 119, 211
Harding, Warren, 35
Hashmi, Ghazala, 163
Hayden, Carl, 55, 64
Heckler, Margaret, 60, 71, 74, 82, 92, 115–118, 125, 165, 181, 200, 219
Henderson, Helen, 169

Hicks, Louise, 82
Holmes Norton, Eleanor, 72
Holtzman v. Power, 116
Holtzman, Liz, 114–118, 181,
    187, 210, 211
Howard Shaw, Anna, 17, 23, 191
Hoyt v. Florida, 64, 102, 196, 201
Hutchinson, Toi, 144, 156
"I Want a Wife," 73, 202
Illinois, ERA ratification 142–57
industrial legislation protecting
    women, 23, 26, 29
International Council of Women,
    49, 197
intersectionality, 46, 152, 156
J.A. Croson v. City of Richmond, 110
Jackson Lee, Sheila, 178
"Jailed for Freedom" pin, 47, 160
Jane Crow, 103, 207
Jayapal, Pramila, 178, 222
Jefferson, Thomas, 171
Jim Crow, 46, 54
Jordan, Barbara, 117–119, 125,
    155, 159, 160, 178, 211, 219
Kavanaugh, Brett, 110, 179
Kelley, Florence, 32–34, 36–40,
    42, 46, 47, 75, 88, 151, 156,
    176, 191, 194–196, 222
Kenyon, Dorothy, 37, 38, 40–42,
    102, 103, 196, 201, 206–208
Kiggans, Jen, 163
Kory, Kaye, 162
Lange, Helene, 49, 50, 197, 198
"legislative graveyard," 65–67, 76,
    80, 85, 165, 168, 176, 183
Lightford, Kimberly, 144, 156
Lochner v. New York, 27–29, 39,
    102, 193

Locke, Mamie, 159, 160, 162, 219
Low-wage work, women, 110,
    145–46, 156–57
Lucas, Louise, 169
Lucretia Mott Amendment, 24
Madison, James, 171, 175, 185
Madison Amendment, *see U.S.*
    Constitution, Twenty-Seventh
    Amendment
male abuses of power, 84, 87, 109,
    110, 114, 116–118, 120, 125,
    142–146, 165, 176, 177, 179
Maloney, Carolyn, 178
maternal mortality, 34–37, 154, 156
maternity leave, 24, 36, 51, 81,
    86, 92, 93, 108, 113, 209
Matthews, Burnita, 25, 29–31, 36,
    193, 194
maximum hours law, 27, 33
May, Catherine Dean, 61, 74
Mayfield, Rita, 144, 150, 151,
    153, 155–157
McClellan, Jennifer, 141, 160–
    162, 187, 219–221
McConnell, Mitch, 88, 204
McGovern, George, 69
McGuire, John J., III, 169
#MeToo, 2, 3, 109, 110, 111,
    141, 142, 144, 145, 146, 153,
    179, 182
Merlin, Angelina, 53
Mikulski, Barbara, 119, 120
Milholland, Inez, 21, 191, 192
military draft, 64, 66, 67, 76, 80,
    82, 84, 90, 104
minimum wages for women,
    26–30, 32, 33, 36, 37, 39, 41,
    156

Mink, Patsy Takemoto, 68–71, 73–75, 77–79, 81, 83, 86, 91, 108, 112, 132, 133, 162, 176, 181, 201–203, 210, 213
"monopoly of jurisprudence by men," 39
motherhood, economic disadvantages, 4, 36, 47, 70, 73, 86, 92, 99, 111, 134, 140, 146, 179; statistics, 92; uncompensated, 25, 73
Mott, Lucretia, 11, 12, 15, 16, 24, 189
Muller v. Oregon, 27, 28, 32, 33, 38, 102, 194
Muller, Curt, 27
Murkowski, Lisa, 174, 222
Murray, Mary, 24, 192
Murray, Pauli, 102, 103, 106, 109, 110, 113, 123, 169, 186, 206–208
National American Woman's Suffrage Association, 16, 21, 33
National Archives and Records Administration, 172, 173, 175
National Association for the Advancement of Colored People (NAACP), 42, 46
National Association of Colored Women, 42
National Association Opposed to Women's Suffrage (NAOWS), 35
National Civil Liberties Bureau, 22
National Consumer's League, 32, 33, 38
National Organization for Women, 72, 101, 141, 202, 214, 219

National Woman's Party, 21, 22, 25, 26, 29, 30, 33, 34, 36, 37, 39, 40, 42, 47, 50, 52, 191–195, 198; arguments in support of ERA, 26–30, 37
Netsch, Dawn Clark, 147–150, 216
Nevada, ERA Ratification, 129–141, procedural devices, 116
Nixon, Richard, 93, 115, 117, 160, 219
Nolan, Mae, 30, 60
Nursing Mothers Accommodation Act, Nevada, 140, 214
Ocasio-Cortez, Alexandria, 115
"our posterity," 10, 11, 183, 188
Parliamentary Procedures, 58, 116, 167, 168, 176
Paul, Alice, 21, 22, 25, 29, 40, 42, 46, 47, 52, 91, 151, 155, 160, 176, 191, 193, 195
Pelosi, Nancy, 178, 179
Phillips v. Martin Marietta, 71, 108, 201, 208
"Pink Wave," 2, 169
pregnancy discrimination, 100, 108, 109, 113, 116, 178, 179, 206, 208, 220, 224
Pregnancy Discrimination Act, 108, 109, 116, 181, 208, 220
Pregnant Workers Accommodation Act, Illinois, 144, 156
Pregnant Worker Fairness Act, Virginia, 170
Pregnant Workers' Fairness Act, Nevada, 140

President's Task Force on
Women's Rights and
Responsibilities, 58, 59, 74,
102, 200
Pritzker, J.B., 144
"pro-family rally," 91
"Put 'Rat' in Ratification!," 18
racial justice, 5, 46, 48, 49, 76,
106, 117, 118, 141, 151, 154,
155, 160
Raker, John E., 16
Rankin, Jeannette, 16, 210
Ratti, Julia, 138, 140
Reagan, Ronald, 163
Reed v. Reed, 101–103, 105, 106,
206–208; Ginsburg Brief,
101–103
Reid, Charlotte, 60
"remember the ladies," 9, 10, 154,
159
reproductive justice, 6, 99, 100,
139–141
revolutionary fervor, 2, 9, 11, 23,
93
Roberson, Michael, 139, 140, 214
Robertson, Alice, 35
Roca, Gilberte, 51, 52, 198
Roem, Danica, 162
romantic paternalism, "put
women, not on a pedestal, but
in a cage," 104
Rudd, Eldon, 119
Schlafly, Phyllis, 83–86, 88, 89,
91–93, 116, 129, 133, 142,
143, 147, 149, 165, 172, 204,
205, 213
Second Continental Congress, 9
Senate Women's Caucus, 144, 215

Seneca Falls, 4, 11, 12, 14, 24,
101, 190
Sessions v. Morales-Santana, 112
sex discrimination, 22, 23, 46,
53, 54, 59, 62, 68, 71, 72, 74,
76, 78, 86, 93, 98, 103–109,
113, 133, 135, 137, 139, 144,
146, 153, 156, 157, 162, 181,
206–209, 215, 217, 223
sex equality, 28, 51, 53, 87, 90,
98, 101, 102, 125, 162, 183
sexual harassment, 74, 109, 135,
144–146, 157, 179 182
Sheppard-Towner Maternity and
Infancy Protection Act, 34–36,
38; opponents, 35, 36
Shipley, George, 85
Siegel, Reva, 139, 140, 185, 187,
192, 194, 206, 214
"Silent Sentinels," 21
Simon, Marcus, 168
Smith, Margaret Chase, 55, 62,
193, 199, 200, 216
Spearman, Pat, 129–135, 139–141,
155, 160, 182, 187, 212–214
Speier, Jackie, 178
St. George, Katharine, 129–135,
139–141, 155, 160, 182, 187,
212–214
Steans, Heather, 143, 144, 147,
150, 156, 157, 182
Steinem, Gloria, 58
Stevens, John Paul, 148, 149
STOP-ERA Movement, 5, 84, 89,
93, 116, 142, 143
Stratton, Juliana, 144–146, 151,
153–156
Strauss, David, 139, 214

Struck v. Secretary of Defense,
  97–100, 101, 103, 104, 107,
  108, 113, 205, 206
Struck, Susan, 97–99
Sturtevant, Glen, 163
Suffrage Amendment, *see U.S.
  Constitution, Nineteenth
  Amendment*
Suffrage Parade, 46, 151, 155,
  160, 191
suffragists, militant tactics, 21, 22
Sullivan, Leonor Kretzer, 88, 89
Sunstein, Cass, 139, 214
Supreme Court, 13, 14, 27–29,
  32, 33, 36, 38, 39, 41, 45, 46,
  69, 71, 79, 93, 98, 100–105,
  107, 108, 110, 112, 113,
  180–120, 125, 130, 132, 139,
  149, 158, 174, 175, 179, 181,
  182, 186, 202, 206, 208–210,
  216–218, 223, 224
Susan B. Anthony Amendment,
  15, 24
Syfers, Judy, 73, 202
symbols, 130, 131
Terrell, Mary Church, 45–51, 53,
  103, 112, 151, 155, 160, 197
Terrell, Robert, 48
tipped workers, 146, 157
Title IX of the Education
  Amendments Act, 74, 75, 78,
  79, 92, 162, 181, 203
Title VII, 92, 108, 203, 207, 209
Tlaib, Rashida, 179, 180
Towner, Horace Mann, 34
Trump, Donald, 131, 179, 211
Trump Administration, Justice
  Department, Office of Legal
  Counsel, 173

U.S. Constitution
amendment process, 109, 118,
  125, 149, 155, 173, 175, 217
Article V, 4, 15, 19, 20, 54, 61,
  109, 118, 122, 125, 137, 148,
  149, 164, 172, 174, 175, 177,
  180, 216, 222, 223; difficulty
  obtaining rights without
  rights, 15, 16, 54, 61
slavery, 10
Fifth Amendment, 28, 33, 78, 99,
  107, 110, 112
Fourteenth Amendment, Equal
  Protection Clause, 5, 13, 14,
  46, 98, 99, 101; gendered
  language, 13, 14; impact on
  legal profession, 13; race-
  conscious affirmative action,
  110
gendered language, 10, 13, 14
Nineteenth Amendment, 1, 2,
  12, 16–18, 20–22, 28, 32–34,
  38–40, 46–48, 61, 101, 164,
  176, 189–192, 194, 216;
  effects on women's labor
  protections, 28; ratification,
  2, 12, 16, 18, 20–22, 34;
  ratification vote in Congress,
  16, 20; seven-year time
  limit, 18; arguments against
  time limit, 18; Tennessee
  ratification, 18
Preamble, 10, 14, 52, 188
Prohibition Amendment, 18, 19,
  34, 119–121, 175, 176, 222;
  seven-year time limit, 18,
  119–121, 175, 176, 222
rights of women, 1–5, 11–14, 23,
  25, 61, 75

Tenth Amendment, 35
Twenty-Seventh Amendment, 175
unequal pay, 141, 180
unequal power, 3, 6, 23, 36, 39,
    52, 62, 87, 106, 109, 110–
    112, 123, 176–179
United Nations Charter, equality
    of the sexes, 45, 51, 54
United States v. Virginia, 107, 111,
    113, 159, 171, 181, 208–210,
    218
violence against women, 4, 6, 74,
    92, 106, 109, 110, 129, 131,
    135, 136, 140, 143–146, 153,
    179
Virginia, ERA ratification,
    158–171; parliamentary
    procedures, 116, 117, 166–
    168, 176; proposed changes
    to parliamentary procedures,
    167, 168; recent legislation in
    support of women's rights, 169
Virginia Military Institute (VMI),
    107, 158, 182, 218
voluntary motherhood, 24, 113,
    140
Wagner, Sue, 136, 137
Wald, Patricia, 121, 122, 211
Wallace, Litesa, 144–146, 151–153,
    155, 156, 215, 218
Watts, Vivian, 162

"We the People," 10, 14, 17, 117,
    118, 120, 125, 160, 171, 176,
    179, 183
Weinstein, Harvey, 109, 142, 143
Wells, Ida B., 46, 155, 218
Wiggins, Charles, 76
Wilson, Woodrow, 21, 22
Wolfgang, Myra, 70, 75, 151, 201
Woman Suffrage Committee,
    15–17, 30
Women Who Make Illinois Run,
    143–146
Women's Joint Congressional
    Committee (WJCC), 33, 34,
    42, 195
Women's March, 2, 3, 131; unity
    principles, 131
Women's Rights Convention, 11,
    12, 190
Women's Strike for Equality
    (1970), 71, 72, 80, 81, 85,
    100, 202; demands, 72
Woodhouse, Joyce, 138
World Antislavery Convention, 11
World War I, effects on women's
    suffrage, 17, 23, 25, 26
World War II, effects on women's
    rights, 5, 45, 51–54
Yale University, fraternity lawsuit,
    110